KILLING ENGLAND

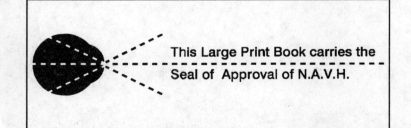

This Large Print Book carries the
Seal of Approval of N.A.V.H.

KILLING ENGLAND

THE BRUTAL STRUGGLE FOR AMERICAN INDEPENDENCE

BILL O'REILLY
AND MARTIN DUGARD

WHEELER PUBLISHING

A part of Gale, a Cengage Company

GALE
A Cengage Company

Farmington Hills, Mich • San Francisco • New York • Waterville, Maine
Meriden, Conn • Mason, Ohio • Chicago

Copyright © 2017 by Bill O'Reilly and Martin Dugard.
Wheeler Publishing, a part of Gale, a Cengage Company.

ALL RIGHTS RESERVED
Wheeler Publishing Large Print Hardcover.
The text of this Large Print edition is unabridged.
Other aspects of the book may vary from the original edition.
Set in 16 pt. Plantin.

**LIBRARY OF CONGRESS CIP DATA ON FILE.
CATALOGUING IN PUBLICATION FOR THIS BOOK
IS AVAILABLE FROM THE LIBRARY OF CONGRESS.**

ISBN-13: 978-1-4328-4438-7 (hardcover)
ISBN-10: 1-4328-4438-5 (hardcover)

Published in 2017 by arrangement with Henry Holt and Company

Printed in the United States of America
1 2 3 4 5 6 7 21 20 19 18 17

This book is dedicated to
all American history teachers
past and present.

Legend

	UNITED STATES/ FRANCE		BRITAIN
Movement			
Highlighted movement			
Retreat			
Infantry/ cavalry			
Earthworks/ fortifications			
Artillery			
Transport ships			
Warships			
Wagons			

COMBATANT NATIONALITIES

United States

Britain

France

MILITARY FEATURES

Clash/event

✕ Previous engagement

PHYSICAL FEATURES

○ City/town

□ Feature

Bridge

Road

River

Forest

Terrain

Wetlands

Burned area

Water

PROLOGUE

The long knives are out.

The face of Capt. Daniel-Hyacinthe-Marie Liénard de Beaujeu is striped in war paint. Primeval forest conceals his French Marines, Canadian militia, and Indian allies as they maneuver into position. Hidden behind boulders and ancient oak trees, they await the massive combined force of the British and colonial armies now marching toward them. Beaujeu's French and Indians are heavily outnumbered. Unlike the British, they don't have cannon that can kill and maim dozens with a single blast of canister shot. Instead, their weapons are those of a nimble guerrilla fighting force: muskets, tomahawks, war clubs to bash skulls, and sharp knives for slicing the flesh

7

and hair from a dying man's head.

Captain Beaujeu clearly sees the dirty crimson uniforms and miter caps of the Forty-Fourth and Forty-Eighth Regiments' Grenadier companies. These foot soldiers at the front of the British ranks are an elite fighting force. As best the French commander can tell, they number about three hundred men. He has scouted the enemy well, and knows that hundreds more British and Americans follow behind them in a thin mile-long column, hemmed in on both sides by the woods.

Beaujeu is stripped to the waist in the manner of his Indian allies. Bear grease smeared on his torso will make him slippery and more difficult to fight when the combat becomes hand to hand. The forty-three-year-old father of nine never tires of defeating the British. Killing them, he has written in his journal, fills him with "joye." His weapon of choice is a musket made at the Tulle Arsenal in Saint-Étienne, France. The Indians under his command, warriors from many tribes, are so enamored of this lightweight weapon that they ask for the "Tulle fusil" by name.*

*Among others: Iroquois, Nipissing, Huron, Abenakis, Odawa, Ojibwa, Potawatomi, Shawnee,

But right now, those guns are silent.

The French and Indians hold their fire as they await the moment when Beaujeu will stand tall in the forest to wave his hat. This is the signal to attack.

Oblivious to the coming ambush, twenty-three-year-old George Washington sits gingerly in the saddle at the very rear of the British column, guiding his horse along the narrow path leading straight into the hidden enemy. Dressed in the blue uniform of the Virginia militia, Washington is in agony. A tall and charismatic young man with large hands and a face marked by smallpox scars, Washington rides atop a pillow to protect his ailing backside from the pain of hemorrhoids. A rumble in his belly signals yet another attack of dysentery, forcing him to abruptly guide his charger into the forest in search of discreet relief.

The young Virginian contents himself with

Delaware, Osage, Sac, and Fox. The Indians preferred fighting for the French because the British were more insistent on confiscating tribal lands so that they might be settled by colonists. The French, on the other hand, controlled their frontier territories with small forts whose military population had little effect on Indian hunting grounds.

the knowledge that the march is almost over: after six weeks and 290 backbreaking miles through the wilderness, the British Army is just one day away from reaching the French garrison known as Fort Duquesne, which it plans to destroy.

Washington's intestinal illness forced him to travel flat on his back in a covered wagon until yesterday. But it is vital that he ride into battle on horseback. Just one year ago he was the officer who fired the first shot in the war between the British and the French. "The volley fired by a young Virginian in the backwoods of America set the world on fire," is how one British historian will describe the incident. Indeed, Washington's decision to attack a small French scouting party, killing all its soldiers, will launch what will become known as history's first world war. In time, the fighting will spread far beyond North America — into Europe, Africa, and even India.*

*George Washington's single gunshot escalated the rivalry between Britain and France, which had been simmering for some time as the two nations jockeyed for world leadership. The Seven Years' War, as it would become known in Europe — or the French and Indian War, as the American portion of the worldwide conflict is known — was at

But that moment of impulse eventually led to public disgrace. Soon after the skirmish, Washington suffered the humiliation of surrendering his Virginia militia to the French at a battlefield not far from here known as Fort Necessity. In order to avoid a wider war, the French allowed Washington and his men to return home, but the stigma of failure still hangs over the ambitious former surveyor. He has returned to this forest as a volunteer, seeking redemption by using his knowledge of the lush woodland trails to assist the British commander, Gen. Edward Braddock.

---

first confined to a series of frontier skirmishes in the American wilderness. Spain entered the war on the French side in 1761, causing the British Navy to seize French and Spanish territories in the Caribbean and Pacific. Portugal, which entered the war on the side of the British, thwarted an attempted Spanish invasion shortly thereafter, leading the French and Spanish to sue for peace. The British victory gave them control of most of North America — though, for a short time. They needed revenue to fund military installations on the newly established western border of the colonies and attempted to raise those funds by taxing their American colonists. Dispute over the legality of these taxes led to the Revolutionary War.

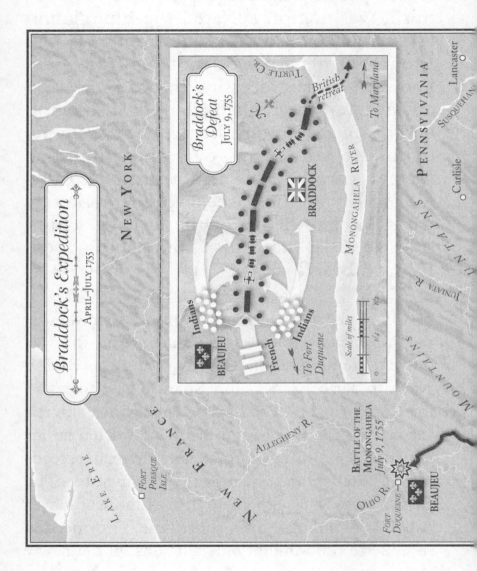

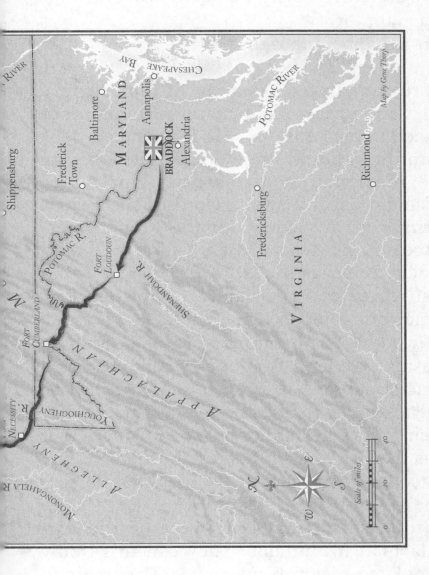

KANAWHA RIVER

CHESAPEAKE BAY

MARYLAND

Annapolis

Baltimore

Frederick
Town

Shippensburg

BRADDOCK

Alexandria

POTOMAC RIVER

Richmond

Fredericksburg

VIRGINIA

FORT
LOUDOUN

Potomac R.

POTOMAC R.

SHENANDOAH R.

FORT
CUMBERLAND

APPALACHIAN

NECESSITY

YOUGHIOGHENY

ALLEGHENY

MONONGAHELA R.

M

N
W   E
S

Scale of miles

0   20   40

Unbeknownst to George Washington, however, the battle he seeks will not take place tomorrow.

It is happening right now.

Three hundred miles away, in Philadelphia, forty-nine-year-old Benjamin Franklin sits naked in his bedroom. He is reading a book with the windows wide open while enjoying the rejuvenation of his daily "air bath." Franklin eagerly awaits word of the British Army's great victory, for the French presence in the Ohio River Valley not only blocks America's westward expansion, but also threatens the safety of the existing American colonies.

Franklin is not alone. From Virginia to Boston, General Braddock's campaign is a cause célèbre. The French and British have been at odds in Europe for centuries. Now their rivalry is shifting to North America. It was the British who first established a string of colonies up and down the Atlantic seaboard, but the French were not easily outdone, settling land west of the Appalachian Mountains. They call this thinly populated region New France. Beginning in Canada, the territory extends from the Great Lakes south through the Mississippi Valley all the way to the region on the Gulf of Mexico known as Louisiana. The border between the French and British colonies is poorly defined. One region in particular, the Ohio River Valley, is highly coveted by the British as a means of expanding their sphere of influence. General Braddock has been sent to America with the singular purpose of taking possession of this land.

But there is also a more tactical reason for the impending battle. The French soldiers in the Ohio River Valley are limited to the garrison at Fort Duquesne. They are in a defensive stance right now, dedicated to keeping the British contained on the coast. But, in time, Fort Duquesne could serve as a jumping-off point for a French assault on the British colonies themselves. If that happens, their Indian allies will be free to loot and pillage colonial farms and towns.

Fears of the French and Indians sweeping into Pennsylvania and Virginia have church-goers ardently praying for the general's success "against our neighboring enemies." Many colonists are so confident of Braddock's abilities that toasts to his victory have already been raised throughout the colonies.

Franklin, however, is *not* ready to celebrate.

The balding postmaster is a few inches short of six feet tall, with broad shoulders and what many consider a very large head. He has been in a common-law marriage for twenty-five years, to Deborah Read, a buxom beauty two years his junior.* He sired an illegitimate son with another woman before their union, and Deborah has given birth to two children, one of whom died from smallpox at the age of four. The gray-eyed Franklin favors a vegetarian diet and appears portly but is in fact muscular due to his passion for swimming. He is an inventor, writer, firefighter, publisher,

*As a young man, Franklin was a boarder in the Read family home. He was seventeen at the time, and Deborah was fifteen. Franklin fell in love with her and requested her hand in marriage, but her widowed mother denied this request because Franklin was financially unstable. Deborah was instead married off to a man named John Rodgers, who turned out to be a thief and ran out on her after two years. Franklin reentered her life soon after. Colonial laws prohibited a divorced woman from remarrying, so instead, the couple declared a common-law marriage in 1730, when Franklin was twenty-four. This arrangement legally bound them to one another, though it was not formally recognized by church or civil officials as a true marriage. They would remain together for the rest of their lives.

postmaster, and scientist.

Most of all, though, Benjamin Franklin is patriotic for a nation that does not yet exist.

Franklin's current focus is protecting "America" from the growing French threat. He seeks to form a union of the colonies that will provide this protection. But instead of seeing him as an ally, the British see him as a gadfly. His efforts to meet with the Iroquois Indians to broker a peace are viewed as interfering with the power of the king.

Despite British animosity, Franklin's ingenuity saved General Braddock's expedition in April, when the general himself declared that he could not proceed into the Ohio River Valley due to a lack of wagons and drivers for hauling the food and munitions vital to supplying his army. Franklin and Braddock met in person in late April, just days before George Washington joined the British cause.

"I happened to say I thought it was a pity they had not been landed rather in Pennsylvania," Franklin will write, "as in that country almost every farmer had his wagon. The general eagerly laid hold of my words, and said, 'Then you, sir, who are a man of interest there, can probably procure them for us; and I beg you will undertake it.' "

Within two weeks, Franklin presented Braddock with 150 wagons and another 259 horses. Among the wagoners is a twenty-year-old outdoorsman named Daniel Boone.*

Franklin is uneasy about Braddock's battle

*Franklin saved the day by posting an advertisement stating that the British required wagons and drivers, and were willing to pay a decent wage. Knowing this would not be enough, the flyer added that the British would take by force whatever wagons they needed, at the loss of compensation. Though written in a whimsical style that was meant to charm farmers into volunteering to relinquish their wagons, the subtext was quite clear. Within two weeks, Braddock was outfitted with two hundred wagons, with Franklin giving his personal bond as security to indemnify the wagon owners in case of any loss. The clash between these independent civilian wagoners and their military superiors would be a major cause of conflict during the Braddock campaign. In addition to Daniel Boone, there was also Daniel Morgan, a hard-drinking wagon driver fond of fistfights who would go on to become one of America's top generals in the Revolutionary War. His hatred for the British was legendary, dating to the time when he received 499 lashes for punching a British officer in 1756.

tactics. He believes the sixty-year-old British general is ignorant about fighting in the wilderness and employs strategies better suited to the empty plains of Europe. Franklin has personally warned Braddock about the Indians' ability to camouflage themselves and strike without warning. He believes the general's plan of traveling through the forest in a single column could lead to a devastating surprise attack.

"These savages may, indeed, be a formidable enemy to your raw American militia," Braddock replied as he dismissed Franklin's advice, "but upon the king's regular and disciplined troops, sir, it is impossible they should make any impression."

Just a few days ago, when two good friends requested that Franklin donate to a fund that would purchase fireworks to celebrate Braddock's coming victory, Franklin was uncharacteristically dour. "Time enough to prepare for the rejoicing," he told them by way of refusal, "when . . . we should have occasion to rejoice."

"You surely don't suppose that the fort will not be taken?" one of his friends asked in astonishment.

"The events of war," Franklin replied, "are subject to great uncertainty."

■ ■ ■ ■

A bare-chested Capt. Daniel-Hyacinthe-Marie Liénard de Beaujeu now rises to his feet and waves his black tricornered chapeau high over his head.

Yet the French and Indians do not immediately open fire. Instead, they move toward the British lines while simultaneously fanning wide until they surround the enemy on three sides.

The center of the French line is a disciplined band of marines well versed in forest fighting. Their uniforms are not the garish red of the British or even the bright blue of the American colonists, but consist of brown moccasins and leggings of a type borrowed from the Indians. Like Captain Beaujeu, many marines are stripped to the waist and slathered in bear grease.

These hardened men now completely block the British advance. A fight is inevitable. Beaujeu has chosen the perfect killing ground to make his stand, offering the British no room to move past the French and toward Fort Duquesne. Indians in the woods outflank the redcoats on the right and left.

Initially, the British are flustered by the

sight of the enemy, but their training soon takes over. Answering with cool precision the command to "fix your bayonets," they slide the seventeen-inch triangular blades over the ends of their musket barrels and march toward their enemy with outward calm. On the inside, however, these young men from England, Ireland, and Scotland are terrified. They fear the French, but not as much as they fear the Iroquois and the Delaware. The horror of getting scalped alive has been a frequent topic of late-night campfire conversation.

"God save the king," the grenadiers shout, forming into three neat lines to fire the first volley. Most shots go wild. Their Brown Bess muskets cannot be aimed accurately at a distance greater than fifty yards, thanks to a lack of rifling grooves in the barrel, so volley fire is the only way to hit any targets at all. Yet the British draw first blood: two young French officers are hit, one shot through the mouth.

The French once again dive for cover. As the grenadiers reload for the second volley, two British six-pound cannon are dragged forward into firing positions. With rehearsed precision, the grenadiers part ranks as the guns are aimed and loaded in their lines, ensuring that none of them is hit by the deadly salvoes of canister shot soon fired at the French.

The effect is immediate. If the greatest fear of British soldiers is being scalped, the French and Indians tremble just as mightily at the mutilation wrought by canister and grape. Each round contains fifty-six balls weighing 1.5 ounces each. These flying pieces of hot, jagged metal now shred limbs and torsos. "Every man for himself," cried out in French, echoes up and down the ridgeline. The Canadian militia, whom Beaujeu has long suspected of cowardice, abandons its position as its men run from the battle. Beaujeu and his remaining men cower behind the ancient oaks and walnut trees, taking advantage of the cover provided by the white smoke from musket fire that now settles over the land like a low cloud.

The British fire a third volley.

A single musket ball pierces the forehead of Captain Beaujeu.

His body slumps to the ground. No one rushes to check for signs of life. Instead, the battle Beaujeu planned so meticulously continues to rage as he lies facedown in the dirt at the edge of a ravine.

The captain's death undoes the French. Even many Indians flee the battle. Not only have the British thwarted the ambush within a matter of minutes, but they have done so without suffering any loss of life. Roaring a cheer of self-congratulation, the grenadiers rush forward to claim their victory — a fatal mistake for many.

Not all the Indians have run away.

Gen. Edward Braddock once bragged to Benjamin Franklin that these native warriors would be no match for His Majesty's Army. The truth is that the Indians are the most experienced fighting force on this battlefield. They have been stealthily observing the British for a month, awaiting this moment of attack. Their knowledge of this landscape and of the tactics required to win the engagement is beyond the comprehension of the pale and blistered soldiers they now face. Even the British officers on horseback, whose bright red uniforms make them such an easy target, are no match for these brave men.

As the British grenadiers race forward with great commotion, the remaining Indians now begin shooting from the right and left sides of the column, unleashing a brutal cross fire that catches the grenadiers completely off guard.

The Indians' next gambit is equally unexpected. Rather than standing in one place to fight, as the British expect from their opponents on the battlefield, the tribes run like deer through the woods, bounding over rocks, hiding behind trees to reload and shoot, then sprinting toward a new field of fire. High-pitched war cries pierce the air, making it seem as if the Indians were everywhere at once. It is a scream the British will never forget, "perhaps the most horrid sound that can be imagined," one account will later read.

The grenadiers fire a fourth round, but that will be their last. Order is soon lost. The neat lines of British soldiers that launched precise volleys into the French lines just moments ago have been replaced by a jumble of terrified men shooting at anything that moves. Indians storm the British lines. The thick white clouds of musket smoke add to the chaos.

Most of these men will never see England again. This they now know. Panicked grenadiers turn and run. Officers attempting to stop them are ignored — some even shot by their own desperate men.

Indians quickly fall upon the stragglers, shouldering their cherished Tulle fusil muskets so they can kill face-to-face. The sickening thud of spiked clubs cracking open skull after British skull combines with the war cries and musket cracks and the whinny of dying horses.

A senior British officer is shot from his horse. As he breathes his last, a junior officer who happens to be his son runs to the rescue, only to be shot dead and fall motionless atop his father's body.

Capt. Robert Cholmley of the Forty-Eighth is also shot from the saddle. He is scalped as he lies wounded. Just eight months ago, before sailing from his home in Ireland to America, Cholmley sensed that this campaign might not end well. "As to my body, where the leaf falls, let it rot," he wrote in his will.

So it is. The veteran officer's corpse will never be buried or moved from this spot. He truly will be left to rot. Perhaps the greatest indignity is Captain Cholmley's final moment of life, as two warriors pull the brain from his head and smear its gray matter on their bodies as a sign of domination.

Cholmley is not alone in his debasement. Blood is everywhere, in streaks on faces and uniforms, pooling on the forest floor. Dead grenadiers litter the earth. Almost every British officer is shot. The peaked miter caps that were once the most distinctive element of the grenadier uniform lie scattered atop the carpet of leaves, knocked from the heads of the dead in the instant before foreheads were sliced and scalps peeled away from the bone with expert precision.*

Each Indian carries a length of cord for handcuffing prisoners, but they have no use for that right now. This is no longer a French-led battle but, rather, a lesson in terror meted out by these hardened warriors — and killing is the only thing on their minds.

George Washington gallops toward the fight.

At first, the distant snap of musket fire seemed a trifle, just British advance scouts

*The practice of taking a human body part as a trophy of war is a global phenomenon dating back thousands of years. It was often customary to present the severed head of an enemy to a king in exchange for a share of the plunder. However, it was impractical to carry human heads for any great distance or period of time, so taking just the scalp became more prevalent. This was done by grasping the victim's hair and making deep cuts into the flesh on the front and sides of the skull before yanking the scalp free. The Indians were not the only side taking scalps during the French and Indian War. The governor of Massachusetts offered a bounty for the scalp of any Indian warrior, woman, or child.

trading shots with Indian outrangers. From his position at the rear of the column, along with the baggage, camp followers, and cattle, Washington seemed safe from harm. "We . . . believed our numbers almost equal to the Canadian force. They only expected to annoy us," Washington later wrote of the confidence displayed by the British and the blue-coated Virginia militia, a hardy band of colonists also known as the "Brave Blues."

But as the sound of shots increased in intensity, followed by bloodcurdling Indian war cries, it became clear that this was more than a mere skirmish. General Braddock instantly ordered his top aides, Washington among them, to spur their horses. They now race up the rocky, uneven road, past teamsters and wagons, and toward the disarray that now characterizes the battlefield.

A favorite Indian tactic is to kill enemy leaders to create confusion among the troops, and it is clear to all who witness Braddock's arrival that he is every bit the British senior officer. It is not just his age and girth that give him away, but also the beautiful white charger on which he rides and the bright red and gold of his clean uniform.

Washington quickly learns that his blue

uniform and breeches also make him a marked man. A musket ball penetrates his coat, embedding itself in the thick fabric but going no farther. His horse is shot out from under him. As the animal collapses in death, Washington is thrown to the ground. He collects the pillow from the saddle and scrambles to his feet, desperate to find a new horse. The smells of carnage attack his senses: gun smoke, excrement, vomit, and urine. Grenadiers racing back from the front have collided headlong with the main body of British soldiers advancing toward the fight. They've formed themselves into clumps of twenty to thirty men, praying that their numbers will protect them. The grenadiers refuse to advance, and General Braddock refuses to order a retreat. The soldiers simply huddle and await their fate. The Indians oblige, shooting men one by one from the protective cover of a nearby ravine.

Meanwhile, a riderless horse trots in panicked circles. Washington quickly grabs its reins. In the midst of the battle, he takes the time to place his pillow upon the saddle. Given the horror of seeing men butchered before his very eyes, the luxury of doing battle atop a cushion seems absurd, but there is no other way for him to fight.

As he mounts the horse, he winces in pain. In his weakened state, the simple act of pulling himself up onto a horse's back requires all his strength. Soon he is astride, and once again galloping through the chaos to encourage the troops. But his efforts are in vain. "Our numbers consisted of about 1300 well armed men, chiefly regulars, who were immediately struck with such a deadly panic . . . that confusion and disobedience of orders prevailed among them," he will later remember.

Washington has long feared this sort of ambush. His time at Fort Necessity one year ago taught him the need for unconventional fighting tactics. He insisted to General Braddock that the elite British troops give up their traditional uniforms and instead fight wearing "Indian dress," in buckskin tunics, leggings, and moccasins, if not for camouflage, then for greater ease of movement. Washington also encouraged Braddock to abandon the traditional straight lines from the British order of battle, allowing the soldiers to fight as small fire teams in the manner of their Indian opponents.

The general ignored him. Braddock enjoys Washington's company, and is delighted to have him on staff, but an undeniable air of disdain defines the attitude of the British toward the colonials, whom Braddock at least considers to be second-class citizens. Washington's charisma, wit, and intellect are greatly appreciated at the dinner table, as is his courage in accompanying the expedition as a volunteer aide-de-camp, but in matters of military strategy, George Washington is considered a precocious fool.★

Washington's hat is shot from his head. Another musket ball nicks his coat. An incredible sort of luck seems to follow him now — the musket balls do not so much as touch his skin. In all, four musket balls will

---

★Washington held the rank of colonel in the Virginia militia in 1754, during his initial foray into the Ohio Country. After being criticized for his military ineptitude and naked ambition on the failed expedition, he resigned his commission. Even if he had not, the hierarchy of the relationship between the British Army and the colonial militias was such that even as a colonel, Washington would have been junior in rank to any other British officer. Nevertheless, it was Washington's hope one day to secure a commission in the British Army. Seeking to gain an influential friend in Braddock while at the same time salvaging his pride, Washington arranged for the volunteer position as the general's aide.

A young George Washington, colonel of the Virginia regiment

strike him today, yet the Virginian will leave this battle unscathed.

His new horse is shot out from under him. Again, Washington is thrown to the ground and hurries to find another mount. Every officer on horseback will be killed or wounded today — all except the young Virginia volunteer.

Washington hurls himself onto a horse and weaves through the chaos, his sword drawn as he screams orders for the British to close ranks and return to the fight. He is disgusted by what he sees. "They ran as sheep pursued by dogs," he will later write. "[I]t was impossible to rally them."

It is equally clear to Washington that the Brave Blues of the Virginia militia are outfighting the British regulars. This is not unexpected. The Brave Blues are battling to protect their families and homes, knowing that if the French and Indians win this engagement, there will be little to stop them from marauding through Virginia.

Yet, rather than encouraging the Brave Blues to continue their successful strategy of fighting behind rocks and trees — "treeing," in the vernacular of the British Army — Braddock loudly denounces the Virginians as "cowards and dastards," and even strikes them with the flat of his sword to force them out into the open.

In the end, few Brave Blues will return home. "They fought like soldiers and died like men," Washington will lament of the fallen.

The handful of Brave Blues who make it

home will bring with them a new spirit of independence: from this day forward, it will be clear that the Americans no longer need the British to fight their battles.

In fact, on this day, it is the British who need the Americans, but even they can't reverse the horrible course of the battle.

In the first hour of combat, the grenadiers are routed.

In the second hour of fighting wagon teamster Daniel Boone cuts his horse loose from its traces and joins a group of unarmed teamsters galloping away from the slaughter. Almost all will live.

In the third hour of combat, Gen. Edward Braddock is mortally wounded by a musket ball. He has had four horses shot out from under him, and is struck in the right arm and lungs as he mounts a fifth. Knowing the battle is lost, and that great shame and humiliation will be heaped upon him, Braddock begs for a pistol so that he might take his own life. His aides ignore him.

The general then calls for George Washington, the one man who knows this terrain better than any of the British.

Ride, Braddock tells Washington. Ride for help.

It is past four in the afternoon. Washington is still weak from illness, and emotionally drained from three hours of battle. The summer heat and humidity have caused him to sweat through his linen shirt and thick wool uniform coat. He is thirsty and hungry, and knows that critical reinforcements and medical supplies are dozens of miles away through the wilderness.

George Washington was new to warfare when he surrendered to the French at Fort Necessity a year ago. Though eager and well meaning, he blundered through that conflict and returned home in disgrace. His courage was never an issue, nor his desire to learn from that debacle. He was sure that volunteering as an aide-de-camp to Braddock might replace that memory with one far more glorious.

But the opposite has happened: Braddock has lost; the British have been routed, almost to a man; and the colonies are now defenseless against a French and Indian attack. There is little glory to be gained from what has happened today. The British captives will be paraded back to Fort Duquesne at twilight — the women to be raped, the men to be burned alive for the amusement of the French and Indians.*

*The lopsided nature of the French and Indian victory over Braddock's army is best viewed

34

Yet, on this day, Washington ceased being a surveyor and Virginia gentleman.

Today, he became a warrior.

Strapping his pillow tightly to his saddle, George Washington obeys Braddock's order.

---

through the number of fatalities. Though exact statistics are unknown, it is estimated that the French and Indians suffered approximately thirty deaths. The British and colonial armies lost more than five hundred. An equal number of British were wounded. Those female members of the British caravan were either wives accompanying their husbands or "necessary women," whose duties were consistent with those traditionally associated with maids. It is believed that thirteen of these women were taken captive by the Indians, among them, one who was clubbed to death on the way back to Fort Duquesne for walking too slowly.

The French later returned to the battlefield and buried their dead. Some were interred where they fell. The body of Capt. Daniel-Hyacinthe-Marie Liénard de Beaujeu was carried back to Fort Duquesne (now the site of modern-day Pittsburgh) for burial. The bodies of the British, however, were left to rot. For three years, the decaying bones of British and colonial soldiers littered the forest. It was only in 1758 that a British force returned to the area and buried them all in a common grave. Among the deceased was Sir Peter

Halkett, shot from his horse early in the battle. His son James was mortally wounded while coming to Halkett's aid and collapsed atop his dead father's chest. Their two skeletons were found in the same position by the burial party. The elder Halkett, a former member of Parliament, was positively identified by a false tooth still embedded in his jaw. Both men were wrapped in the tartan cloth of their Scottish homeland and laid to rest in a ceremony featuring drum and pipe.

1

Philadelphia, Pennsylvania
June 16, 1775
8:00 A.M.

George Washington is out for blood.

Twenty years almost to the day after Braddock's Defeat, as the infamous battle in the Ohio River Valley has come to be known, the six-foot-two Virginian pushes back his chair and rises to his feet. Seventy-year-old Benjamin Franklin watches him from across the cramped Assembly Room here in the Pennsylvania State House. Delegates to the Second Continental Congress sit in high-backed chairs, their papers splayed before them on cloth-covered tables, waiting to hear if Washington will accept the new title he has been offered.

At the head of the room on this oppressively humid Friday morning, overseeing the proceedings, sits John Hancock, the

37

wealthiest man in Massachusetts and president of the Congress. A man of medium height and build, he is thirty-eight and soon to be married, with a baby already on the way. Born the son of a clergyman, Hancock was sent to live with a rich uncle at the age of seven, after his father had died and his mother could no longer care for him. The uncle had no children of his own, so Hancock was raised to take over the family's highly successful import-export business. In time, Hancock added to his growing wealth by becoming a smuggler of wine, tea, molasses, and tobacco. His duties as president of the Congress are slight — most often, mediating debate. On days when the arguments become loud enough for people outside the tall windows ringing the Assembly Room to hear what is being said, Hancock might insist that they be kept closed. But this morning, thanks to the temperature and thick morning air, they are wide open.*

*Construction on the Pennsylvania State House began in 1732 but was not completed for more than twenty years. At the time, it was one of the most ambitious buildings in the colonies. In 1824, the Assembly Room was rechristened the "Hall of Independence," which was later shorted to "Inde-

Sitting on the aisle next to the second row of desks is Benjamin Franklin. He is weary but attentive, his impish sense of humor nowhere to be seen. Just six weeks ago, he returned home from eleven years in England. Unfortunately, his wife, Deborah, who had remained in Philadelphia due to fear of ocean travel, had died during Franklin's absence. Shortly before last Christmas, she was felled by a stroke. Her husband got the news while living in a small brick row house between Charing Cross and the Strand, in London.

As much as he misses his wife, it is not her passing that lays the biggest burden on Franklin's heart. His original purpose for sailing to London had been to act on behalf of his home colony, seeking to establish a

---

pendence Hall," a name that became synonymous with the entire building. On February 22, 1861, President-elect Abraham Lincoln visited Independence Hall on his way to Washington, DC. Four years later, on April 22–24, 1865, Lincoln's body lay in state in the same room on its way back to Illinois for burial. More than eighty-five thousand mourners filed through to pay their respects. A bronze marker indicates the spot where another fallen American president, John F. Kennedy, spoke while visiting Independence Hall on July 4, 1962.

closer relationship between Pennsylvania and the British Crown. But the effort was soon overshadowed by England's exploitative policy of taxing the American colonies to pay British debts. Onerous legislation such as the Molasses Act, Sugar Act, and Townshend Acts forced the Americans to pay duties on everyday amenities such as rum, paper, paint, and glass, with all the revenue flowing to England — all to pay for the same frontier defenses the colonies already provided for themselves. The colonists believe this to be illegal.

Even worse, there was no attempt to allow the colonists a voice in Parliament, leading many to fume that "taxation without representation" was a form of slavery.

The Intolerable Acts of 1774 went a step further, punishing the people of Massachusetts by abolishing their provincial government and installing a British general as the colony's new governor.

At first the enraged colonists responded by actually beating tax collectors. With rebellion in the air, Franklin's focus changed. Instead of just Pennsylvania, he found himself representing all the colonies as a diplomat, working tirelessly to keep the peace.

Franklin is not a timid man. He knows

there is a time and a place for war. In 1755, shortly after Braddock's stunning annihilation left the colonies wide open to French and Indian attack, more than four hundred white settlers were slaughtered and scalped in Pennsylvania. It was Franklin who led the call for a state militia to defend the people. His pleas were ignored until the bodies of those dead settlers were brought by wagon to Philadelphia and dumped on the steps of this very statehouse.

Two days later, Franklin had his army.

In his efforts to prevent war between England and America, Franklin has made every effort to be impartial. "In England," he once wrote of the criticism thrown his way, "I am accused of being too much an American, and in America of being too much an Englishman."

Now, despite his diligent efforts, war has come. On April 19, 1775, shortly after he boarded a ship for the voyage home to America, the Battles of Lexington and Concord in Massachusetts saw the first casualties of a conflict that would eventually become known as the Revolutionary War.*

*In England, it will be known as the War of American Independence.

41

■ ■ ■ ■

On this very day, north of Boston, twelve hundred colonial soldiers are hastily building defensive fortifications on the hills of the Charlestown Peninsula. Breed's Hill and Bunker Hill offer a commanding view of Boston, a city of fifteen thousand people and long a hotbed of loathing toward the British. The Crown has occupied Boston since 1768, as it tightened restrictions in the most rebellious of colonies, controlling the ebb and flow of daily life while carefully monitoring the growing divide between "patriots," as the rebels call themselves, and the Loyalists. There has been bloodshed as a result of this friction, most notably the Boston Massacre in 1770, when British soldiers fired into a patriot mob, killing five men. Currently, a force of six thousand regulars is garrisoned within Boston's one-square-mile limits.*

Were it not for a thin stretch of land known as the Roxbury Neck connecting it to the Massachusetts coastline, Boston would be an island. Colonial troops under

*"Regulars" are so-called because they are career soldiers who serve on a daily basis rather than being called out only when needed.

Artemas Ward control access to the Neck, forming a narrow barrier preventing the British from marching out of Boston and expanding their control of the surrounding towns. Yet, while the English may be contained, they are by no means cut off. They control Boston, which means that English ships come and go with impunity, resupplying the regular army garrison and preventing the military siege that would see British food and ammunition choked off. The Massachusetts Colony has no navy to contest these vessels, many of which are armed with cannon. Thus, a stalemate has existed for months between the two forces — and continues to this day, despite the skirmishes at Lexington and Concord two months ago.

If the British were to take control of Bunker Hill and Breed's Hill, the colonists would lose a key strategic position. From their lofty summits overlooking Boston Harbor and the city itself, the colonists can fire cannonballs — which is why the British have spent the last three weeks secretly plotting an invasion of the Charlestown Peninsula, to capture those heights. But just two days ago, on June 13, the rebels got word of the British plans. Working day and night, they have been preparing redoubts from which to fend off the redcoats. Six feet high, made of earth, with wooden platforms on the interior from which men can stand to fire their muskets, the square-shaped fortifications are protected from assault by ditches around their perimeter.

Early on the morning of June 17, British warships fire on Breed's Hill and Bunker Hill, to little effect. The emboldened colonists endure a sweltering day in the sun as they await the next move from the English. Soon, they spot longboats rowing soldiers from Boston over to the Charlestown Peninsula. The flotilla is massive, ferrying some fifteen hundred grenadiers and light infantry across the harbor. Some of the colonists quietly desert, retreating back toward Cambridge rather than facing sure death. Those who choose to remain will long remember the confusion of that day, as the local militia volunteers mill about with a lack of military discipline, even as the British regulars fix their bayonets and prepare for the attack. The mere sight of them is daunting: hundreds of red-coated soldiers stand abreast, lining up in four neat rows, prepared to launch a full-frontal assault on the hastily built colonial defenses. When American snipers fired from buildings in the town of Charlestown, British cannon responded with red-hot shot, setting fire to the city and casting great plumes of smoke into the air.

Yet it is the colonists who win the early stages of the fight, thanks to the strength of their defensive positions. Shooting with a sniper's precision, they pick off the English with ease. Many grenadier and infantry units lose almost all their men, some with "only eight or nine men a company left," in the words of one English observer. It appears to be a stunning repeat of Braddock's Defeat, a comparison made all the more apparent by the fact that the British commander, Gen. Thomas Gage, served side by side with George Washington at that battle as another aide to Braddock.

The first British attack stalls when the light infantry, attempting to turn the American flank, is decimated by fire from a barrier on the shoreline. A second assault fares only slightly better. The British entered the battle believing the colonists would run at the first smell of gunpowder. Their arrogance has been costly, the grenadiers' advance slowed by fences and other obstacles that disarray their columns and allow them to be cut to ribbons by the fortified colonial positions. Dead redcoats lie sprawled in the dense grass just outside the American fortifications. The wounded and the dying cry for help, but their pleas go unanswered.

As afternoon turns to evening, however, the colonists run out of ammunition. Only then does the tide of the battle turn toward the British. The colonists' muskets, used more often for hunting dinner than killing men, lack bayonets. So, as the professional soldiers come over the parapets during the third English assault in late afternoon, the combatants resort to hand-to-hand fighting, and the battle swings toward the English.

Having no other choice, the colonists retreat, leaving Breed's Hill and Bunker Hill to the British. They flee toward Cambridge where they will have safety in numbers, some getting caught by British bayonets but most escaping. The retreat is orderly and precise, saving the lives of hundreds of colonists and preventing their imprisonment. And while they have lost what will become known as the Battle of Bunker Hill, the men of Massachusetts have extracted a fierce toll: almost eight hundred wounded and more than two hundred dead, including a large number of officers. Most astounding: almost half of all British soldiers entering this battle are now casualties.

Sir William Howe, a British general newly arrived from England, will report this shocking news back to London: "When I look to the consequences of it, in the loss of so many brave officers, I do it with horror — the success is too dearly bought."

All the fighting in Boston will take place tomorrow. Right now, the Continental Congress is deciding who will form and lead the American army. "Resolved," the minutes of its June 15 meeting read, "that a general be appointed to command all continental forces raised or to be raised, for the defense of American liberty. That five hundred dollars a month be allowed for his pay and expenses."*

Though the salary is lavish, the obstacles to success are many. Enthusiasm for the fight is high throughout the colonies, but most potential soldiers prefer to remain close to home, serving with their local militia, taking orders from friends and relatives. The idea of fighting in a Continental Army, obeying the directives of strangers, and waging war hundreds of miles from their families is distasteful. It will be the role of the new general to convince those uneducated and unsophisticated men that accepting his commands is in their best

*More than fifteen thousand dollars per month in modern currency.

interest.

Then, of course, there is the harsh penalty for failure.

If the new commander in chief can successfully raise, train, feed, clothe, and equip an army, he must still find a way to defeat the British regulars, widely considered the world's greatest fighting force. Should he lose, this new general will not merely be placed in captivity as a prisoner of war, he will be treated as a traitor to the British Crown and hanged for high treason.

This will not, however, be an ordinary hanging.

High treason is considered the greatest capital crime a man can commit against the king of England. The punishment is extraordinary, ensuring a slow and hideous death. It will begin when the accused is tied to a horse and dragged to the gallows. He will then be hanged by the neck, but cut down before he dies so that he remains alive for what comes next, which is the slicing open of his abdomen and the burning of his intestines as they dangle outside his body. Only then will this general have his head cut off. His corpse will then be cut up into four parts, all of which will be delivered to the king. But the punishment will not end there. All lands and monies will be confiscated from this unlucky man's estate. His wife and children will be forever forbidden from purchasing property or owning a business. And, of course, if the general's wife should also be accused of treason for conspiring with her husband, she will be burned alive.

Ben Franklin no longer has a wife, but as he looks around the cramped Assembly Room on this June morning, he is well aware that simply attending this seditious meeting to discuss waging war against the Crown is grounds for high treason. It is not just the new general who stands to stretch a rope, but every single delegate in the room. Simply traveling to Philadelphia to attend the Congress was an act of great courage, for a recent smallpox epidemic in the city killed three hundred men, women, and children.* With no assurances that the outbreak has passed, the delegates entered the city to take part in the uncertain business of forging a nation.

*Philadelphia's population at the time was approximately thirty thousand. The bulk of the city was located along the waterfront, while the area now known as Independence Hall was several blocks inland, close to what was then the city's outskirts.

The problem facing these men now, even after war has broken out, is that Georgia, not yet believing fully in the cause of independence, has refused to send a delegate to this convention. In other words, the thirteen colonies are still unwilling to stand together as one to fight for their common future.

It is Franklin who will sound the ominous reminder of their fate if this does not change: "We must, indeed, all hang together — or most assuredly we will all hang separately."

Despite the long odds against defeating England, a number of men have stepped forward to apply for the generalship. Candidates include the slovenly British-born lieutenant colonel Charles Lee, a man with a temper so fierce that during the French and Indian War, the Iroquois nicknamed him Ounewaterika, "Boiling Water." Lee is missing two fingers, thanks to a dueling accident, and has a passion for prostitutes that will one day be his undoing.

Another candidate is Artemas Ward, a fiery, heavyset forty-seven-year-old Bostonian who is presently commanding the forces at Bunker Hill. Ward, who suffers frequent bouts of ill health, enjoys a reputation as a military leader so illustrious that Massachusetts has appointed him commander in chief of "the Grand American Army," as the collection of local militias has been nicknamed by the press.

However, the most popular choice is the genteel John Hancock. Despite a lack of military experience, the Massachusetts native feels that his service as president of this Congress entitles him to be appointed commander in chief. He is a man born to privilege, fond of expensive wine, dancing, and the pursuit of life's many pleasures. Rather than simply travel on horseback, for instance, Hancock drives a carriage pulled by six matching bay-colored horses. His mode of dress is shocking in its garishness: "He wore a coat of scarlet, lined with silk, and . . . a white satin embroidered waist coat, dark satin small clothes, white silk stockings, and shoes with silver buckles," one observer wrote.

John Hancock presumed he would be given the title of commander in chief as thanks for his serving as president of this Congress. In fact, he presumes many things, thinking himself worthy of almost every great honor. Ironically, Hancock is not in favor of colonial independence. He is a hardened Anglophile who spent four years in London learning to run the House of Hancock, the family business that revolves around the sale of British goods to the colonies — in particular, whale oil. His loyalty to the British throne led him to attend the London funeral of King George II in November 1760, and then remain in England for the coronation of the current monarch, George III, ten months later.

In truth, Hancock has more to lose than almost any other man in this room. His livelihood depends on the freedom of the high seas, allowing his ships to smuggle Dutch tea and French molasses into the colonies. The outbreak of war will see an end to that. John Hancock will never be a pauper, but he will also never see the heights of wealth he knew before the disruption in trade caused by the war with Great Britain.

There are, in fact, three deeply divided factions within the Second Continental Congress, all with separate ideas about America's future. The more conservative group longs for a return to traditional ties with England. The most radical group, led by John Adams, argues for complete independence — although they rarely discuss this in public, for the notion is so outlandish as to border on heretical. The most popular faction, of which Hancock is a member, wants to maintain ties with England but considers the British Parliament corrupt and duplicitous, and believes it has no authority in the colonies. These men want America to report directly to George III, whom they see as their ally and dear friend. Hancock believes a strong military statement might achieve that end.

Because Hancock is not totally in favor of separation, delegate John Adams of Massachusetts is uncomfortable with him forming a Continental Army and leading it into battle. He is also of the belief that the support of the southern colonies is vital to defeating the British. Rather than select Ward or Hancock, both of whom hail from Adams's home state, Adams has persuaded his cousin, the fiery Samuel Adams, to help him nominate George Washington as the man to lead the Continental Army. Washington is known for his military bearing and rational behavior. The fact that he hails from Virginia will definitely bring about a tighter colonial alliance.

Thus, two days ago, John Adams stood to address the delegates. He and Hancock have known each other since childhood, and it was Hancock's father who baptized the newborn John Adams in 1735. As a beaming Hancock looked on, believing his friend was about to nominate him, the loquacious Adams opened his remarks by speaking of the "state of the Colonies" and "the need to appoint a general."

Then Adams shocked the room, stating that "a gentleman from Virginia" should lead the new army.

Suddenly, John Hancock's demeanor changed.

"I never remarked a sudden or more striking change of countenance," John Adams would later write about Hancock. "Mortification and resentment were expressed as forcibly as his face could exhibit them."

As the room exploded into debate, George Washington immediately left so he would be out of earshot as the delegates discussed the matter.

The following day, another motion was made to name the forty-three-year-old Washington commander in chief. A newcomer to the Continental Congress, Thomas Jefferson, seconded the motion.*

*The man who nominated Washington was the remarkable Thomas Johnson of Maryland. Forty-two at the time, Johnson would later go on to lead troops in the Revolutionary War, serve as the first governor of Maryland once it became a state, serve as a justice of the U.S. Supreme Court, and

In a letter to his wife, Martha, Washington will declare that he never lobbied for the job, stating that "far from seeking this appointment, I have used every endeavor in my power to avoid it."

That is not true. Franklin and the other fifty-five delegates have been quite aware of Washington's burning desire to lead the rebel army, primarily out of boredom. Washington needs action. His ambition is impossible to ignore. Nowhere has this been more in evidence than in his choice of clothing. Every day since arriving in Philadelphia one month ago, the forty-three-year-old Virginian has dressed in a blue military uniform quite similar in design to his battle dress at Braddock's Defeat. No other delegate dresses in this manner. And although that battle took place twenty years ago next month, the uniform is a reminder to everyone that Washington is a seasoned warrior. It was he who oversaw Braddock's burial those many years ago, and then ordered the remaining British soldiers to trample back and forth over the dirt to hide the grave from the French and Indians, lest they

---

insist that a new national capital known as "Federal City" be renamed in honor of George Washington.

exhume the body.

Washington has done well for himself militarily since Braddock's Defeat, returning to the Ohio River Valley as part of another British force in 1758, this time winning the battle and wresting territory from the French.

He has also climbed the social ladder. Also in 1758, he rekindled his love for a wealthy, dark-eyed, British-born member of Virginia society, the beautiful twenty-eight-year-old Sally Fairfax. Washington's passion for the fairer sex is well known, with his friends even giving him the nickname "the stallion of the Potomac." However, his status as a planter and surveyor saw him rebuffed by two wealthy young women in his early twenties. In the case of Sally Fairfax, the affection was mutual, yet the affair was doomed from the start, for Washington was not wealthy enough at the time to be a suitable match — more important, Sally was already married, to one of his good friends.*

*Although there is no proof the couple consummated their relationship, Washington openly professed his love to Mrs. Fairfax in writing. "The world has no business to know the object of my love, declared in this manner to you," he stated in a secret letter to Fairfax while engaged to Martha

Instead, Washington took the widowed Martha Dandridge Custis for his bride in 1759. The marriage elevated Washington into the highest levels of colonial society. This was no accident. Washington was so keen to woo the rich young widow that he took a break from his military career in March 1758 to pay a visit to her home, just eight short months after the death of her husband. Martha was smitten by the tall man who arrived at her house that day with his reddish-brown hair carefully powdered. Nine days after their first meeting, he proposed. Soon after, Martha ordered a wedding dress from a shop in London. The dress itself was modest, as a reminder that she had just ended a time of mourning. She also purchased purple slippers for the occasion, as a symbol of the new joy she had found with the gallant Washington.

Custis. Sally Fairfax visited Washington and Martha frequently after their marriage, but moved to England with her husband, George William Fairfax, in 1773. She remained there long after Fairfax's death. In 1798, Washington wrote her, urging a return to Virginia, reminding her of "those happy moments, the happiest of my life, that I have enjoyed in your company." She ignored him, dying alone in England in 1811.

One foot shorter and eight months older than her second husband, the plump and pretty Martha is known for her charm and iron will. Her home is called White House, a Virginia tobacco plantation of 17,500 acres holding more than three hundred slaves. But George and Martha choose to live at a smaller estate, one passed to Washington upon the death of his half brother, Lawrence. Mount Vernon, as it is known, is a 6,500-acre parcel of land that requires more than one hundred slaves to function smoothly.* The combined population of all thirteen colonies is 2.5 million, of which 500,000 are slaves — one in five people. At the time of the Second Continental Congress, George Washington owns 135 men, women, and children; his wife's slaves are her separate property.†

*In 1759 Mount Vernon was approximately 3,170 acres. Over the next thirty-plus years, Washington added various parcels of land that increased the size to almost 7,600 acres.

†Shortly after Washington's death, a series of suspicious fires was set at Mount Vernon. This led many to believe that his slaves were growing restless. Martha granted them their freedom on January 1, 1801, and many said it was because she feared for her life. However, by law, she could not

The sixteen years of retirement from the military since the French and Indian War have been a time of prosperity for Washington. He has become one of the wealthiest men in the colonies. The one great disappointment in his life is that he has not fathered any children. He refuses to admit that he is the problem, blaming it instead on Martha. But the truth is that Washington is likely sterile due to his teenage bout of smallpox.*

Back in Philadelphia, Washington is a man in need of a challenge. Wealth and power

---

free the slaves she had inherited from her first husband forty years earlier. These individuals were passed down to her heirs upon her death.

*Martha was first married to Daniel Parke Custis, twenty years her senior, when she was just eighteen years old. He died in 1757 after seven years of marriage. Martha gave birth to four children during that time. However, even in an age when fewer than 60 percent of children lived to the age of twenty, the deaths of her two oldest children before they turned five was a staggering loss. Martha's two remaining children, John Parke "Jacky" Custis, and Martha Parke "Patsy" Custis lived to see her marry George Washington. However, Patsy died of seizures in 1773 at the age of seventeen. Jacky Custis died in 1781 at the age of twenty-six.

are not enough. He is a man of action. He remembers the lessons in drill and tactics he learned during his time with the British Army. He knows where to place troops on the battlefield and how to exploit an enemy's weaknesses. This belief in himself gives Washington an inner strength that is evident to the delegates. "He seems discreet and virtuous," notes Connecticut lawyer Eliphalet Dyer, "no harum scarum ranting swearing fellow, but sober, steady and calm."

John Adams, a man known for his dour outlook, is also taken with Washington's disposition. "Something charming to me in the conduct of Washington. A gentleman of one of the first fortunes on the continent, leaving his delicious retirement, his family and friends, sacrificing his ease, and hazarding all in the cause of his country!"

So, just as George Washington once rode through the night to gain assistance for General Braddock's defeated army, he has now made the decision to put his life on the line fighting the British.

The vote has been counted.

The choice is unanimous.

Washington will have his chance to defeat England on the battlefield. "As the Congress desire it, I will enter upon the momentous duty, and exert every power I possess in their service, and for support of the glorious cause," he tells the assembled delegates as he accepts his command.

Then, in a move that the frugal Ben Franklin admires tremendously, the wealthy and powerful Washington says he will do it all for free.

"As to pay, Sir," Washington continues, "I beg leave to assure the Congress, that, as no pecuniary consideration could have tempted me to have accepted this arduous employment, at the expense of my domestic ease and happiness, I do not wish to make any profit from it."

General Washington leaves for Boston in the morning.

Three weeks later, on July 8, the Georgians finally decide to send delegates to Philadelphia and formally ally themselves with those fighting the war against England.

2

London, England
October 26, 1775
11:15 A.M.

King George III has had enough.

From within the plush confines of his golden royal carriage, the tall and youthful thirty-seven-year-old monarch rehearses the speech he will give from a throne in the House of Lords in one hour's time. The opening of Parliament, over which he will preside this morning, normally takes place later in the year. But because of the situation in America, George III has ordered that the event be held earlier.

The king will soon don royal robes of crimson velvet trimmed in the soft white winter fur of a stoat.* A gray ceremonial wig and a crown festooned with diamonds

*Also called ermine. A stoat is a member of the weasel family.

King George III

will adorn his blond hair. To the thousands of cheering loyal subjects witnessing his journey through the streets of London, their sovereign rides in apparent luxury, seated within the satin and velvet confines of the four-ton state coach. But the gaudy carriage has steel wheels and a Moroccan leather suspension so ineffective that riding inside is like "tossing in a rough sea," in the words of one of the king's sons.

The journey might be easier if his queen,

Charlotte, were at his side, for he cherishes her and treasures her support. The couple lives at Buckingham House, an estate next to St. James's Park in London.* They are thought by many to be a boring couple, fond of gardening and a frugal lifestyle. George agreed to marry Charlotte before even meeting her, understanding his traditional duties — he needed a wife.

George III chose Charlotte to be his bride because she had been born in northern Germany, like his own ancestors. The courtship was bizarre. An emissary sailed from England to present Charlotte's dying mother with a contract, written in Latin, stating that Charlotte would depart immediately for England, convert to the

*The official royal residence was St. James's Palace, but George III found it confining. He purchased Buckingham House in 1761, so named because it had once belonged to the Duke of Buckingham. The estate was also called the "Queen's House" because of Charlotte's deep affection for the property. The structure was greatly expanded in the nineteenth century. For a time, it was proposed that it house Parliament after a blaze in 1834 destroyed the Palace of Westminster. Instead, it became Buckingham Palace, the official royal residence to this day.

Anglican Church, and never involve herself in politics. Elisabeth Albertine of Saxe-Hildburghausen, a noblewoman eager to see her eighth child married, agreed to the contract but died before the British diplomat arrived in Germany. It was left to Charlotte's brother Adolphus Friedrich IV to sign on his mother's behalf.

Charlotte left for England immediately, never to return home again. Upon disembarking from the yacht *Royal Charlotte* after a stormy ten-day voyage from the North Sea port of Cuxhaven, she was whisked to London, where she met the king at the garden gate of St. James's Palace. The date was September 8, 1761. Charlotte spoke no English, and George was put off by her homely appearance, but the contract had already been signed.

They wed at nine o'clock that evening — Charlotte was just seventeen years old.

Two weeks later, in a lavish coronation at Westminster Abbey, George III was officially crowned king and Charlotte his queen. In their short time together, they had already become quite comfortable with each other, thanks to George's fluency in the German language.

During the coronation ceremony, one famous poet in attendance, Thomas Gray, noted that the couple did not act in a royal manner. They were so famished from the long day of festivities that all pretenses disappeared. Despite their meal being served on golden plates, the king and queen, in the words of Gray, ate "like farmers."

Royal expectations aside, George III is a lightning-fast eater who is fastidious about his weight. Breakfast is usually just bread and butter served with tea. Fruit is always on hand for snacking during the day. Dinner is served at 4:00 p.m., and is a simple portion of mutton, soup, vegetables, and a pudding, all washed down by barley water. Charlotte and George do not entertain often, but when they do, it is common for guests to race through their dinner, for etiquette prevents them from continuing the meal once the king has finished his last bite.

George III has come to love Charlotte deeply, despite initial concern about his bride's beauty. Their marriage will be long, and he will never be unfaithful. This is a highly unusual commitment for a British king. George is well aware that his grandfather and father both strayed from the marital bed, and he is intent on setting a different example for his children — of which there are many. Charlotte, who learns to speak English with a heavy German accent and likes to regale her husband with performances of "God Save the King" on the harpsichord, has been pregnant almost every moment of their fourteen-year marriage. The couple now has ten children. At this very moment, Charlotte is three months along with their eleventh, a princess. All told, she will bear fifteen royal heirs.

Charlotte's appearance is of mixed ethnicity, and despite many rumors, her African lineage will not become a matter of public discussion for more than two centuries. Going forward, however, whichever king or queen sits on the British throne will share Charlotte's African bloodline.*

*The roots of Charlotte's African lineage are unclear. Thanks to the intermarrying of Europe's royal families, it was not uncommon for houses from far-flung lands to be joined. Thus, Charlotte is thought to be either a distant descendant of the black Portuguese noblewoman Margarita y Castro de Sousa, or of Portuguese king Alfonso III and his mistress Mourana Gil, who was of Berber descent. Although portrait artists during her lifetime softened Charlotte's features to make them more British, one physician with close ties to the royal family stated for the record that she had the face of a mulatto. A poem written to commemorate Charlotte's wedding to George III

■ ■ ■ ■

Since the costly English victory at Bunker Hill three months ago, there have been no further battles between the British and George Washington's Continental Army. But through a long, wet summer, which has now turned into a cold, wetter autumn, George III has fumed about the American uprising. It could not have come at a worse time for him. The British people have begun to doubt his authority, equally shocked at the colonists' unruly behavior and the army's inability to stop it. On September 14, when the transport ship *Charming Nancy* arrives in Plymouth, England, carrying the wounded British survivors of Bunker Hill, newspapers report the shocking sight of "some without legs and others without arms, and their loose clothes hanging on them like morning gowns."

Making the *Charming Nancy*'s arrival even worse is the presence of sixty widows and children of men lost at Bunker Hill. They

---

included these lines alluding to her appearance: "Descended from the warlike Vandal race, She still preserves that title in her face."

are devastated.* The ship itself reeks of squalor and rotting flesh, an aroma so powerful that it can be smelled before the ship docks. The British may have won the Battle of Bunker Hill, but it is obvious that the victory came at a great price.

Soon, the returning soldiers began sharing their battlefield memories, explaining how the best-equipped and most highly trained army in all of Europe was nearly defeated by a ragtag bunch of colonists who lacked a clear chain of command. They told of the British general William Howe being so confident of triumph that a servant rode into battle at his side with a bottle of wine to slake the general's thirst. They also described the bravery of their American op-

*British regular army soldiers often traveled with their families. Wives did washing, worked as nurses, and sold alcoholic beverages. Children were allowed to remain with their fathers until the age of fourteen, when they were turned out to make a living for themselves. The widows of Bunker Hill, like all women who had lost a husband in combat, might remain with the army if they had gainful employment but were entitled to passage back to Great Britain if they chose, as did the women returning home on the *Charming Nancy.*

ponents, who refused to fire until the British were just fifty yards from their breastworks, thus ensuring massive slaughter of the tightly packed redcoat columns.* Officers were a favorite target of the colonial militias because of their brightly colored uniforms and the shiny gorgets protecting their throats.

But it was the horror of the third and final assault on the colonial positions that signaled to the people of England that the Americans had every intention of fighting to the bitter end. The rebels eventually retreated after they ran out of ammunition, with many of them shot in the back as they

*The phrase "don't fire until you see the whites of their eyes" is said to have been coined at Bunker Hill by Continental Army colonel Israel Putnam. This myth was propagated by nineteenth-century writer Mason Weems, the same man who concocted the legend about George Washington chopping down the cherry tree. In fact, the rebels were told to wait until they could see the tops of the gaiters the British troops wore around their ankles. Gaiters worn in America were black. Only those of the foot guards in London were white. In any case, "whites of their eyes" was first uttered by Prince Charles of Prussia in 1745 and Frederick the Great in 1757.

fled. But those who remained wreaked havoc on the British when their lines were finally breached. Despite the futility of that moment, when all was obviously lost, the Americans threw rocks at the attackers and swung the butts of their muskets as war clubs. British bayonets made quick work of those colonists, slaughtering so many in such a short period of time that the redcoats had to climb over the bodies of the dead to continue fighting the living. One British officer summed up the fighting this way: "[we] expected rather to punish a mob, rather than fight with troops that would look us in the face."

Shortly before the *Charming Nancy*'s return to England, George III issues A Proclamation for Suppressing Rebellion and Sedition. He acknowledges that the colonists have been "misled by dangerous and ill designing men, forgetting the allegiance which they owe to the power that has protected and supported them." He then goes on to authorize atrocities, including murder, allowing British troops to "use their utmost endeavours to withstand and suppress such rebellion."

Although King George III is usually a measured man, he is ruthless about imposing British power. Two years ago, the oppressive British Tea Act of 1773 made British tea available in the colonies at a lower price, after tax, than any other imported tea. The colonists saw through this scheme, recognizing that buying this inexpensive tea would mean paying taxes without parliamentary representation, and would set a precedent for further taxation.

Rather than give in, American colonists dressed up as Indians, raided three British ships in Boston Harbor, and dumped their cargo of tea in the water to protest, an act so flagrant that Parliament passed what have become known as the Coercive Acts.

It was Prime Minister Lord North's intent to make an example of Massachusetts in an effort to discourage other colonies from fomenting rebellion. The port of Boston was closed until the destroyed tea was paid for, thereby punishing the entire city for the acts of a few. The Coercive Acts also stated that British officials who faced criminal charges could be tried outside of the colony — meaning that witnesses would be unlikely to attend such a trial. Troops could be housed in any available vacant buildings and were to be fed at the expense of the colonial government. Finally, and perhaps most important, the Massachusetts colonial charter was revoked, in an attempt to give the British government direct control of the colony. It has been twelve years since Great Britain has waged war, but its attempts to strangle Boston and its inhabitants is akin to a military siege. If Parliament has its way, that raucous rebel town will learn the hard way that England is its master.

The plan backfires. The Coercive Acts (known in America as the Intolerable Acts) are far too punitive. It is clear that Britain no longer believes the American colonists are entitled to the same rights and privileges accorded free men and women in England. The people of Massachusetts create their own government, in defiance of Parliament's authority. Instead of distancing themselves from the besieged people of Boston, the other colonies band together and form the First Continental Congress. There, the true seeds of sedition are sown.

The Battles at Lexington and Concord, and now Bunker Hill, are proof that a direr form of punishment is required to control the Americans. For King George, a tipping point has been reached, one from which there can be no return. He is a strict man. The rebels are children who must be slapped, if necessary, to bring them to heel.

"I am of the opinion that once these rebels

have felt a smart blow, they will submit," George has informed his good friend John Montagu, Fourth Earl of Sandwich and First Lord of the Admiralty. Thus, the king refuses even to read the "Olive Branch Petition" sent by the Continental Congress as a last attempt at reconciliation.

Now, on this very morning, the man the rebellious colonists once considered their benefactor wants nothing less than their total destruction. George III is a deeply spiritual person, prone to spending hours in prayer. He does not see the rebels as virtuous. Nor does he condone the argument that Parliament has no power to levy taxes upon the colonies. American dissenters believe that because they have no voice in the House of Commons, they have no obligation to pay taxes. King George III is adamant that British colonies obey and provide support to the motherland — and that they not be entitled to *any* representation. Reports that American colonists see themselves as equal to British subjects have enraged the king. He is having none of that.

So now he must act — George III means to declare war.

This declaration is not an act of insanity — though, in time, the heavy amounts of arsenic in the ceremonial wigs the king wears each day may be a reason his urine is turning a vibrant blue and he is losing his mind.* George III's actions are a statement of power. He controls thirty-one colonies around the world, some of them gained due to the explorations of Capt. James Cook, who has recently returned from a second circumnavigation of the globe. That voyage brought the newly discovered continent of Australia under the king's power.

The loss of the American colonies would be a crushing blow. As an island nation, England is highly dependent on the natural products of its colonies to ensure its wealth. Should the American rebellion be successful, other highly profitable colonies such as Canada and the West Indies might follow suit. Also, rival nations such as Spain and France might see England as weak and pursue their own colonial ambitions more

*Arsenic (from the Greek word for "potent") was once considered a medicine. It was long used to treat syphilis, asthma, and eczema. It is still in use today as an aggressive treatment for acute leukemia. During his reign, George was often given a medicine known as James Fever Powder, which contained high levels of arsenic. A powder form of arsenic was also sprinkled on the royal wigs to protect them from decay and insects.

aggressively.

The loss of the American colonies, in other words, would kill England as the world now knows it.

"We shall be reduced to a miserable little island," British writer Horace Walpole will state about the prospect of losing America. "We shall lose the East Indies as Portugal did, and then France will dictate to us more imperiously than we did to Ireland."

King George is the most powerful man in the world — and he means to remain so.

The House of Lords is a narrow room with the king's ceremonial throne at the far end. King George III takes his seat as the red-robed peers now look on, waiting to hear why their sovereign has called this early meeting.

"The present situation of America, and my constant desire to have your advice, concurrence and assistance, on every important occasion, have determined me to call you thus early together," George tells them. As a child, he was often depressed and somber. In adulthood, that demeanor has given way to a powerful air of steely determination.

"The rebellious war now levied [has] become more general, and is manifestly carried on for the purpose of establishing an independent empire. I need not dwell upon the fatal effects of the success of such a plan. The object is too important, the spirit of the British nation too high, the resources with which God hath blessed her too numerous, to give up so many colonies which she has planted with great industry, nursed with great tenderness, encouraged with many commercial advantages, and protected and defended at much expense of blood and treasure."

Then, in words designed to strike fear into the heart of George Washington, King George III makes clear his intentions — and, in so doing, makes it equally clear that America now stands alone.

"It is now become the part of wisdom, and (in its effects) of clemency, to put a speedy end to these disorders by the most decisive exertions. For this purpose, I have increased my naval establishment, and greatly augmented my land forces; but in such a manner as may be the least burthensome to my kingdoms.

"I have also the satisfaction to inform you, that I have received the most friendly offers of foreign assistance."

The king finishes his speech to rousing cheers.

Three thousand miles away, George Washington has no idea of the horror that is coming his way.

3

Dorchester Heights, Massachusetts
March 4, 1776
5:42 P.M.

His Excellency Gen. George Washington is apprehensive.

The evening air thunders with rebel cannon. Flames belch from the cast-iron barrels with each blast, illuminating the sky over Boston Harbor. Washington watches with approval, mounted on the back of Blueskin, a spirited white half-Arabian horse who sometimes grows skittish at the sounds of battle.* Within moments, after eight months of waiting, Washington hopes to

*At a time when superior equestrian skills were required of all true gentlemen, Washington was known for his prowess on horseback. He was fond of leaping fences and galloping across fields during daylong fox and stag hunts. The general had two primary mounts during the Revolutionary

79

deliver a cruel and hopefully deadly blow to the British Army.

Despite the welcome presence of his beloved Martha, who has traveled from Virginia to be with him at his headquarters in Cambridge, the Massachusetts winter has been a long and bitterly cold challenge for the general. Shortages of cannon, muskets, and gunpowder have limited his ability to wage war on the British forces who occupy Boston. The soldiers in his army are deserting in droves, done in by a winter so cold that men actually freeze to death on guard duty. Nevertheless, Washington imposes strict discipline on his troops, hoping to counter the boredom of the months-long stalemate with the British Army.

The initial euphoria of being named commander in chief has long since passed for Washington, replaced by the fear that he has made a very big mistake.

"I have often thought how much happier

War, Blueskin and Nelson, a chestnut gelding who was known for his calm under fire. Washington rotated the daily use of the two horses in order not to overwork them. He also refused to whip his mounts, and made it a habit to visit their stables first thing every morning to check on their well-being.

I should have been if, instead of accepting a command under such circumstances, I had taken my musket on my shoulders and entered the ranks," he has written to a friend.

Four times since July, Washington has presented to his council of war detailed plans to attack Boston. And four times the council has voted him down.* During a February cold snap Washington was consumed with a far-fetched scheme to send thousands of troops across the frozen waters of Boston Harbor but was overruled by his more practical-minded generals.

Yet, that plan was doomed to failure, as Washington was overruled by his more practical-minded generals. Cannon on British warships anchored offshore would have

*Rather than rely solely on his own wisdom, and recognizing the need for good advice before making major decisions, Washington convened a council of war. Its members consisted of Maj. Gen. Charles Lee, Maj. Gen. Artemas Ward, and four other men who would rise to prominence as generals in the Continental Army: farmer William Heath, lawyer John Sullivan, physician John Thomas, and Maj. Gen. Nathanael Greene. Washington was not bound by their decisions, but he tended to defer to the council.

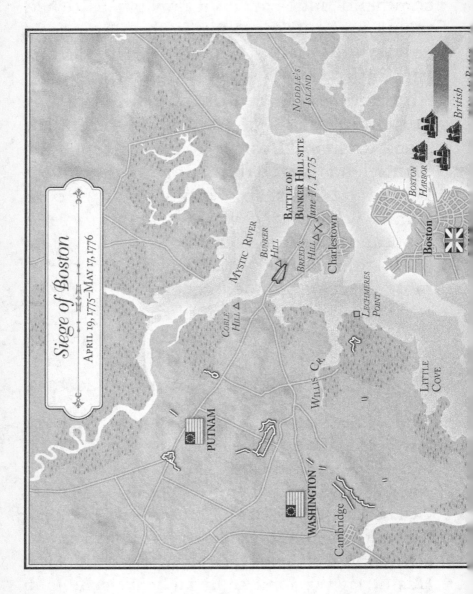

Siege of Boston

APRIL 19, 1775–MAY 17, 1776

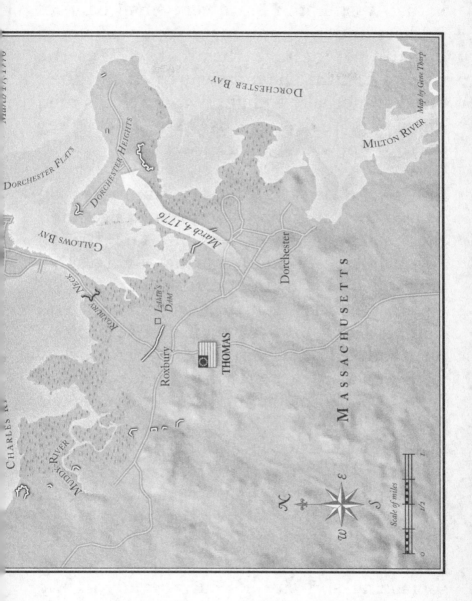

March 17, 1776

DORCHESTER BAY

MILTON RIVER

Map by Gene Thorp

DORCHESTER FLATS

DORCHESTER HEIGHTS

GALLOWS BAY

ROXBURY NECK

LAMB'S DAM

Dorchester

Roxbury

March 4, 1776

THOMAS

MASSACHUSETTS

CHARLES R...

MUDDY RIVER

N
W   E
S

Scale of miles
0   1/2   1

made short work of his army. The hard truth is that Washington has a very small band of soldiers under his command, many of whom do not yet believe they can defeat the mighty British. The only way to change their minds is actually to fight. Washington's men know that their cause is just — now they need to know that their leader is able.

For two days, beginning at midnight on March 2, American cannon have pounded the besieged city of Boston. The British Army has responded in kind, firing salvo after salvo at the American artillery batteries atop Cobble Hill, Lechmeres Point, and Lamb's Dam. Such exchanges have become purposeful. The Americans fire because they want to keep the British pinned down in Boston and to remind the five hundred redcoats hunkering within their Bunker Hill fortifications that they can go no farther.

The British fire back to assure the Americans that any attempt to attack Boston on the ground will be answered in force.

On nights when there is no shelling, rebel gunners can hear the sounds of tavern socializing and city life carrying across the bay on the wind. On nights when their cannon fire so often that the barrels glow, these same men hear the distant screams of women and children being driven from their homes by crashing cannonballs. As if that anguish were not enough, some patriot artillerymen wonder if those screams are those of *their own* wives and children. Women are already playing a crucial role in the war effort, managing homes and businesses while their husbands man the front lines. The women had little choice in this matter, just as the men who are rebelling had no choice but to leave their families behind in Boston, there to endure the hardships of life under British martial law.

The harsh rigor of British tyranny rose to new heights two years ago, in 1774, when the British Parliament passed the punitive Boston Port Act. This law closed Boston to all commercial shipping until the city made complete restitution for the cargo dumped in the harbor during what has become known as the Boston Tea Party. Overnight, shipwrights, sailors, coopers, and dock laborers who formed the majority of Boston's workingmen lost their jobs.

"It is now a very gloomy place," one Boston resident wrote to friends in England. "The streets are almost empty and many families have departed."

That was just the first exodus. One year later, in April 1775, the British expelled thousands of patriots after the skirmishes at Lexington and Concord. Entire families, suspected of rebel activity, were forced to leave their homes, not knowing if they would ever return. The causeway connecting Boston to the mainland became choked with these instant refugees, men and women leading their children while pulling carts laden with all their earthly possessions. Most spent that summer roaming the countryside in search of work and a place to sleep. By winter, homes throughout the colony became hostels for the displaced. Following a plea by the colonial government, it has become common for Massachusetts homeowners to invite refugees into their homes. Some kind souls even provide lodging for two or three entire families.

Among them is thirty-one-year-old Abigail Adams. "Every town is filled with the distressed inhabitants of Boston," she writes to her husband, John, still serving as a delegate to the Second Continental Congress in Philadelphia. The Adamses live on a farm in the town of Braintree, due south of Boston but close enough that cannon fire keeps Abigail awake at night. "It would make your heart ache to see what difficulties and distresses the poor Boston people are driven to," she writes her husband.

Abigail Adams herself knew such loss. Her mother and her niece died of smallpox within weeks of each other in October 1775.

But it is not just American patriots who face hardship. Citizens of Massachusetts still loyal to King George are also being forced from their homes. As those being evicted from Boston jam the causeway on their way out of town, British Loyalists travel in the opposite direction, headed *into* Boston, to find sanctuary after months of being abused by fellow colonists for their allegiance to the king.

Whether patriot or Loyalist, most displaced families long to return home once hostilities end. They can only pray that their vacant houses will not be vandalized and the remainder of their possessions not plundered.

Those prayers will go unanswered. In Boston, despite orders prohibiting the looting of private property, British soldiers make it a habit to enter abandoned homes and take what they like.

It is even worse for the Loyalists. Massachusetts patriots are already in the process of permanently stripping homes and businesses from their possession. They can never come back again.

■ ■ ■ ■

The Boston that George Washington now sees is a closed city, a collection of destroyed homes and filthy boulevards inhabited by a starving, war-weary populace eagerly praying for summer. The only way in or out is with a special pass.

Survival takes many forms. For ladies of the night, there is no difference between patriot and Loyalist. Though the British soldiers may be short on food, they are still getting paid. The prostitutes of Boston ply their trade in the red-light district known as "Mount Whoredom," risking not just syphilis and gonorrhea, but the spread of lice that comes with intimate human contact.* Throughout the city, the dirty snow is covered in human waste. Garbage fills the streets, fueling an epidemic of "diarrhea, dysentery, food poisoning, malnutrition, pleuritical disorders, respiratory infections, arthritis, rheumatism, scurvy, and typhoid-typhus," in the words of one resident.

In September 1775, Gen. Thomas Gage receives news from England that he has

*Incredibly, Mount Whoredom is now one of Boston's most affluent neighborhoods, Beacon Hill.

General William Howe

been relieved of command because of his failures at Lexington, Concord, and Bunker Hill. The new commander in Boston is Gen. William Howe, a dark-haired, brooding, extremely wealthy forty-six-year-old career soldier who spends most nights in the arms of a Boston Loyalist's wife.*

Elizabeth Loring is blond, blue-eyed, and at age thirty-one has just given birth to her first son. Despite having a newborn at home, Mrs. Loring gambles and drinks most evenings at General Howe's side, sometimes losing enormous sums in a single hand. One local paper describes her as a "brilliant and unprincipled woman," while Howe's staff simply calls her "the Sultana." Mrs. Loring's husband has learned how to accept the gossip about his wife's affairs, and ignores those who call him a cuckold.†

*The actual extent of Howe's relationship with Mrs. Loring is uncertain. Allegations began in New York in early 1777; although they were both in Boston before that, it is not certain whether their affair began there. The authors of this book have used the version of events put forth by most modern writers.

†It was not uncommon for British generals to leave their spouses at home and take a mistress while away at war. Sometimes these affairs were in the open, as with the unmarried Howe and Mrs. Loring. Other times, the consorts were disguised as "cousins" and took up residence at a general's headquarters. However, the case of Mrs. Loring became such a public distraction that it attracted

And for good reason. The British government has rewarded Joshua Loring Jr. well. Born in Hingham, Massachusetts, in 1744 and raised as a staunch British Loyalist, Loring was appointed to the lucrative position of Boston's vendue master and auctioneer, which allowed him to earn commissions on the sale of captured goods. "He fingered the cash," one British observer will later write, "the General enjoyed madam."

The British general is over six feet tall, like his foe George Washington. Howe's courage under fire has never been questioned. As commander in chief, Howe is responsible for the entire population of Boston, military and civilian, and the city is a chaotic place after residents have fled and refugees have poured in. In November, as the weather gets colder and troops must be moved from encampments into quarters, he makes the difficult decision to send three hundred civilians out of the city and into American lines.

---

the attention of both the Continental Army and the British Parliament. American general Charles Lee said of Howe, "He shut his eyes, fought his battles, drank his bottle and had his little whore." Parliament condemned Mrs. Loring as a "Cleopatra to this Antony of ours."

"Destitute of almost everything . . . in the most miserable and piteous condition," George Washington wrote of these men, women, and children who were sent on boats to the mainland northeast of the city.

Meanwhile, Howe and his officers socialize, spending their nights attending concerts and plays, drinking, and gambling. One general, "Gentleman Johnny" Burgoyne, spends much of the winter writing and producing well-attended theatrical plays before he is finally ordered home to London.

British regular soldiers are not as refined. They battle the boredom of winter garrison duty in the manner of occupying armies since the dawn of war: getting falling-down drunk, chasing whores, and repressing the locals. Drinking has long been a staple of life in Boston, despite its Puritan origins. Yet the debauched behavior of the British soldiers is so appalling that it is a common worry among local women that it will have an adverse effect on their children. Those fears pale in comparison with the threat of greater abuses, for even though martial law is in effect and the punishment for rape is death, it is impossible to prevent crime in a garrison of ten thousand bored, opportunistic soldiers.*

One British officer will write home describing the British attitude toward violently defiling American women: "A girl cannot step into the bushes to pluck a rose without

*British soldiers enlisted for life, with terrible pay (the modern equivalent of twenty cents per day) and cramped living conditions. Thus, the need to maintain strict discipline to prevent mutiny was paramount. Even during the siege of Boston, General Howe inflicted severe punishments upon British soldiers for breaking the rules. Methods of discipline ranged from whippings to hanging, depending on the offense. Hangings were carried out on the Boston Common, for all to see. If the punishment was flogging, the accused was stripped to the waist, tied to a tree or post, then lashed across the back with a whip known as a cat-o'-nine-tails. The name comes from the number of knotted cord tentacles attached to the whip handle. It was not uncommon for a soldier to receive several hundred lashes. It was considered bad form to cry out or flinch during this punishment, so soldiers very often crushed a lead bullet between their teeth while being whipped, to counter the pain. In some extreme cases, the lashings were administered over the course of several days, which would not allow the wounds to close before the administration of more punishment,

running the most imminent risk of being ravished, and they are so little accustomed to these vigorous methods that they don't bear them with the proper resignation, and of consequence we have the most entertaining courts-martial every day."

Beyond the fortified city, the entire Boston Harbor is ringed by artillery — all except a set of low, barren hills at the windy southern entrance. This area is known as Dorchester Heights. Just as Bunker Hill and Breed's Hill control the high ground to the north of Boston, so the Heights overlook the city from the south.

Both the British and Americans keep a sharp eye on this vital tactical location, but it remains unoccupied. The base of the heights is a collection of farmhouses, fields, and orchards, but the hillsides are completely exposed, making it easy for either

---

thus making the ordeal far more painful. The cat-o'-nine-tails would become covered in blood during a whipping. When not in use, the "cat" was very often kept in a bag made of coarse crimson cloth. The color was deliberate, meant to blend with the blood seeping through the fabric. The act of removing the whip from this storage pouch gave rise to the term "cat's out of the bag," as a method of referring to a revelation.

side to bombard any troops erecting fortifications. Even if the slopes weren't so vulnerable, the cold winter has frozen the soil to a
depth of two feet, making it impossible to
build foundations.

Even more than Bunker Hill, possession
of the Dorchester Heights, in the words of
heavyset British general Henry Clinton, is
"absolutely necessary for the security of
Boston."

General Howe, commander of British
troops in Boston, is even blunter. He promises that any rebel attempt to fortify the
Heights will be met "with our full force."

For good reason. Should George Washington take control of Dorchester Heights, the
high ground will allow his gunners to
bombard the British day and night, while
simultaneously closing the southern entrance of Boston Harbor to all British shipping. The British Army would then be
almost completely cut off. Any British ship
trying to run the blockade would be within
reach of the American guns.

Most Americans sympathetic to the rebel
cause have fled across the causeway. The
majority have settled in towns nearby, such
as Braintree and Weymouth, while others
have fled Massachusetts entirely, to make a
new life far from the fighting. What remains

in the city are British soldiers and colonists loyal to the king, suffering through the most wretched winter they have ever known.

It's not just the single-digit temperatures and biting winds that have taken their toll, nor the blizzards that turn a ship into a "cake of ice," in the words of one British admiral. Something as simple as writing a letter becomes a challenge, as the cold freezes ink inside quills.

The misery is made all the more unbearable by Washington's military siege. He has deprived Bostonians of almost every amenity. The cattle that once grazed on Boston Common were slaughtered months ago, their grazing land replaced by a campsite for British troops. The vegetable gardens of summer are now covered in a deep layer of snow. What scant food that exists is greedily claimed by the wealthy and elite, leaving little for the poor and dying, soldier and citizen alike.

Early in the winter, before the harbor iced over, it was possible for British ships to resupply the city with food, rum, and winter clothing. The frozen harbor, the foul weather, and the American privateers so fond of hijacking British cargo now make that impossible.

"The distresses of the inhabitants and

troops in Boson exceed the possibility of description," one soldier writes in his journal. "They are almost in a point of starvation, for want of food or fuel. The inhabitants, totally destitute of vegetables, flour and fresh provisions, have actually been obliged to feed on horse flesh, and the troops confined to salt provisions, by which means they have become sick."

The British contempt for the civilian population, even those loyal to the king, is total. Citizens are beaten for no reason, the cries of the suffering almost completely unheard by the occupying forces.

Firewood has become the essence of life. The city's trees have been chopped down, rows of church pews ripped out, and entire houses demolished to quench the need for kindling.

Even worse than the cold and starvation is the smallpox. The disease is epidemic in Boston, taking far more lives than the war. Highly contagious and incredibly painful, smallpox starts with a flu-like fever and then develops into a rash with sores that cover the mouth, throat, and inside of the nose. Bleeding from the gums, orifices, and eyes occurs next. Soon, every part of the body, even the palms of the hands and the soles of the feet, are covered in painful bright red pustules. As the infection enters its second week, the victim begins to reek of decay and the pustules pop. There is no cure for smallpox, though some lucky victims recover. Others go blind. Many simply die.

George Washington is well acquainted with the blinding headaches and crippling back pain that can precede the outbreak of smallpox sores, having survived his own scare with the killer disease decades before.*

*Washington contracted smallpox in 1751, while visiting Barbados with his half brother. The two men had traveled to the Caribbean island seeking a cure for Lawrence Washington's tuberculosis. On November 17 of that year, the nineteen-year-old George was stricken with smallpox. He endured three weeks of suffering before the illness passed, but in the process, he became an ardent believer in smallpox inoculation, a highly controversial practice at the time. It involved placing a small amount of pus from an infected victim into an incision on the body of a healthy person. This would result in a mild form of smallpox, one that could sometimes be fatal, but when successful, it gave the individual a lifetime of immunity from the disease. Thus, in 1776, as Martha Washington came to stay with her husband in Massachusetts, the general vigorously urged her to get inoculated.

He is so concerned about the epidemic spreading to his troops that he will not allow any individual fleeing Boston to come in contact with his army, knowing smallpox can be transferred by something as simple as a handshake.

Washington understands that the British may be making an even more deliberate attempt to use biological warfare against his troops. "By recent information from Boston, General Howe is going to send out a number of the inhabitants in order, it is thought, to make more room for his expected reinforcements," Washington writes to John Hancock during the course of the winter. "A sailor says that a number of these coming out have been inoculated, with design of spreading the smallpox."*

General Washington is now personally responsible for the siege of Boston. This makes him accountable for the suffering now being experienced by its inhabitants,

---

Despite great misgivings, she did, with no ill effects. It should be noted that Lawrence Washington's trip to Barbados was unsuccessful. He died of tuberculosis upon his return to Virginia in 1752.
*There is a widespread, though unsubstantiated, belief that Washington used biological warfare against the British in this same manner.

British troops, Loyalists, and their families.

But Washington does not care.

The general is known as a man of compassion. Yet, as one soldier writes, "General Washington possesses an inflexible firmness of purpose, and is determined that discipline and subordination in camp shall be rigidly enforced and maintained."

Washington has shot soldiers for desertion, flogged men who disobeyed orders, and once even erected a forty-foot-tall gallows to remind troops what would become of them if they did not do their duty.

In a letter recently circulated among his troops, Washington made it very clear what would happen to any soldier refusing to do his duty: "If any man in action shall presume to skulk, hide himself, or retreat from the enemy, without the orders of his commanding officer, he will be instantly shot down as an example of cowardice."

So, if the general has no problem treating his own men in this manner, he surely doesn't give consideration to the British and their supporters enduring the deprivation brought on by the military siege.

In fact, Washington's bold new plan of action will make their lives even more unbearable.

■ ■ ■ ■

The strategy begins to unfold just after dark
on March 4. After two days of firing, the
British have become desensitized to the
sound of American cannon. They do not
expect an American ground attack, and they
plan no offensive action of their own. As the
rebel guns begin firing again, the British fire
back as usual. In doing so, they play into
George Washington's hands. The deafening
pounding of the cannon now conceals the
sound of hundreds of rebel infantrymen
sprinting toward Dorchester Heights. Strategically placed sheaves of hay lining the road
provide a protective screen, allowing the
rebels to move into position without being
seen or heard.

Washington himself conducted some of
the reconnaissance for this risky mission —
and for good reason. The Continental Army
has just come into possession of fifty-nine
British cannon and mortars captured in
upstate New York. The general now plans to
place them atop the Heights.*

*American troops under Gen. Benedict Arnold
earned America's first victory of the Revolutionary War by capturing the British-held Fort Ticonderoga on May 10, 1775. Twenty-five-year-old

101

The infantry is soon followed by an unlikely force of twelve hundred men driving
teams of oxen pulling carts piled high with
prebuilt log fortifications. A full moon will
provide all the light they need to transport
these loads to the summit of Dorchester
Heights and set them in place. The night air
is unusually warm, letting both men and
animals labor without the hindrance of biting wind or a snowstorm.

At the base of the heights, a low haze
settles over the infantry as they cut down
orchards and use the toppled trees to form
a defensive line. But the real work takes
place as the oxen slowly drag their heavy
loads up the hillside. As Washington
planned, the clank of harnesses and yokes is
muffled by the nightlong cannon fire. The

Henry Knox from Boston, a bookstore owner who
had yet to receive his commission in the Continental Army, boldly suggested the idea of retrieving
the captured guns from Ticonderoga and dragging
them to Boston by ox-drawn sleds. Washington
put Knox in charge. The nearly impossible three-
hundred-mile journey through thick winter snow
and ice took fifty-six days, but Knox successfully
arrived in Boston on January 25, 1776 — complet-
ing one of the most impressive military missions
in American history.

men do their best to maintain silence, lest a sharp word carry across the water to Boston and alert the British.

"The whole procession moved on in solemn silence, and with perfect order and regularity," one eyewitness will write, "while the continued roar of cannon serves to engage the attention and divert the enemy from the main object."

A first load of fortifications reaches the bluff top and is set in place. Then the oxen are guided back down the hill for another. While they are gone, a second rebel group, armed with pickaxes, goes to work on the frozen soil, slowly breaking up chunks of rock-hard earth that will fill spaces between the logs in the hastily erected fortifications. Fresh hay will be added, pressed into the gaps to form a solid seam that will prevent even a sliver of British canister and grape from passing through.

By 10:00 p.m., the fortifications are durable enough to withstand British cannonballs. And still the Americans solidify their stronghold, working to exhaustion. At 3:00 a.m., a force of three thousand men relieves the first shift. The pace quickens with the approach of dawn. Storage barrels are filled with rocks and sand — in case of a surprise British attack, the impromptu weapons will be rolled down the slopes at the advancing army.

As the first rays of morning sun break the darkness over the Atlantic Ocean, the oxen no longer drag fortifications up the hill.

Instead, they haul cannon.

"These are the preparations," one soldier will write in his journal, anticipating that the British will send men across the harbor to do battle "for blood and slaughter."

The battle never comes.

"My god," a stunned General Howe exclaims as he studies the new fortifications: "These fellows have done more work in one night than I could make my army do in three months." Howe's admiration is quickly replaced by action. He orders the rebels' fortifications to be tested with a withering cannon barrage.

But, as Howe perhaps already suspected would happen, the British guns do little damage — most cannonballs are deflected, and cause little fear among the Americans. Throughout the long night of digging and the day of cannonading, just two rebel soldiers lose their lives.

Even as the British pound the hillside, Washington gallops Blueskin up Dorchester Heights to congratulate his troops. "His

Excellency General Washington is present, animating and encouraging the soldiers, and they in turn manifest their joy, and express a warm desire for the approach of the enemy," one soldier will later write.

George Washington has his first great victory — and he has yet to lead his men into battle.*

General Howe is not a fool. He knows his army will be destroyed if Washington continues to bombard the city. In return for a British promise not to burn Boston to the ground shortly after the occupation of

*Washington himself required his soldiers and officers to call him "Excellency." The term, now frequently associated with popes and kings, was once more commonly used to signify status within an organization. The term often precedes another title, thus "His Excellency General George Washington," signifying that Washington was separate and superior from the other generals in the Continental Army. It was a source of deep frustration to Washington that he was looked down upon by the British military leadership. Using this title was yet another way to show that he was their equal. Despite this, General Howe, in particular, refused to acknowledge Washington as anything other than a contemptuous rebel.

Dorchester Heights, the Americans allow a flotilla of British ships to line up at the docks and load eight thousand redcoats in a humiliating evacuation of the city. Many of these men have lived in Boston long enough to take wives and start families, so these dependents are let on board as well.

Hundreds of nonmilitary civilians who consider themselves Loyalists, and who swear fealty to the king in spite of the rebellion, also find their way into steerage. Among them are Boston's leading bankers, lawyers, preachers, shipowners, and politicians. These proud men who once dictated the ebb and flow of the city's daily life will never again be welcome to return.*

Also on the ship are Elizabeth Loring and her husband, Joshua. They will follow Howe's army, he being appointed to the important and well-salaried post of commissary of prisoners in New York, she becoming the focus of accusations that Howe never put his all into fighting the American war.

George Washington is not just driving

*Massachusetts passed a Banishment Act in 1778, prohibiting the return of certain individuals who once lived in the colony and expressed an abiding loyalty to the king.

away the British Army. He is ripping the Loyalist heart and soul out of Boston — and with great relish. There is no room for disloyalty in his world. On March 17, 1776, his army marches across the neck into Boston as a drum and fife play "Yankee Doodle." It is a song the British have long used to deride the Americans as buffoons, but which the rebels have instead adopted as a badge of honor. In time, it will become their anthem.

As the British fleet sails out into the Atlantic, Washington realizes he will have to confront his enemy in another place. King George is not going to cede the fight easily.

Washington does not know where the next battle will take place.

He suspects it will be in New York City.

4

Thomas Jefferson is thinking about death.

His personal losses are overwhelming, but now, as a congressional delegate, he has to put his pain aside.

It is almost a year since Congress named George Washington commander in chief, and three months since British troops fled Boston. The thirty-three-year-old Jefferson sits in a high-backed Windsor chair near the oak fireplace in the Assembly Room, torn between the personal grief that would have him home in western Virginia instead of in this sweltering chamber and the destiny that demands he be in Philadelphia to hear all that will transpire today.

So far, it hasn't been much.

This morning's session began an hour ago.

The red-haired Jefferson, who stands six feet two inches tall and has a face dotted in freckles, quietly listens to the agenda items, beginning with the shipowner seeking restitution for lost cargo. This is the grinding daily business of Congress. Or, in the words of the outspoken John Adams of Massachusetts, "drudgery of the most wasting, exhausting, consuming kind."

Jefferson remains quiet throughout the discussion. He is prone to extreme introversion, so he is comfortable with solitude and silence. He is a brilliant writer but is not adept at public speaking, often stumbling over the same words in speech he so easily employs on the page. These failings might be a detriment to most political careers, but Jefferson succeeds thanks to a quick mind and intense focus. In the three weeks since his arrival in Philadelphia, his fellow representatives have taken note of his understated genius. John Adams considers the young Virginian to be "prompt, frank, explicit, decisive."

Those qualities are not on display at this moment. Jefferson barely notices as the sloop owner's appeal ends and a new agenda item is introduced, this one concerning the procurement of defective gunpowder in South Carolina.

The athletic-looking Jefferson knows this drudgery will soon end. Moments from now, his fellow Virginia delegate, Richard Henry Lee, will rise to his feet and make a startling pronouncement. Lee's words will have nothing to do with mindless minutiae or trivial agenda items. Rather, the stentorian Virginian will cut to the very quick of why this Continental Congress exists in the first place, challenging each colony to vote one way or the other on America's most divisive issue: independence.

Considered radical and even unthinkable one year ago, the subject can no longer be ignored.

So far, the war against Britain has been waged in the hope that King George will rescind his punitive actions against the colonists. As of this moment, the Americans are still considered British subjects, despite their rebel status. Many would be happy to remain that way.

A vote for independence changes everything. Any form of colonial allegiance to Britain will cease. No longer will the struggle be about respect — from this day forward, it will be a quest for freedom.

In the mind of George III, this choice has already been made. "The die is now cast," he told British prime minister Lord North when the rebellion first flared. "The colonists must either submit or triumph."

But, to many colonists, it is not that simple. There have been British colonies in America for almost two hundred years.* Americans have a deep emotional bond to Britain that reflects this long history — and in many cases, their own ancestry. To sever that tie would be to turn their backs on the century upon century of English tradition that forms the essence of who the colonists are as a people. Thomas Jefferson himself, whose mother was born in London, traces his ancestry "back in to the early mists of Scottish and English history."

The truth is that no one knows what will happen once independence is declared. The colonies have no idea how to govern or tax themselves. Like petulant children, they don't know where they are going or how they will get there — all they know is that they can no longer tolerate British oppression.

Thus, the great divide. Only seven colonies currently favor independence. New Jersey, New York, Pennsylvania, Delaware, Mary-

*The Jamestown colony was founded at the mouth of Chesapeake Bay in what is now Virginia, on May 14, 1607.

Thomas Jefferson

land, and South Carolina are either completely loyal to the Crown or wavering about whether to break with England.

If it is to be seriously pursued, all thirteen must vote for independence. Any division among the colonies will undermine the rebellion.

The path is clear: all thirteen colonies must now consider themselves states.

As Thomas Jefferson watches from his chair, Richard Henry Lee rises to his feet. His left hand is wrapped in a black silk handkerchief, to conceal the absence of four fingers lost in a hunting accident. The words he is about to state are a poorly kept secret, having been drafted for him at the pro-independence Virginia Convention in Williamsburg three weeks ago. He will read them word for word.

Lee is a powerful man, a forty-four-year-old planter and legislator from one of Virginia's most esteemed families. Descended from generations of Lees in the British Midlands, he feels a strong connection with England. But since arriving in America one century ago, the Lees have established an even greater connection with their new homeland.*

Richard Henry Lee clears his throat. The room grows silent. Thomas Jefferson leans in, the better to hear.

"Resolved," Lee begins, "that these united colonies are, and of right ought to be, free and independent states; that they are absolved from their allegiance to the British crown, and that all political connection

*It is ironic that, eighty-five years after Richard Henry Lee made the case for an independent American nation, another Lee from the same bloodline, Confederate general Robert E. Lee, waged war to cut the nation in two.

between them and the State of Great Britain is, and ought to be, totally dissolved."

John Adams immediately seconds Lee's motion. The Assembly Room explodes into angry debate. Thomas Jefferson holds his tongue, allowing windy orators such as Adams and Lee to make the arguments for independence. The great windows on two sides of the room are closed, despite the rising June temperature. This is not an issue for passersby on the gravel walkways outside to overhear.

If he wanted, Jefferson could stand and join the fight. He is an avid reader, devoting himself to absorbing the literature circulating throughout the colonies about the pros and cons of independence — in particular, Thomas Paine's *Common Sense,* published just a few months ago.* If Jefferson desired to make a statement in favor of indepen-

---

*Paine, a recent immigrant from England, published the pamphlet anonymously on January 10, 1776. He argued not only that America had a right to independence, but that continued servitude to England was illogical. Five hundred thousand copies of *Common Sense* were sold in America, France, and England in its first year of publication. It is still in print.

dence, he would have a great deal to add to the discussion.

But the Virginian says nothing. Still, throughout the debate, he takes meticulous notes, filling page after page in neat script, recording every idea put forth.

Like Benjamin Franklin, who is absent from the Congress due to an attack of gout that makes it difficult for him to walk, Jefferson has an extremely active mind. His thoughts can flit from politics to the weather to global exploration in an instant. He is a creature of habit who begins each day by rising before the sun, no matter how late he has gone to bed the night before. Breakfast is coffee, fresh bread, and ham. But he does not eat until he soaks his feet in cold water, convinced this is good for his health.

Jefferson then records the morning temperature and wind speed in an ivory-colored notebook he keeps with him at all times. He also records the afternoon temperature at precisely four o'clock each day. Even now, as he sits amid the great cacophony of the independence debate, Jefferson's pockets are filled with implements to satisfy his curiosity: notebook, thermometer, pencil, compass, and even a pocket-size globe. In spring, Jefferson makes note of the date on which particular flowers bloom. Once autumn comes, he will record the migratory patterns of birds.*

By then, Jefferson hopes to return home to his five-thousand-acre plantation, Monticello. His absence is felt quite keenly now, thanks to a series of tragedies, beginning with the drowning death of his sister Elizabeth two years ago. That was followed by the loss of his seventeen-month-old daughter Jane, who was named for his mother.

Then, just nine weeks ago, Jefferson's mother, Jane Jefferson, suffered a stroke and passed away within the hour. Though born into privilege, she had lived a hard life, giving birth to ten children and burying her husband when she was just thirty-seven. Jefferson's father had been a force of nature, an oversize man who surveyed and settled western Virginia, then rose to the rank of colonel in the state militia and served in the House of Burgesses, Virginia's legislative body. As a young boy, Thomas Jefferson

* Jefferson used the same notebook throughout his life. It is on display at Monticello, which is now a museum. He recorded every daily observation in pencil, then transferred those notes into books pertaining to each subject (weather, garden, etc.). He then erased the notations in his notebook and reused the pages.

spent many an evening in Peter Jefferson's study, listening intently as his father taught him about the classics, literature, voyages of discovery, and surveying. Their close relationship inspired a lifelong fascination with learning for young Thomas, who was just fourteen when his father died. Peter Jefferson's will dictated that Thomas not come into his inheritance until he was twenty-one, and his relationship with his mother deteriorated in those seven years.

Jefferson resented her deeply, believing her to be an angry, violent, domineering woman. Part of the problem was that Jane Jefferson was so fixated on running the family plantation after her husband's death that she sent her son away to boarding school during the week. Young Thomas took that as rejection.

Throughout his life, he very rarely mentioned his mother, but at one point he observed, "Anger and violence and rage deform the female figure. A turbulent woman disgraces the delicacy of her sex."

When it came time to choose a wife, then, Jefferson purposely selected a spouse who manifested the opposite behavior. The auburn-haired Martha is a petite beauty known for her gentle nature and her compassion — traits Jane Randolph Jefferson's

117

son did not often see his mother display.

And yet, her sudden death shattered Thomas.

He was incapacitated for a full month, racked by blinding migraine headaches that left him unable to leave Monticello. These "paroxysms of the most excruciating pain" began "every day at sunrise and never left me until sunset."

Jefferson's grief abated when he arrived in Philadelphia, but now other worries confront him. His relationship with Martha is intense and loving, full of wine and music. Friends and colleagues allude knowingly to the frequency of their connubial pleasure, with many a joke about Jefferson's absences from Congress attributed to his passion for Martha.

She is frail, though, suffering from undiagnosed diabetes. The Jefferson family physician, Dr. George Gilmer, is forced to visit Monticello far too often. Shortly before Jefferson departs for Philadelphia, Martha learns that she is once again pregnant — a condition that has taken a hard toll on her in the past. The weight gain of pregnancy and the high blood sugar brought on by diabetes increases her chance of miscarriage.

Now twenty-seven, Martha Wayles Skelton Jefferson was married at the age of eighteen and widowed by the time she was twenty. Her first husband, Bathurst Skelton, knew Thomas Jefferson during their time together at the College of William and Mary. He died after a brief illness, leaving Martha to raise their infant son alone. John, as the child was known, died three years later, while she and Thomas Jefferson were courting. Six months later, on New Year's Day 1772, Martha married Thomas. She became pregnant almost immediately.

Martha Jefferson (or Patty, as her husband has nicknamed her) has pale blue eyes, impeccable manners, an easy laugh, and lily-white skin that she protects from the sun by never venturing outside without a bonnet or scarf. She and Thomas are fond of playing music together, her soprano harmonizing with his tenor as she plays the harpsichord and he the violin. Martha was once the more romantic of the two, but during their time together, his oft-cynical intellectual nature has softened into a deep and abiding passion for life.

Martha and Thomas are third cousins. More unusual is that she is the half sister to six Monticello slaves, thanks to her late father's dalliances with domestic servant Betty Hemings. The youngest of these is

Sally, who will later become an infamous figure in Jefferson's life, and is now just two years old.*

Precisely thirty-eight weeks and four days after the Jeffersons' wedding date, their daughter Martha came into the world. She was nicknamed Patsy, to distinguish her from her mother. There is no cure for or protection from diseases such as whooping cough, measles, scarlet fever, and mumps, so of the six children born to Thomas and Martha Wayles Skelton Jefferson, only this daughter and Mary Jefferson, who will be born in 1778, live to adulthood. The other four babies will all die of childhood illnesses before the age of two. The Jeffersons' only son will live just seventeen days.

Given how easily illness and infection can take a life, and how much tragedy he and Martha have known in their young lives, Thomas Jefferson is understandably nervous about his wife's current pregnancy while he works in Philadelphia. She writes him at least once a week, but if that reassuring letter does not arrive on schedule, Jefferson is

*Though the Hemings lineage at Monticello is easily traced, some chose to spell their last name with two *m*'s. Biographers alternate the spelling, depending upon individual preference.

overcome by anxiety.

As he sits in this increasingly stuffy room, Jefferson has much on his mind. But the best way to avoid morose thoughts is to remain busy.

The congressional debate over independence spills over from Friday to Saturday, through the Sunday recess, and finally into Monday, June 10. All the while, the tall Virginian remains silent, taking page after page of notes. Finally, when it is clear that the delegates need to step back and let the idea breathe, the Congress agrees to take a three-week break from the issue. On July 1, they will revisit the topic of independence once again.

Jefferson is pleased with the decision. "It appearing from the course of these debates that the colonies of New York, New Jersey, Pennsylvania, Delaware, and Maryland were not matured for falling from the parent stem, but that they were fast advancing to that state, it was most prudent to wait awhile for them, and to postpone the final decision to the first of July," he observes.

Jefferson's time as a spectator now comes to an end. On June 11, he is asked to articulate Lee's resolution in a written document. If the Congress votes for independence on July 1, this "declaration," as the British refer to public pronouncements of this nature, will explain the decision to the world. John Adams recommends that Jefferson write it.

"What can be your reasons?" a shocked Jefferson asks.

"Reason first," Adams responds. "You are a Virginian, and a Virginian ought to appear at the head of this business. Reason second, I am obnoxious, suspected, and unpopular. You are very much otherwise. Reason third, you can write ten times better than I do."

"Well," Jefferson responds in acceptance, "if you are decided, I will do as well as I can."

Thus, as Martha Jefferson remains home alone, soon to lose their unborn child to miscarriage, Thomas Jefferson stays in Philadelphia. He sequesters himself in the second-floor rooms of a new brick house on Seventh and Market Streets. His favorite slave, Jupiter, has just gotten married and requested that he be allowed to remain behind at Monticello. Instead, the man who will shave, dress, and serve Jefferson's meals each day is Robert Hemings, the light-skinned fourteen-year-old offspring of Jefferson's father-in-law and slave Betty Hemings.

Thomas Jefferson spends the last two

weeks of June 1776 putting quill to paper in the stuffy upstairs parlor of his rented lodgings. He sits at a small wooden table draped in a white cloth as he writes. A fireplace is to his left. A grandfather clock across the room chimes the hours.

Atop the table rests Jefferson's portable mahogany desk. He is right-handed, and thus keeps an inkwell and a set of extra quills to that side of the hinged writing surface. The same task awaits him each morning: to craft a convincing moral and ethical argument in favor of separating from England.

Racked by personal tragedy, and accompanied only by a slave boy, Thomas Jefferson carefully assembles the 1,337 words that will go down in history.

The "Declaration of Independence" is born.*

*Of the hundreds of slaves Thomas Jefferson will own in his lifetime, Robert "Bob" Hemings was the first he set free, most likely sometime around 1799. After leaving Monticello, Hemings owned a livery business in Richmond, Virginia, until his death in 1819. Bob's life as a freedman, however, was not easy. At some point, he had both his hands shot off during an attack later in life.

5

Benjamin Franklin is suffering.

Limping slightly, the aging diplomat accepts the well wishes of his fellow delegates as he takes his seat at a table reserved for the Pennsylvania delegation. Franklin has been away from Congress for two weeks, dealing with his latest attack of gout, but he has managed to stay busy during the absence. This past weekend, he pored over Thomas Jefferson's latest draft of the Declaration of Independence, offering comments and suggesting a line or two that might be clarified. Franklin, along with John Adams, has suggested changes throughout the writing process. If all goes well, the plan is to present the declaration to Congress formally this coming Friday.*

Perhaps then, the "Doctor" can truly get some rest. Though he is fitter than his corpulent appearance might indicate, Franklin is seventy years old, and the past few months have been a time of mental and physical hardship unlike any he has known.

Benjamin Franklin was born in Boston on January 17, 1706, the tenth son of an English-born soap maker and his second wife. By age ten, he was put to work helping his father boil soap, cut candlewicks, and fill dipping molds with animal fat.

"I disliked the trade," Franklin wrote in his autobiography, "and had a strong inclination for the sea, but my father declared

*Congress appointed a committee of five men to craft the Declaration of Independence: Jefferson, Franklin, Adams, Robert Sherman of Connecticut, and Robert Livingston from New York. Jefferson was chosen to do the actual writing because of previous documents he had written on the subject of independence. He then ran the document past the rest of the committee for a critique. Franklin's insight was highly regarded, but there were some who thought the author, printer, and political theorist might have tried to insert too much humor into the document if he had been the writer.

against it. However, living near the water, I was much in and about it, learnt early to swim well, and to manage boats — and when in a boat or canoe with other boys, I was commonly allowed to govern, especially in any case of difficulty. Upon other occasions I was generally a leader among the boys, and sometimes led them into scrapes."

Josiah Franklin, fearful that his headstrong son would indeed run away to sea, noticed Benjamin's love for reading and apprenticed him to his older brother James, a printer recently returned from London with his own press.

A formal legal contract was required before the relationship could take place. Benjamin Franklin signed the terms of his indenture at the age of eleven, formally binding him to work for his brother until the age of twenty-one. He would not be paid a wage until the final year of his apprenticeship. If he tried to escape, he would be arrested, and even jailed.

This servitude led to the first great relational divide of Benjamin Franklin's life.

Soon after Ben's arrival, James founded the first independent newspaper in the colonies, the *New England Courant*. Young Benjamin begged his brother for the chance to publish an article of his own in the paper.

Time and again, James refused. So, posing as the widow "Silence Dogood," the teenage Benjamin slipped articles penned in her name under James's door once every two weeks. Not only did the *Courant* run the "letters," but the observations of Silence Dogood became enormously popular. The widow's true identity became the subject of intense curiosity. Men even wrote to the *Courant* proposing marriage to Widow Dogood.

After fourteen Silence Dogood letters, Benjamin confessed to his brother that he was the author. James Franklin had long been annoyed and jealous of his younger brother's charisma and fondness for independent thinking. So, rather than applaud Benjamin's resourcefulness, he beat him.

"My brother was passionate, and had often beaten me, which I took extremely amiss; and, thinking my apprenticeship very tedious, I was continually wishing for some opportunity of shortening it," Franklin would later write.

Despite that, Benjamin remained loyal, running the *Courant* on his own when James was arrested that same year for printing articles deemed offensive to Boston's religious community. But once again, instead of thanking his brother for keeping the business up and running, and printing articles in James's defense, James continued to punish his younger brother with a beating.

Fed up, Franklin escaped.

"I sold some of my books to raise a little money," Franklin would later write of the voyage by ship that took him from Boston, "and as we had a fair wind, in three days I found myself in New York, near three hundred miles from home, a boy of but seventeen . . . with very little money in my pocket."

Escape brought independence, but Franklin never forgot the beatings that made him run. Writing of James, he would later note, "I fancy his harsh and tyrannical treatment of me might be a means of impressing me with that aversion to arbitrary power that has stuck to me through my whole life."

Franklin would write those prophetic words in 1757, at the age of fifty-one, almost twenty years before King George and Parliament bullied America into war.

Overcoming the beatings of the brutal James Franklin, young Benjamin found the inspiration to live a life of independence, unrestricted by the standard expectations that so often prove the downfall of lesser men.

In 1730, at the age of twenty-four, Benjamin Franklin became a master printer in his own right. In that same year, now living in Philadelphia, he entered into a common-law marriage with the plain and industrious Deborah Read. And whether coincidence or not, this arrangement allowed him to evade formal indictment for the crimes of "bastardy" and "fornication" — which carried a fine of ten pounds and, in some cases, a public whipping.

For the next four decades, Franklin nurtured his growing celebrity in the colonies, all due to his printing business and the articles he wrote to fill the journals he circulated. He published the widely read *Pennsylvania Gazette,* along with a collection of homespun wisdom he named *Poor Richard's Almanack.*

The Doctor also indulged his passion for science and invention, conducting experiments in electricity and designing a stove that provided efficient heat for a small home. He named it after himself, but refused to take out a patent in order that the Franklin stove become widely used. In an amazing series of public-oriented initiatives, Franklin founded Philadelphia's first library, postal service, hospital, and volunteer fire department. He even redesigned the city's streetlights so that they would burn more efficiently. His election to the Pennsylvania Assembly in 1751 began the natural progression from civic leader to national figure.

Despite the mental rigor of publishing, inventing, indulging his curiosities, and founding a colonial militia, Ben Franklin has never lost his affection for the fairer sex.* "Neither a fortress or a maidenhead

---

*In 1745, Franklin wrote the essay, "Advice to a Young Man on the Choice of a Mistress," in which he acknowledges the lustful "violent natural inclinations" living within all men. He suggests that if a man should decide to take a mistress, she should be an older woman because "there is no hazard for children" and "they are more prudent and discreet in conducting an intrigue to prevent suspicion. The commerce with them is therefore safer with regard to your reputation." Franklin concluded that "in the dark all cats are grey, the pleasure of corporal enjoyment with an old woman is at least equal, and frequently superior, every knack being by practice capable of improvement." Franklin took this advice to heart in his relationship with Margaret Stevenson during the fifteen years he rented a room from her in London. She was his own age, and their relationship was often considered one of husband and wife. However, Franklin often forgot his own instruction. In 1767, a good friend of his recounted walking in on a

will hold out not long after they begin to parley," is one of the many amorous comments he writes in *Poor Richard's Almanack.* Deborah, who runs the postal service when her husband travels, turns a blind eye as Franklin stays out late most nights in the taverns drinking rum and enjoying dalliances with women who are sometimes decades younger. Twenty-three-year-old Catharine Ray made him sugar plums as he arrived in Boston at Christmas to inspect the local postal network. They then traveled together to Rhode Island through deep snow, and kissed in a snowstorm, "pure as your virgin innocence, white as your lovely bosom," as Franklin would later describe the scene in a letter to Catharine upon his return home to Philadelphia.

One political enemy will even pen a verse about Franklin's infidelities.

Franklin, tho' plagued with fumbling age,
Needs nothing to excite him.
But is too ready to engage
When younger arms invite him.

Later, living in England, Franklin will fall

---

sixty-one-year-old Franklin kissing and fondling "a young lass sitting on his lap."

not only for his landlady, Margaret Stevenson, but also her daughter, eighteen-year-old Polly. Their relationship will continue to the moment of his death, with Polly sitting at Franklin's bedside as he breathes his last.*

But, above all, Benjamin Franklin loves the American colonies.

The septuagenarian spent most of the winter and spring of 1776 traveling to Montreal in a vain effort to convince the Canadians to send a representative to Congress and join the struggle for independence. The

---

*Polly Stevenson was just eighteen when Franklin first moved into her mother's home, and he was instantly attracted to her intelligence and curious mind. The relationship between Ben Franklin and Margaret Stevenson was romantic, but that between him and Polly Stevenson was likely never more than filial. For many years after his return to America in 1775, it consisted solely of transatlantic correspondence. In all, she and Franklin exchanged 170 letters. Polly married a British surgeon in 1770. When he died from sepsis contracted while dissecting a cadaver, Franklin encouraged her to bring her three children to America to live with him. She did so, remaining in Franklin's home until his death.

journey took him through miles of wilderness and involved deep snow, poor roads, and poor sleep in makeshift accommodations each night. Franklin's body broke down from the deprivation and hardship, and he was afflicted with gout, boils, and severe dizziness. For a time, he thought he might die.

"I begin to apprehend that I have undertaken a fatigue that at my time of life may prove too much for me, so I sit down to write to a few friends by way of farewell," he wrote to good friend Josiah Quincy on April 15.

Though Franklin did eventually make it to Montreal, the mission failed. His return trip in May brought yet another setback when he was unable to convince the Native American tribes of Canada and New York to join the rebellion.*

*Franklin spoke with representatives of the Seven Nations of Canada, the same tribes from the Saint Lawrence River Valley that had fought alongside the French in the French and Indian War. They were on their way home from a council with the Six Nations, a confederation of tribes in New York and the Great Lakes region. The purpose of that council was to discuss whether the Native Americans would stay neutral in the war between Britain

Yet, despite the enormous anguish Franklin endured on that fruitless journey, his physical pain is nothing compared to the emotional suffering he is experiencing because of the great rift with his illegitimate son, William.*

It is a grief that is about to get far worse.

For the past thirteen years, the colony of New Jersey has known just one governor: William Franklin. In 1762, Benjamin Franklin arranged the royal appointment by King George for his son. William is forty-five years old and well understands that he has

---

and the colonies. As of Franklin's meeting, no decision had been made on the matter. The Seven Nations of Canada later joined the fight on the side of the British. The Six Nations of the New York and Great Lakes region divided their loyalty, with tribe often fighting tribe as one side fought for the British and the other for the Americans.

*William Franklin's date of birth is uncertain, but historians place it between September 1730 and March 1731. In his autobiography, Benjamin Franklin said of his sexual encounters at that time: "that hard-to-be-governed passion of youth hurried me frequently into intrigues with low women that fell in my way." Perhaps for this reason, the name of William's mother remains unknown.

made good thanks in great part to the father whom he so closely resembles.

In a letter to his father in September 1758, William pronounced himself "extremely obliged to you for your care in supplying me with money, and shall ever have a grateful sense of that with the other numberless indulgences I have received from your paternal affection."

There was a time when Benjamin and William Franklin were as close as a father and son could be. In William, Benjamin found his most trusted confidant and ally. Their bond began in William's childhood, when Benjamin doted on the child, buying him a pony and hiring the best and brightest tutors in Philadelphia to educate him. Thanks to his father's intercession, William secured plum jobs as a clerk for the Pennsylvania Assembly and comptroller of the American postal service. A friend once said of their relationship that Benjamin was William's "friend, his brother, his intimate, and easy companion."

The greatest bond father and son shared was their passion for England, and a deep belief in the need for loyalty to the crown of George III. When Benjamin Franklin sailed to England in 1757, the twenty-six-year-old William at his side, one purpose of the trip was to petition the king to give Pennsylvania the designation "royal" colony, like her neighbors New York and New Jersey.* Naturally, Benjamin Franklin hoped to be named royal governor when this new status came to pass.

Franklin had already shown himself loyal to the Crown through his assistance of General Braddock in 1754, and exulted in his royally appointed role as head of the American postal service. Benjamin Franklin once said of George III that he could "scarcely conceive a King of better dispositions, of more exemplary virtues, or more truly desirous of promoting the welfare of his subjects." In 1762, the British returned

*The thirteen colonies were broken up into three distinctions: royal colonies (New York, New Hampshire, New Jersey, Virginia, North Carolina, South Carolina, Georgia), proprietary colonies (Maryland, Pennsylvania, Delaware), and charter colonies (Massachusetts, Connecticut, and Rhode Island; Massachusetts would later become a royal colony). Royal colonies were administered by officials chosen by the king; charter colonies were self-governed, with rights and privileges granted to them through a written contract with the king; proprietary colonies were lands deeded to an individual by the king, with full governing rights.

the affection when Oxford University presented Benjamin Franklin with an honorary doctorate for his accomplishments in science.

Even as relations between America and England deteriorated, both Franklins believed that loyalty to England and the throne was an act of patriotism. "You can never place yourself in a happier situation than in your ancient constitutional dependency on Great Britain. No independent state ever was or ever can be so happy as we have been, and might still be, under that government," William wrote to the New Jersey legislature in 1776 in defense of his Loyalist views.

"Their government will not be lasting," he added of the Continental Congress. "It will never suit a people who have once tasted the sweets of British liberty under a British constitution."

The young Franklin has never wavered from that belief.

Benjamin Franklin's love for England, however, came to an abrupt end on January 29, 1774. He was working relentlessly to prevent war when word of the Boston Tea Party reached London.

As the colonial agent to Parliament for Massachusetts and Pennsylvania, he was summoned to appear before an elite group of royal advisers known as the Privy Council. The meeting took place late on a Saturday afternoon, in an octagonal room in Whitehall Palace known as "the cockpit." Centuries before, when Henry VIII ruled the land, he enjoyed cockfights and drinking in this same room. Its eight walls now house a theater, but are still designed so that the eye is drawn to the action at the very center of the room.

After returning to London in 1764, Franklin reveled in behaving like a proper English gentleman. He purchased fine suits and wigs. He delighted in the shipments of buckwheat, cranberries, and tart green Newtown Pippin apples Deborah sent from home, but he also drank strong coffee with the intellectuals at St. Paul's Coffee House. His writing style was British to the core, trained by reading and then rewriting articles by British writers Richard Steele and Joseph Addison. He was a fellow at the Royal Society, the nation's most esteemed intellectual body, thanks to winning the Copley Medal for his experiments in electricity.*

And yet, as Franklin was led into the

*The Copley Medal was the eighteenth-century

cockpit, wearing for the first time a simple crimson-and-yellow suit made of Manchester velvet, he was every bit the American.* Gone was his powdered wig. Instead, the top of his head was bald. The strands of hair that grew from the side of his skull dangled to his shoulders, rather than being pulled back and tied. In London, a man of such appearance was considered a bumpkin — even a "Yankee Doodle" — an American so simple and unsophisticated that he thought that placing a single feather in his hat made him appear a world traveler with knowledge of glamorous indulgences such as Italian macaroni.

Franklin did not care. At five foot nine, he was not tall, but he stood ramrod straight, unafraid of the attacks that were sure to come.

He was directed to a long table at the center of the room. He stood next to a

---

equivalent of the Nobel Prize, though focused exclusively on science.

*Manchester velvet was made of printed cotton, not the shiny and more expensive silk velvet. It is also commonly known as "corduroy." Franklin would have worn this as a nod to the burgeoning textile industry in northern England, and also as a sign of practical fiscal conservatism.

fireplace, where he could see the galleries packed with some of the most powerful men in England. Adding to the carnival-like air, many of these "gentlemen" had brought their wives, so that they might enjoy the spectacle of a decent man's public humiliation. Among the crowd were philosopher Edmund Burke; Prime Minister Lord North; and Lord Hillsborough, the former secretary of state to the colonies, whose disdain for Ben Franklin is widely known. Member of Parliament Horace Walpole once described Hillsborough as "a pompous composition of ignorance and want of judgment."

Yet men such as Hillsborough now stood in judgment of Benjamin Franklin.

Led by Solicitor General Alexander Wedderburn, the Privy Council insulted Franklin for about an hour. Wedderburn was known as one of the great orators of his time, and he put those skills on display as he pounded on the table for dramatic emphasis while vilifying Franklin as the *true* conspirator behind the troubles in Massachusetts. The primary issue was a scandal known as the Hutchinson letters, in which postmaster-general Franklin diverted letters Massachusetts governor Thomas Hutchinson had written to the British government requesting a greater British military presence to quash colonial rebellion. Franklin showed the letters to his fellow dissidents under the condition that they not be made public. John Adams, however, published Hutchinson's writings in the *Boston Gazette* in June 1773. Hutchinson was forced to flee to England for his safety. It was only later, after three innocent men were accused of leaking the documents, that Franklin stepped forth to reveal his duplicity.

Franklin never moved a muscle, remaining silent and composed, a thin smile pasted on his lips. He stayed that way even when the gallery erupted in taunts, heckling, and mocking laughter.

"The Doctor . . . stood conspicuously erect, without the smallest movement of any part of his body. The muscles of his face had been previously composed as to afford a placid tranquil expression of countenance, and he did not suffer the slightest alteration of it to appear," Fellow American Dr. Edward Bancroft, one of Franklin's only allies in the cockpit that day, would later write.*

*Bancroft is a fascinating character. Just thirty-one in 1776, he was already an accomplished physician, chemist, adventurer, and author, writ-

"He kept his countenance as immovable as if he had been made of wood."

When asked if he would like to make a statement in his own defense, Benjamin Franklin demurred. He would have none of that. As he exited the cockpit, Franklin attempted to convey the appearance of stoicism and of being unsettled by the attack. Yet, as a man acutely aware of the power of his good reputation, he found such public humiliation devastating. He had lost all status in London, of that he was sure.

From that moment forward, Franklin's fondness for all things English vanished.

It would take time, but the Doctor would get his revenge against those famous faces in the gallery who'd mocked him. He made a vow never again to wear the spotted velvet suit until that moment arrived.

Two days later, King George added insult to injury. A letter was delivered to Franklin's home on Craven Street, informing him that the king no longer had use for his services

ing the treatise *Essay on the Natural History of Guiana* in 1769. Franklin not only assisted in getting his fellow American elected to the Royal Society, the world's leading body for scientific discourse, but he also hired Bancroft to spy on Britain's top leaders.

as deputy postmaster-general in America. Enraged, Franklin wrote to his sister Jane that the attacks would only make him stronger: "Intending to disgrace me, they have rather done me honor."

The painful split with William began soon after. Franklin hoped his son would step down as royal governor of New Jersey once he heard how badly his father had been insulted. But William refused to leave his post. Franklin seethed, writing to his son that he was disloyal, a "thorough courtier."*

Upon Dr. Franklin's return to America from London, the split between father and son grew worse. At the time, Americans identified themselves as either patriots or Loyalists.

Benjamin Franklin, however, will soon be known as a superpatriot.

William went in the opposite direction, resolute in his loyalty to King George. He began sending intelligence reports to the British Army, even writing to inform them

*By definition, a courtier is an individual who spends a great deal of time in the royal court. In its most pejorative meaning, however, it is an insult hurled at members of the royal court who seek personal advancement through fawning, flattering, and other obsequious behavior.

of his father's journey to Canada.

William had become not just an embarrassment to his father, but also an ally to his enemies, the many who spread rumors that the Doctor was himself a spy for King George. For a deeply prideful man like Franklin, the personal attacks instigated by his son were searing.

So, when the Congress finally moved to take away William's governorship, Benjamin Franklin did nothing to stop them. When the New Jersey militia enforced the removal by placing the younger Franklin under house arrest, Benjamin Franklin once again refused to intercede, despite having advance knowledge that William would be arrested and taken to prison.

In Benjamin Franklin's mind, his son no longer existed.

Now, on June 24 in Philadelphia, Secretary Charles Thomson, the Irish-born Philadelphian who records the minutes of every session, apprises the Continental Congress of William's current situation.

At 10:00 a.m. on Friday, June 21, two members of the New Jersey Provincial Congress arrived at the former governor's lodgings with orders to transport him to their governing body for questions. William refused. An armed guard of more than twenty men was required to take him away.

Just as when his father was led into the cockpit, William appeared before the assembled members of the Provincial Congress to explain his behavior. The stakes, however, were much higher for William Franklin. Instead of merely losing his reputation, like his father, he stood to lose his freedom — and perhaps his life.

Nonetheless, William remained haughty during the ensuing interrogation, even when his inquisitor, the Scottish-born John Witherspoon, alluded to his beginnings as a bastard. When questioned about his Loyalist stance, William refused to explain himself, calling the Provincial Congress a powerless and illegal governing body.

William was taken from the room and returned to house arrest. A motion was then passed that he be removed from New Jersey altogether and sent to prison in another colony.

This required the permission of the Continental Congress.

Thus, in Philadelphia, three days after William's questioning, congressional secretary Charles Thomson now reads the transcript of William's interrogation. To underscore why such an interrogation was deemed

145

necessary, the New Jersey request describes William as "a virulent enemy to this country, and a person that may prove dangerous."

The appeal concludes "that said William Franklin be confined in such place and manner the Continental Congress shall direct."

Once again, Benjamin Franklin refuses to help his son.

The Congress dictates that William be bounded over to Governor John Trumbull of Connecticut for incarceration. William will soon be confined to a series of prisons, among them a hellhole in Litchfield, Connecticut, with a filthy, rat-infested dungeon usually reserved for men sentenced to death. He will sleep on a straw mat that reeks of urine, sweat, and human filth. His cell will be without bed, chair, or toilet. But most damaging of all, he will be alone, held in solitary confinement in order that he might have plenty of time to consider his actions.

"I suffer so much in being thus buried alive, having no one to speak to day or night," he will write from prison, "and for the want of air and exercise, that I should deem it a favor to be immediately taken out and shot."

It gets worse.

William Franklin will lose every tooth and all his hair from malnutrition. In agony because his wife is dying, he will petition George Washington directly, asking that he be temporarily freed to be with his ailing wife.

But, behind the scenes, Benjamin Franklin will intercede. At his direction, Congress will vote that William not be paroled to be by the side of his beloved Elizabeth as she breathes her last.

The harsh treatment of his son will haunt Benjamin Franklin his entire life. But the Doctor feels his actions are justified: "Nothing has hurt me so much and affected me with such keen sensations as to find myself deserted in my old age by my only son; and not only deserted, but to find him taking up arms against me, in a cause wherein my good fame, fortune and life were at stake," he will later write to his son directly.

This is the dark side of Benjamin Franklin: those who cross him will pay a price.

6

New York City, New York
June 28, 1776
11:00 A.M.

Soon the noose will take another life.

Twenty thousand New Yorkers are now aware that George Washington has Sgt. Thomas Hickey's death warrant. Much of Manhattan has come to watch the disgraced soldier hang by the neck until dead. Men, women, and children; black and white; rich and poor — all have traveled to Washington's military encampment.* They came on foot, horseback, pushcart, or by carriage to indulge in colonial America's favorite form of mass entertainment: public execution.

On this warm Friday morning, some spectators even enjoy a picnic. Others

*The site of Hickey's gallows is currently the corner of Chrystie and Grand Streets, on Manhattan's Lower East Side.

stumble across the greenery of the common, very drunk despite the early morning hour. Pickpockets, of which there are many, enjoy a busy and prosperous day.

These are Thomas Hickey's last moments as a terrestrial being, but there is little sympathy for him. Some in the crowd call out to the condemned man, asking him to account for his sins. But most hecklers are more delighted to taunt the handsome Irishman on his slow procession to the hangman's rope.

Washington stands near the gallows, which he has purposely set atop a hill for maximum spectator viewing. Columns of soldiers stand in formation on three sides, there to serve as eyewitnesses to the execution. On Washington's orders, construction of the gallows was the Quartermaster Corps' first duty upon making camp at this large open field two months ago. Once the British sailed away from Boston in March, destination unknown, Washington marched the Continental Army to Manhattan, where he believes the British will attack next.

Washington's hair is still a youthful reddish-brown. His new Continental Army uniform is blue, although darker than the Virginia hue for which he was once known. The general spent the morning writing let-

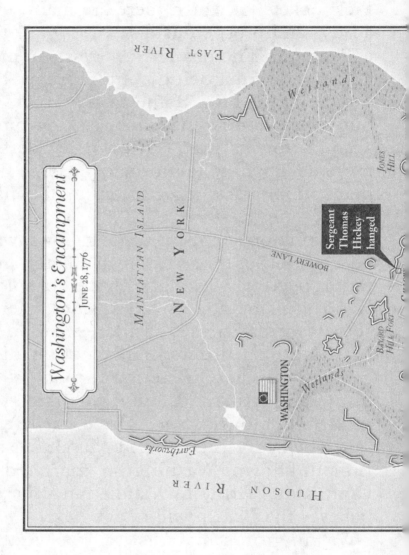

Washington's Encampment
June 28, 1776

EAST RIVER

Wetlands

JONES
HILL

MANHATTAN ISLAND

NEW YORK

BOWERY LANE

Sergeant
Thomas
Hickey
hanged

Bayard
Hill Fort

WASHINGTON

Wetlands

Earthworks

HUDSON RIVER

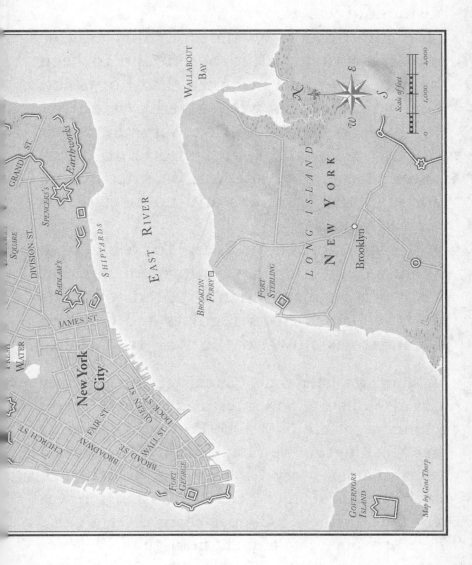

WALLABOUT BAY

LONG ISLAND

NEW YORK

Brooklyn

FORT STERLING

BROOKLYN FERRY

EAST RIVER

SHIPYARDS

GRAND ST.

Earthworks

SPENCER'S

DIVISION ST.

SQUARE

BADLAM'S

JAMES ST.

WATER

New York City

FAIR ST.

QUEEN ST.

WALL ST.

DOCK ST.

BROADWAY

BROAD ST.

CHURCH ST.

FORT GEORGE

GOVERNORS ISLAND

Scale of feet

0   1,000   2,000

N
W   E
S

Map by Gene Thorp

ters and conducting official business, knowing that this hanging is part of the messy business of war.

On any other day, the enormity of this public spectacle would be enough to keep the general's mind occupied. But not today. That's because his wife, Martha, is on her way back to Mount Vernon, Virginia, which is both a relief and source of grief to Washington. He is glad she will be safe, but he will miss the comforts and counsel of his beloved wife.*

Martha is leaving New York because Washington's spies have informed him that a Royal Navy fleet laden with tens of thousands of British Army regulars and German auxiliaries is now on the way to the city

*A story was later widely circulated that a soldier named William Cooper testified before a secret committee of the New York Provincial Congress that Washington was having an affair with a woman named Mary Gibbons, and by doing so, put himself in danger. "General Washington was very fond [of her]," Cooper charged. "He came there very often late at night in disguise." The accusation was a widely circulated British invention, intended to discredit Washington. In fact, no one named William Cooper testified before the secret committee.

from Canada and could arrive as early as tomorrow. The general has fortified Manhattan as best he can, but in all likelihood his small army will be vastly outnumbered. The untested Continental Army will soon reveal whether it is battle ready.

Washington knows that in Philadelphia the debates over independence continue, with a five-man committee in the process of writing a formal declaration of freedom.

But none of that will matter unless he finds a way to defeat the British.

Seen in that light, the hanging of Sergeant Hickey is a mere sideshow, but a vital one — it sends a powerful message to all in attendance.

Washington studies the approaching prisoner. Hickey — five foot six, dark-haired, thickly set — is sobbing. He still wears the distinctive blue wool jacket and white breeches of Washington's "Life Guards."*

*Washington's bodyguards were known by several names, among them the Life Guards (common with enlisted members), Washington's Life Guard, the Commander-in-Chief Guard, and Washington's Body Guard. In the general order of June 27, 1776, sentencing Hickey to death, they are referred to as the "General's Guards." Their official title, however, was "His Excellency's Guard."

Thomas Hickey has spent two weeks in a jail cell. The buttons and stripes have been cut from his coat as a ritual act of stripping his rank. The loss of stripes means he is no longer *Sergeant* Hickey, but a mere private.

Just three months ago, Hickey was hand-picked to serve as one of Washington's personal bodyguards. But with General Howe's army and navy just days away from sailing into New York Harbor, Hickey had a change of heart. He joined a daring plot to assassinate Washington and deliver the city over to the British. Now he is about to become the first soldier in American history to be executed for treason.

Washington signed his death warrant with no reservations, for Hickey has shown himself to be a liar, a thief, a braggart, and a traitor — a man who betrayed not just the American colonies but General Washington himself.

The Irishman has long flirted with the gallows. Hickey is a complicated man, trusted by powerful leaders but loyal only to his own ambitions. He first came to America

---

Whatever the name, the bodyguards' motto was "Conquer or Die," and the unit served Washington faithfully throughout the war. First formed in March 1776, they were disbanded in June 1783.

during the French and Indian War, fighting as a soldier in the British Army. Hickey's charisma and efficiency were noted, and he was removed from the ranks to serve at a higher level. By war's end, he was personal assistant to top British general William Johnson, a brilliant tactician whose fondness for Mohawk beauties led him to father mixed-race children by multiple women and take a Mohawk as his common-law bride for the last fifteen years of his life.

Johnson died of a stroke in 1774, leaving Hickey without the status and protection that once accompanied his service to the general. However, rather than return to duty as an ordinary British soldier, he defected to the American cause.

In March 1776, General Washington, realizing the need for men to guard him, his official papers, and the Continental Army's treasury, sent an order asking for a very specific sort of soldier. They were to be individuals of "sobriety, honesty, and good behavior . . . from five feet, eight inches high, to five feet, ten inches; handsomely and well made," he specified, writing in the third person. "There is nothing in his eyes more desirable, than cleanliness in a soldier, he desires that particular attention may be made, in the choice of such men, as are neat, and spruce."

Despite being too short for Washington's specifications, Hickey was among eighty men handpicked for this elite squad. Soon, he became a favorite of the general. But the duties of a Life Guard did not carry the prestige the Irishman had enjoyed while working for General Johnson. Very often, the guards were nothing more than Washington's servants, performing mundane household chores at the general's headquarters. Hickey grew bored. Close daily proximity to General Washington and a lingering allegiance to the British cause made him an easy mark for Loyalists seeking conspirators to assassinate His Excellency.

The ringleader was New York royal governor William Tryon, a British subject and avowed Loyalist.* Tryon fled the city as Washington's army approached in April, taking refuge aboard a seventy-four-gun British ship of the line anchored off the coast, HMS *Duchess of Gordon.*

The American forces lack a navy, leaving Tryon safe aboard the vessel, and giving him

---

*Despite his pro-British leanings, Tryon is remembered in New York City to this day. He is the namesake for Fort Tryon Park in Upper Manhattan, and for Tryon Avenue in the Bronx.

ample opportunity to receive those visitors who rowed out to greet him.* Tryon became so successful at using these guests to send messages to the Loyalist community that Washington himself informed Congress of Tryon's ongoing influence.

"The encouragements given by Governor Tryon to the disaffected, which are circulated no one can tell how; the movements of this kind of people, which are more easy to perceive than describe," Washington wrote.

Tryon was not just exhorting his followers; he was planning a massive campaign to win the war. His messages traveled into Connecticut and as far north as Massachusetts. His plan was simple: kill George Washington, kill the rest of Washington's generals, and then conduct guerrilla warfare in New York City once the British Army arrived. Cannon would be spiked, powder magazines would be set ablaze, and bridges would be destroyed to prevent the arrival of patriot reinforcements.

*The Continental Navy was formed on October 13, 1775. (This date is still celebrated as the birthday of the U.S. Navy.) However, the small force was defensive in nature, and no match for British ships of war.

Rumors of the plot swirled for more than a month. "The friends to liberty are to a man convinced, that the Tories will take up arms, when encouraged by the appearance of any royal troops," noted one of Washington's top generals, Charles Lee.

Tryon recruited New York mayor David Matthews to join his cause, and contracted with a local gunsmith to procure weapons. He enforced a strict code of secrecy, letting few conspirators know the names of others involved.

Tryon's plan might have worked, had it not been for Thomas Hickey.

Washington's bodyguard was arrested on charges of possessing counterfeit money. While in prison, he bragged to jailhouse informant Isaac Ketchum that he had received money from Tryon and was recruiting other Life Guards to join the fight. He bragged that he would personally take up arms on the great day when the British arrived.

Hickey's trial took place two days ago, on June 26. It seemed he had little to fear — every other accused man sentenced that afternoon received a release from prison or a short sentence. But four eyewitnesses testified that Hickey tried to recruit Life Guards to join Tryon's plot. And Hickey's role in the plot, it was revealed, would have required him, personally, to kill George Washington, and then destroy artillery and ammunition.

Hickey admitted to joining Tryon, though only as a precaution, stating that "if the enemy should arrive and defeat the army here, and he should be taken prisoner, he might be safe."

With little doubt of his treachery, Hickey was convicted of "Sedition and mutiny, and also of holding a treach'rous correspondence with the enemy, for the most horrid and detestable purposes."

The Irishman was sentenced "to suffer death."

"The General approves the sentence," Washington wrote in an order that afternoon, "and orders that he be hanged to morrow at eleven o'clock."

Washington could have ordered that the Irishman be shot. A firing squad would have done the job nicely. Hickey would have been forced to kneel next to a coffin, and then been shot in the head by twelve of his fellow soldiers.

But firing squads are anonymous affairs that take place at ground level. Few soldiers would witness the execution, let alone civilians. This is why Washington prefers a hanging. In fact, he likes that mode of execution very much. Capital punishment makes for excellent theater. As with all military executions, the general means to make an example of the traitor. The swinging corpse will serve as "a warning to every soldier in the army" who might consider desertion or treason.

Washington has ordered that the death procession be made as public as possible. As the crowd lines Hickey's path to the gallows, he is trailed by a chaplain, there to hear his confession and offer a spiritual message to the crowd; a provost marshal, to oversee the execution; and more than a hundred uniformed armed guards leveling sharpened bayonets — lest the condemned try to escape. A cadre of drummers sets the procession's slow pace, beating tattoo on the ominous "dead march."

As Hickey walks ever closer to his execution, the sound of the drums seems to grow louder, but that is only because the crowd has become quiet.

It is all as Washington planned.

While the general's intention is to put the fear of God in those soldiers who would plot treasonously or desert their post, His Excellency also has a much more immediate motivation for this public execution.

160

The city is deeply divided. Pockets of Loyalists are everywhere. A statue of King George occupies a prominent position on Bowling Green, at the southern tip of Manhattan. The monarch is nine feet tall and made of lead and gold, sitting atop a proportionally large horse. A fifteen-foot-high marble pedestal supports the two. Modeling it after an Italian statue of Roman emperor Marcus Aurelius, sculptor Joseph Wilton desired that it might "metaphorically assume and actually aspire to the wisdom and grandeur of the ancient stoic leader and thinker."

In fact, the opposite has occurred. As colonial unrest has risen, George has become a very negative sort of inspiration. So much so, that Loyalists recently placed a black wrought-iron fence around the statue for its protection, fearing vandals would destroy it.

Even now, Loyalist spies wander through this hanging ceremony, counting troop tents, artillery pieces, and cavalry horses.

As Washington sees for himself at this moment, a public execution brings the community together. If only during this procession and in the moments when Hickey kicks spasmodically at the end of the rope, the divisions between patriots and Loyalists will cease. The good people of New York will watch one thing and one thing only: the death of Thomas Hickey.

The Irishman takes his final steps to the gallows, where a rope with a hangman's noose dangles from a crossbeam.

The traitor is forced to step into the back of a horse-drawn cart. As Washington looks on, Hickey gazes out at the masses that have gathered to watch his execution. It is a scene that fills him with false confidence. He stops crying.

Utter silence settles over the crowd. All eyes are trained on Hickey. Parents tell their children to pay attention.

The officer of the day reads aloud Hickey's death warrant. His voice carries over the crowd, distinct and damning.

A calm defiance settles over Hickey as the noose is looped over his head and cinched tightly around his neck — though not so tightly as to cause rope burns *before* the hanging itself, for this is considered inhumane.

The chaplain offers to pray with Hickey, or perhaps to hear his pleas for penitence, but the condemned man mocks the clergyman for being a heartless opportunist. He sends the chaplain away.

For his last words, Hickey sneers that his accusers may be the next to die.

There is no blindfold. Hickey's eyes are wide open and his jaw firmly set as he awaits what will come next.

The horse is spurred. The cart leaps forward. Hickey tumbles out the back and stretches the rope.

For the very lucky, the force of the drop is enough to snap the neck, killing the person instantly. But it rarely works like that. Thomas Hickey strangles to death very slowly. His hands are tied, preventing his arms from instinctively clawing at the rope that has already wrenched his larynx away from his trachea, obstructing his desperate attempts to breathe. Simultaneously, the rope squeezes shut his carotid arteries, preventing blood flow to his brain.

Hickey's legs kick spasmodically as the air is forced from his body. The crowd gasps as his eyes begin to pop from his skull, his lips and nose turn purple.

The spectators know what comes next, and now focus their stares on Hickey's white uniform breeches. Within seconds, his sphincter muscle is deprived of oxygen, forcing him to defecate. His pants also bulge outward in front, as his penis becomes erect from the rope placing enormous pressure on the brain's cerebellum.

The crowd looks for these nuances, having seen them at other executions. This is part of the show. Women gasp and cover their mouths, and men close their eyes at the horror. Yet, few look away for very long.

Finally, the kicking stops. Hickey's dead body swings, its pendulum arc growing shorter until it swings no more.

Rain or shine, Hickey's corpse will dangle from this rope for a day or even a week — until General Washington feels the time is right to cut him down. A pit will be dug at the base of the gallows, the rope will be cut, the deceased will drop unceremoniously into the earth, and dirt will then be thrown on top of him, there to remain until the next hanging. At Hickey's own request, no prayers will be said over his body.

As the crowds begin to disperse, Washington mounts Blueskin and gallops back to his headquarters at Richmond Hill, an estate formerly owned by a British Army paymaster.* He is troubled by Hickey's execution, and the fact that other conspirators plotting his assassination have not been found. But as the people of New York clog

*Currently the corner of Varick and Charlton Streets in Lower Manhattan.

the narrow streets on the way back to their homes, the fate of the colonies weighs heavily on Washington's shoulders. The general is left to ponder how many of these citizens will stand behind him when the world's most powerful army and navy invade their city within a few short days.

Public executions are not the most poetic way to bring a city together.

Gathering thousands of people to watch a young man soil himself while strangling to death is also not the most spiritual way to father a nation.

But the fate of American independence does not yet rest upon moral platitudes — right now it depends entirely upon military victory.

Washington needs support.

This is war.

And George Washington will do whatever it takes to win.

The next morning, June 29, 1776, colonial scouts race to inform George Washington that the Royal Navy is sailing into New York Harbor. White sails fill the horizon as far as the eye can see, they tell the general.

The British have arrived.

Soon, there will be more death.

165

7

Thomas Jefferson will soon commit treason.

Thick clouds of horseflies fill the Assembly Room as Congress finally ends its second consecutive long day of debate. The time has now come to cast a vote for or against independence from England. The weather outside is hot and sultry, forcing custodian Andrew McNair to open the tall windows to let in a breeze. But with the fresh air come the horseflies, courtesy of a stable next door. The flies swarm the cloth-covered tables, biting the delegates through the thin stockings covering their lower legs.

One week ago, Jefferson submitted his version of the Declaration of Independence for review by his peers. He is proud of his way with the written word and the elegance with

166

which he crafted the document. The Virginian believes that his Declaration has a clear voice and makes a compelling argument for freedom. Yet he knows that the outcome doesn't belong to him. The case he makes for independence will be scrutinized by congressional subcommittees, which will dissect his words line by line and make their own changes.

Jefferson is not at all happy about this upcoming edit, particularly from men whose writing skills are not his equal. But that is part of the frustrating business of Congress. Every action must be put to a vote, no matter how petty or insignificant it might seem.

The vote at hand, however, is obviously different. Within moments, the term *colony* may no longer define the territories these men represent. Yet a simple majority will not carry the day. By rule of this Congress, all thirteen colonies must unanimously choose independence. If just one votes "nay," there will be no Declaration. Jefferson's three weeks of careful writing will have been wasted.

Each colony is allowed to cast one vote. However, the number of representatives at the Congress is based upon the size of the territories, so there are more representatives for New York than, say, Delaware. Thus, the majority within each colonial delegation decides which way it will vote. Many are split. Each of the men in this room love America, but not all are convinced that a break from England is best.

Yesterday, as thunder hammered Philadelphia and a driving rain pelted the Assembly Room windows, Pennsylvania's John Dickinson delivered a lengthy argument to the Congress, stating that a vote for independence was "premature." It was Dickinson who led the movement one year ago to send George III the Olive Branch Petition promising full support for British superiority in the colonies. The king refused to accept, let alone endorse, the document, but Dickinson has not let go of his loyalty. A separation from England, he told Congress yesterday, would invite an attack by Spain or France. Or, worst case, might even cause a civil war between the colonies themselves.

So, yesterday, when it came time for each delegate to cast his vote, the pale and painfully thin Dickinson stood up and stated his choice: nay. Three other members of the seven-delegate Pennsylvania contingent cast a similar vote. Benjamin Franklin was among the dissenters on the losing side.

In all, nine colonies voted in favor of independence. Two delegations, South

Carolina and a deeply divided Pennsylvania, voted against.*

Delaware split its vote, one to one. The colony actually has three delegates, but the thin, cancer-ridden Caesar Rodney is not in Philadelphia, due to obligations with his colony's militia.

New York abstained, its delegates clearly fearful of an English occupation. Should they vote in favor of independence, only to have the British capture New York, they will certainly be put to death.

South Carolinian Edward Rutledge, who at age twenty-six was the youngest member of Congress, requested a second and final vote the following day, in the hope that the members of his delegation could be swayed to change their minds. Now, as the Congress prepares to take its final vote, Jefferson cannot help but notice that a new momentum

*The four South Carolina delegates were originally ordered by the governor and his advisers to vote against independence because they hoped for reconciliation with Britain. But these instructions were rescinded as patriotic fervor grew. Thus, it was somewhat surprising that, on July 1, the South Carolinian delegation got cold feet, still believing that independence was premature and decided to vote no.

fills the room. Last night, as many delegates were drinking at the City Tavern,* the news arrived from New York that more than one hundred British warships now filled the harbor. It is, in fact, the largest invasion force of the century, an assemblage of men and warships designed by King George to crush the rebel movement.

Hearing that devastating news, John Dickinson made a bold statement: still unwilling to vote for independence but knowing that the future of the nation depended upon a unanimous vote, he has stayed home. Rather than debate this matter in Congress, Dickinson has now chosen to fight the British as a member of the Pennsylvania militia. His

*In an era before there was such a thing as hotels, City Tavern on Second Street was what many delegates chose as their lodgings while serving in Congress. Three stories tall, with spacious meeting and drinking areas where the members could debate politics, it was described by John Adams as "the most genteel tavern in America." The Second Continental Congress had a standing reservation for a dinner for all delegates every Saturday night. City Tavern was leveled in 1854, then meticulously rebuilt by the National Park Service in 1975, in time for America's bicentennial. It is still a thriving business.

conscience will not allow him to vote for independence, but that same conscience cannot endure the wholesale slaughter of American patriots.

Dickinson's defection from the vote means that Pennsylvania is no longer aligned with the king.

For Thomas Jefferson, independence is the only choice. This is not an emotional decision, but one based on his belief that all men are "endowed by their Creator with certain unalienable rights, that among these are life, liberty and the pursuit of happiness," in his own words. All men, that is, except slaves.*

*Slavery was legal and condoned in all thirteen colonies, but by 1776 only Georgia and South Carolina still allowed the importation of slaves. Many members of Congress, including Thomas Jefferson, not just owned slaves but also sold them as a form of commerce. However, the issue of slavery was making many Americans uncomfortable. One of them was Jefferson. He blamed King George for bringing slavery to America. His original language in the Declaration concerning freedom caused considerable debate in Congress, particularly from Georgia and South Carolina. It was later modified to avoid the slavery issue. The

Jefferson believes that power is achieved by overwhelming argument. Thus, he has chosen to begin the Declaration of Independence by using reason to state what must be done:

When, in the course of human events, it becomes necessary for one people to dis-

---

congressional delegates deleted the following paragraph:

He [George III] has waged cruel war against human nature itself, violating its most sacred rights of life and liberty in the persons of a distant people who never offended him, captivating & carrying them into slavery in another hemisphere or to incur miserable death in their transportation thither. This piratical warfare, the opprobrium of infidel powers, is the warfare of the Christian King of Great Britain. Determined to keep open a market where Men should be bought & sold, he has prostituted his negative for suppressing every legislative attempt to prohibit or restrain this execrable commerce. And that this assemblage of horrors might want no fact of distinguished die, he is now exciting those very people to rise in arms among us, and to purchase that liberty of which he has deprived them, by murdering the people on whom he has obtruded them: thus paying off

solve the political bands which have connected them with another, and to assume
among the powers of the earth, the separate and equal station to which the laws of
nature and of nature's God entitle them, a
decent respect to the opinions of mankind
requires that they should declare the
causes which impel them to the separation.

The Virginian is proud of these words. He
crafted them knowing that King George
might himself someday read them, and that
the hope for colonial independence depended upon their precision and logic. But
he is also aware that they are just words on
a piece of paper. Unless Congress casts a
unanimous vote in favor of independence,
the king will prevail.

Despite the small breeze blowing through
the open windows, the muggy Philadelphia
heat is intense. Jefferson, who methodically
grooms himself with a washcloth each

---

former crimes committed against the Liberties
of one people, with crimes which he urges them
to commit against the lives of another.

Although those words disappeared from the
Declaration of Independence, Jefferson kept them
in his private library.

morning, now sweats through his linen shirt and cravat.* His coat and vest are not snug on his lank, lean frame, but the summer humidity makes them feel heavy against his skin. It is likewise for the other delegates, some of whom use the excuse of slipping away to use the congressional privy at Fifth and Chestnut to make a quick stop at a local tavern.

John Hancock calls for a final vote on

---

*The modern practice of bathing or showering by submersion was not widely practiced in America until the nineteenth century. For this reason, the room for conducting daily ablutions was known as a privy instead of a bathroom. In the absence of flush toilets, an individual either used a chamber pot or an outdoor privy. For the latter, it was necessary to dig a trench deep into the ground outside a building for use as a toilet, line the hole with bricks, then fit a wooden seat over the opening. "Bathing" in 1776 consisted of cleaning the face and hands with a cloth wetted in a small washbasin in one's bedchamber. Once the act of cleansing by submersion in water eventually became a common practice, there was great debate over whether cold or hot water was better for the body. Cold-water bathing was considered a form of personal strength, while the use of warm water was seen as a sign of indulgence.

independence. Jefferson is focused, his quill pen poised to take his usual careful notes.

Secretary Charles Thomson calls the roll, beginning with the delegation from New Hampshire. Suddenly, Delaware representative Caesar Rodney strides into the room.* His boots are spattered in mud, his riding coat drenched with rain. Rodney is an odd-looking man. In the words of John Adams, he is "tall, thin and slender as a reed, pale; his face is not bigger than a large apple, yet there is sense and fire, spirit, wit and humor in this countenance."

When Rodney received word at midnight about the split Delaware vote, he saddled a horse and rode eighty miles, braving lightning and cloudbursts, determined to break the tie in his delegation.

Rodney is pale and hungry. His face is ravaged by the cancer in his jaw that is slowly

*The story of Rodney's ride to Philadelphia is cloaked in mystery. There is disagreement about the moment Rodney arrived, whether he rode in a carriage or on horseback, and the specific route he followed from Dover to Philadelphia. In *John Adams,* historian David McCullough gives the moment of Rodney's arrival as roughly 9:00 a.m., when the doors to Congress were about to be closed so the session might begin.

killing him. Too exhausted to stand, he is led to the Delaware delegation's table and slumps into a high-backed chair to await his turn.

State by state, Thomson calls the roll.

The Assembly Room is otherwise silent.

Each of the state's delegates stands when his name is called. New Hampshire immediately votes in favor of independence. Then Georgia. When Delaware is called to cast its vote, delegate Thomas McKean helps Rodney to his feet. McKean has cast a vote in favor of independence once again. George Read of Delaware has again voted no.

Rodney breaks that tie. The midnight rider may be on the verge of collapse, but he cannot help but stray beyond a simple "aye" or "nay" in casting his historical vote. "As I believe the voice of my constituents and all sensible and honest men are in favor of independence," Rodney states clearly, "my own judgment concurs with them. I vote for independence."

Pennsylvania then votes "aye." Delegate Robert Morris has joined John Dickinson by failing to attend the session. In their absence, Benjamin Franklin guides the Pennsylvania vote.

In a surprising effort to align themselves

with the majority and make the Declaration unanimous, South Carolina changes its vote.

New York once again abstains. This Loyalist stronghold is the most important British colony in America.

With twelve votes for and zero votes against, the decision is considered unanimous.

Charles Thomson carefully tabulates the votes. Thomas Jefferson sits just a few feet away as the secretary hands the results to Hancock. The president of the Second Continental Congress then reads them aloud.

"Resolved," the record will read, "that these united colonies are, and of right, ought to be, free and independent states. That they are absolved from all allegiance to the British Crown, and that all political connection between them and the state of Great Britain, is, and ought to be, totally dissolved."

The Assembly Room explodes in cheers. The excited delegates rise as one to congratulate one another on this historic moment.

John Adams, the man who dreamed of independence long before it was considered practical, writes home to his wife, Abigail, in Boston: "Ought to be commemorated as the Day of Deliverance by solemn acts of devotion to God Almighty. It ought to be solemnized with pomp and parade, with shows, games, sports, guns, bells, bonfires, and illuminations from one end of this continent to the other from this time forward forever more."*

Thomas Jefferson, his vision validated, breaks his usual stoicism. A broad smile crosses his face as he shakes the hand of Benjamin Franklin. The two men are not personally close but have deep respect for each other.

John Hancock pounds his gavel to restore order.

Thirty-one days later, at 9:00 a.m. on August 2, Thomas Jefferson bears witness as his Declaration of Independence is formally signed by the members of Congress. News about the vote severing Ameri-

*Adams's vision proved to be true, but not on the date the Bostonian intended. The July 2 vote for independence was a poorly kept secret in Philadelphia, with the delegates trying to keep it quiet until the final wording of the Declaration of Independence could be approved. This took place on July 4, which is why that is now considered America's Independence Day.

ca's relationship with England has ricocheted around the colonies. Printed copies of Jefferson's final document have been read aloud in public squares near and far. The people of Philadelphia have used it as an excuse for bonfires and hard drinking. In New York, after George Washington reads it aloud to his troops, an excited mob tears down the oversize statue of King George in Lower Manhattan. The monument is then melted down and the lead formed into thousands of musket balls, which will be fired upon the British as they fight the Americans for control of New York City.

Despite the revelry, Thomas Jefferson is still anxious. He is eager to leave the Congress to be with his wife, Martha, who has become very ill. And the Virginian is hardly pleased at what Congress has done to his original Declaration. Their line-by-line rewrite is so tedious, in Jefferson's estimation, that he has printed out his own original version to show friends as a reminder of how the Declaration should have read.*

There is nothing, however, that Jefferson can do about that now. It is time to formally sign the Declaration of Independence. John

*Jefferson will not publicly take credit for writing the Declaration for more than twenty years.

Hancock signs first, in a big looping script so large that many will joke that he was trying to ensure that King George can read his name without the use of glasses. One by one, the other delegates step forward. They sign north to south, right to left, so that the last delegation to sign is that of Georgia. Thomas McKean is the last man to put his name on the document.

The process is informal, with some men signing illegibly, such as Thomas Heyward Jr., from South Carolina. Others, such as Samuel Adams from Massachusetts, sign their common name. In Adams's case, his signature will go down in history as just "Sam Adams."

When it comes his turn to sign, Jefferson rises and stands in line directly behind Richard Henry Lee, the man who began the process by proposing independence on June 8. Lee signs in the fourth column. Jefferson takes a pen and affixes his signature directly below Lee's, forever aligning them as fellow Virginians at a moment in time that will change the world.

Each man who signs has just committed an act of treason against the Crown. His life, family, and property are now in dire jeopardy. In time, the British will ride to Monticello in search of Thomas Jefferson, and those fears will be realized.

Right now, though, the prospect of terror is secondary to Jefferson's anguish over Martha. He will find himself bereft throughout the month of August, desperate to return to her side.

Finally, as September arrives, Jefferson can take no more. His work here is done. He resigns from the Congress and rides home to Martha.

But for the warriors who must risk their lives in battle to see Jefferson's vision become reality, the struggle for independence has just begun.

In CONGRESS, July 4, 1776.

The unanimous Declaration of the thirteen united States of America.

8

Brooklyn Heights, New York
August 22, 1776
Evening

George Washington can only wonder when and where the British will attack. Severe lightning and summer storms have devastated New York over the past few days, killing several citizens. It is a time of worry and preparation for the general, who is determined to hold the city at all costs.

Throughout July and August, a stalemate has existed between the rebels and the British, with the Americans holding Manhattan Island and Brooklyn Heights, while the British have remained on the other side of New York Harbor, at a sparsely populated place called Staten Island. The British forces number thirty-two thousand men — a figure almost twice that of New York City's population of eighteen thousand.

Washington is unsure as to whether the main attack will be on Manhattan or Brooklyn. Thus, the summer has been spent building forts and redoubts in both locations. His army preferred Manhattan, where prostitutes and gin houses were plentiful. Brooklyn was more of a wilderness, but here Washington ordered the construction of eight fortresses and instituted a "scorched earth" policy by removing all grain and cattle from outlying areas to deprive the enemy of their use.

The rebel army swung pickaxes and shovels as they excavated the defensive trenches and berms that will protect them from a British invasion. They chopped down trees for a hundred yards in every direction, creating a barren killing zone where no redcoat would be safe from fire. Sharpened tree trunks project from redoubts, there to impede British soldiers who make it through the fields of fire. They've scattered thick copses of branches known as an abatis around the earthworks to entangle British soldiers. Finally, cannon have been situated within each fort for maximum killing effect. Thirty rounds of ammunition are stacked near each artillery piece, ready to be fired.

George Washington knows the artillery will soon be put to use — it is only a matter of time until the British attack.

That time is now.

It is Thursday, August 22, and the British fleet sails unopposed to Brooklyn, landing fifteen thousand British troops and five thousand German mercenaries called Hessians. Six hundred New York Loyalists and eight hundred escaped slaves quickly join the British cause.

A spy erroneously reports to General Washington that the number of invading troops is half that many, leading the general to believe that the invasion is a distraction from a second, larger attack. Thus, Washington divides his army, leaving a portion on Manhattan and sending just six thousand troops to Brooklyn.

"The enemy have now landed on Long Island," George Washington exhorts his troops on August 23.* "The hour is fast ap-

*Brooklyn is located on the southern tip of Long Island, which stretches from the East River to Montauk Point, a distance of 118 miles. Long Island is also 23 miles wide at its broadest point, making it the largest island in the contiguous United States. The name "Brooklyn" was given to the locality by the Dutch who originally settled the region. It was termed "Breuckelen," after a

185

proaching in which the honor and success of the army, and the safety of our bleeding country, will depend."

The general concludes by reminding his solders to "Be cool, but determined; do not fire at a distance, but wait for orders from your officers — It is the general's express orders that if any man attempts to skulk, lay down [sic], or retreat without orders — he be instantly shot down as an example."

With careful precision, the British set up camp. Soon, a sprawling city of white tents covers the southern plain of Brooklyn. There, the British prepare for the imminent battle — drilling, polishing muskets and bayonets, cleaning artillery barrels, and marching in formation. British regulars are

---

town in Holland. When the British took control of the area in 1687, the spelling was Anglicized. New York's Staten Island, along with the Flatbush and Yonkers districts, also take their names from the Dutch. Manhattan was named by the Lenape tribe, who termed it "Manahatta" — or "hilly island." The name "New York" was given to the region on September 8, 1684, after the British defeated the Dutch for its control. It was named for the Duke of York, who went on to become King James II, a widely reviled monarch who was eventually forced off the throne and died in exile.

routinely commanded to shave, bathe, and change their clothing. Discipline is paramount.*

The American soldiers, on the other hand, show an utter lack of discipline. Hunting shirts and tomahawks are more common than military uniforms, and deep rivalries exist among the various colonies. Thanks to poor sanitation habits, a large number of the American troops now suffer from dysentery. These are not the men who fought for Washington six months ago in Boston, for almost all those soldiers returned home after their short service. Instead, Brooklyn is defended by a motley assemblage of soldiers from all walks of life: farmers, manual laborers, and the unemployed. Many are shoeless. The average age is twenty, with some younger than fifteen and others well past forty. Most are poorly trained in the art of warfare. Among them

*The British troops, who despise the Americans, fear what will become of them should they be taken captive by the colonists. Many English believe the Americans to be cannibals. A rumor circulates throughout the British ranks that Americans are fond of slitting open a man's body to stuff it with dry wood, then setting the wood afire as a form of torture.

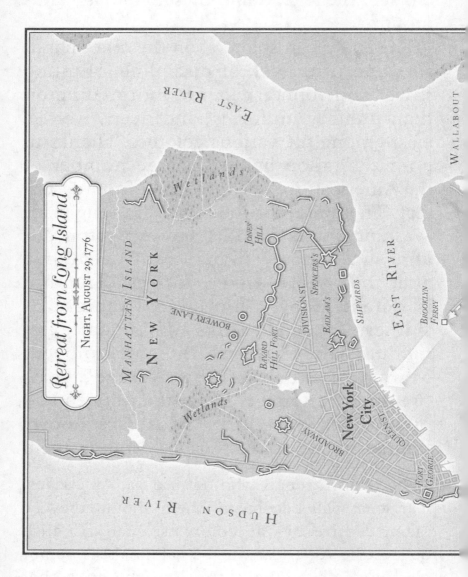

JAMAICA ROAD

FLATBUSH ROAD

NEW YORK

Map by Gene Thorp

L O N G   I S L A N D

HOWE

FORT PUTNAM

FORT GREENE

FORT BOX

Brooklyn

OLD STONE HOUSE

WASHINGTON

GOWANUS CREEK

GOWANUS COVE

Scale of miles

0   1/4   1/2

N

E

S

W

BUTTERMILK CHANNEL

GOVERNORS ISLAND

RED HOOK

FT. DEFIANCE

are fortune seekers drawn to the war by an offer of a steady paycheck, the possibility of a postwar land grant, or simply a steady meal. Few are socially prominent in their home communities. Most, in the eyes of America's more financially successful colonists, are expendable.

Between the British lines along the southern shore and the American defenses in Brooklyn Heights runs a rocky ridge four miles long, covered in a thick forest of ash, oak, and chestnut trees that provide cover for the defending rebels.

After four days of preparation, the British march. They leave campfires burning to make it appear to the American scouts that nothing is afoot. Only the "necessary women" and other camp followers remain behind to tend the flames. The moon is not yet full and the night air is chilly as they advance slowly and silently toward the American lines. The force soon splits, with one column advancing directly toward Brooklyn Heights while a larger column, numbering fourteen thousand light infantry, cavalry, and artillery, begins a long, looping pivot around the back of the American lines. Their goal is to advance through Jamaica Pass and then attack the rebel forces from the rear.

It is this second column that gives British general Howe pause. Sending such a large body of men on a lengthy flanking maneuver is a risky gamble on his part, but should it succeed, the Americans will be at his mercy. The British lack accurate maps of the countryside, so when a British column passes a small settlement at 2:00 a.m., the general steps into the local tavern and rouses the owner and his family.

"General Howe and another officer were standing in the barroom," the tavern owner's son, William Howard Jr., will later remember.

Howe wears a thick tweed cloak and asks for "a glass of liquor." After taking a drink, he demands that Howard guide his army through the night.

"We belong to the other side, General. And can't serve you against our duty," Mr. Howard replies.

"You have no alternative," Howe replies coolly. "If you refuse, I shall have you shot in the head."

Thus, led by William Howard and his son, the British continue their silent march. The moon sets at 3:00 a.m., allowing the British to advance cautiously through Jamaica Pass, an undefended portal over the ridgeline.

When five American scouts fall in alongside them, mistakenly believing in the darkness that the British are rebel soldiers, the Americans are easily taken prisoner. In all, the second British column marches nine miles before sunrise. General Howe's bold gamble to flank the American lines has succeeded.

Upon hearing the news, George Washington races across the East River from his Manhattan headquarters.

What follows is a day of continuous fighting, with the surrounded American troops battling desperately against a fighting force superior in numbers, weaponry, and discipline. The British adopt a tactic of allowing the Americans to fire a volley, and then rushing into their ranks to bayonet them as they reload. One group of Americans breaks in terror and finds its way blocked by a thick marsh. Under a hail of British bullets, many become mired in the muck and can no longer run. They are shot down. Others in this same group reach the safety of deeper water, only to drown.

All the while, George Washington rides along the American lines, demanding that the troops fight "like men, like soldiers."

"Good God," he adds, "what brave fellows I must this day lose."

Then comes a crucial mistake. At a time when General Howe could press the attack and seize the entire area of Brooklyn, he orders a halt to the fighting. The American casualties now number in the thousands, but the British have lost fewer than one hundred men.* Howe is determined to wait for yet another moment of advantage, so that he might finish the slaughter while minimizing his losses. He lacks ladders for scaling the American redoubts and tools to cut away the sharpened stakes jutting outward from the rebel fortifications, and he needs more artillery to begin a proper siege.

These requisitions will take time. But the conditions on the East River will prevent the Americans from getting away by boat. The image in Howe's mind is that thousands of rebel soldiers are dug in and prepared to fight. Now is the time for patience. The British general withdraws his troops to a small clearing beyond the range of American muskets and makes camp.

George Washington has made a decision: he

*General Howe's official dispatches put the number of American casualties at 3,300. He estimates the British dead, wounded, and captured to be 367.

and his army will run.

The date is August 29. Hard rain and a stiff northeast wind rake the East River. The general pulls his long black wool cape tightly around his shoulders in a vain attempt to find comfort. Standing atop the steps leading down to the Fulton Street ferry, Washington is exhausted from two days and nights in the saddle. His thoughts are not on his own misery but on the fate of the thousands of men now gathering on the beach below him. A hastily assembled flotilla of rowboats and sailboats lines the shore, waiting to spirit the demoralized colonial troops from Brooklyn to the safety of Manhattan. Yet George Washington's army can go nowhere until the weather turns in its favor and the river calms.

It has been a brutal forty-eight hours. The colonial rebels entered the battle confident in the strength of their chain of defensive fortresses. But because of the success of Howe's brilliant and risky nighttime march, the enemy was able to place thousands of soldiers behind those forts. By noon on the first day of fighting, the British attacked from three sides and were clearly winning the engagement.

The slaughter was so intense that one unit from Maryland had no choice but to launch a suicide attack. The British column was commanded by a man whose name would soon become well known to Americans: Lt. Gen. Charles Cornwallis.

The men of the First Maryland were led by a bold major whose name would soon be lost to history: Mordecai Gist.

At dawn, Gist's troops numbered two thousand, but by noon on the first day of battle, just four hundred men remained in the field. Rather than cower and await their inevitable capture by the much larger British force, the farmers, fishermen, and merchants turned soldiers, upon Gist's order, hurl themselves at the highly trained British regulars.

At first, the plan worked.

The British were stunned, not expecting such an audacious maneuver. However, they quickly recovered, responding to the frontal assault with cannon fire, directed from a defensive position known as the Old Stone House.*

The men of Maryland were felled by the dozens. Those who remained alive were

*The Old Stone House survived the battle. From 1883 to 1891 it would serve as the clubhouse of a baseball team that would become known as the Brooklyn Dodgers.

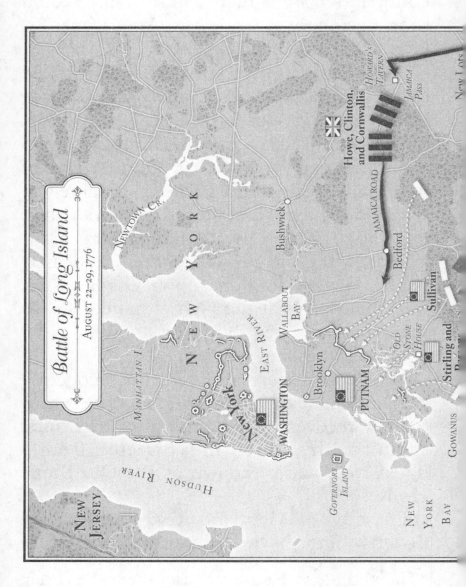

Battle of Long Island
AUGUST 22–29, 1776

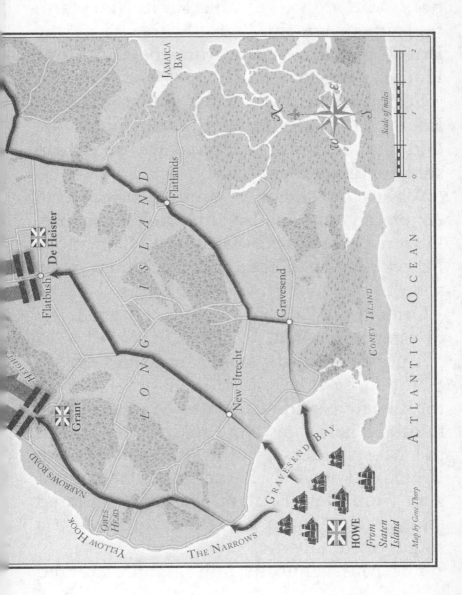

JAMAICA BAY

N

S

Scale of miles

FLATLANDS

LONG ISLAND

De Heister

Flatbush

HEIGHTS

Grant

NARROWS ROAD

Yellow Hook

OWLS HEAD

THE NARROWS

New Utrecht

Gravesend

CONEY ISLAND

GRAVESEND BAY

HOWE

From Staten Island

ATLANTIC OCEAN

Map by Gene Thorp

forced to step over their dead friends to press the fight. Yet the First Maryland regrouped, six times in all, to charge the British and drive them from the Old Stone House — twice.

Still, Cornwallis's force was too large. Each time the Marylanders captured the Old Stone House, a new wave of British soldiers drove them back.

When the skirmish finally ended, 256 Americans lay dead on the field of battle. Dozens more were wounded. Still more Marylanders had been taken prisoner, many soon to die on British prison ships.

Only ten Maryland rebels escaped the disaster unscathed.

Among those was Maj. Mordecai Gist.*

Not to be outdone in their bravery were the ill-fated soldiers of the Massachusetts militia. Their lines were just to the east of the Marylanders', holding a vital path to Brooklyn known as Battle Pass. The contingent from New England was four hundred strong, their battle flag emblazoned with a single word: *Liberty.*

The Massachusetts militia soon squared

---

*Gist, who would go on to fight and to survive the war, named his two sons Independent and States.

off against the units of Hessian regiments anchoring the center of the British line.* The Hessians attacked from the south, up a country lane known as Flatbush Road.

The Liberty flag flew high, but the idealistic ambitions of the Massachusetts soldiers were quickly overrun by the tactical skill of the veteran Hessian soldiers.

Faced with defeat, the remaining men from Massachusetts tried to surrender.

They raised their hands, standing still in the face of the enemy. Soon, several hundred New Englanders were surrounded by a circle of Hessian bayonets. The British had warned the Hessians that the American rebels would put to death any soldier they captured. Thus, the Hessians were intent on

*Hessians came from two German regions known as Hesse-Kassel and Hesse-Hanau. Other German auxiliaries came from Brunswick, Anspach, and other states, but the collective term Hessians has endured. These German states possessed their own professional armies. In fact, Hesse-Kassel's major export was the *Soldatenhandel* ("soldier business") — the leasing of their soldiers to other nations. The amount the British paid for using Hessians in the Revolutionary War covered the equivalent of thirteen years' tax revenue for the Hesse-Kassel region.

doing the same. Making matters worse for the Massachusetts brigade, the Hessians had been drinking all day from canteens filled with water and rum — fueling their hatred for the rebels.

Thrusting their pointed blades, the Hessians tightened the circle, stabbing and hacking at any man who tried to escape. Some rebels were run through and pinned to a tree. The Massachusetts rebels put up a valiant fight, kicking and punching and swinging their muskets toward the bayonets.

But it was futile. Finally, the rebels began pleading for their lives.

The Hessians showed no mercy. Every one of the Massachusetts patriots was slaughtered. American bodies bloated as the August morning grew warm. Flies swarmed the corpses, though not before the Hessians plundered the enemy dead for any sort of wealth. Then the Germans moved on, leaving the bodies of the men from Massachusetts to rot as they pressed their attack through Battle Pass and into Brooklyn.*

Despite the enormous casualties, the Americans are not overwhelmed by the British.

*More than three hundred men from Massachusetts died at the hands of the Hessians that day.

The rain saves them. It pours down all through the afternoon and night. Muskets become useless as the flints and power are drenched. "All the time the rain came falling with an uncommon torrent," one American soldier will write. "The guns of the whole army are whetted [*sic*]."

The earthen berms and redoubts behind which the Americans cower become nothing but mud and waist-deep puddles. There is nowhere to take cover from the elements, so men doze standing up or simply lie down to shiver in the muck. At daybreak the following morning, the British artillery opens fire, adding to the misery. But the attack does not come. The weather forbids it.

Thus, the stalemate remains for two long days. George Washington prepares for a British siege, and orders that the wounded be taken by boat to Manhattan as soon as possible. But on the evening of August 29, things change. Rather than endure a British attack, which no doubt will end in the capture and imprisonment of him and his entire army, Washington decides the time has come to send his force back to the fortifications on Manhattan Island.

Better to retreat, and live to fight another day, than to hang by the neck until dead.

The general's plan to ferry nine thousand

men, wagons, horses, and cannon across a turbulent tidal river in the dead of night is not just audacious; it is downright foolish. Washington opposed retreat until this afternoon, when his council of war told him he had no other choice. Now that it has begun, the general is at the mercy of the wind, tides, rain, and, most of all, darkness. All will be lost if the retreat is not concluded by sunrise, when the British will see for themselves that the Americans are on the run. Victory will be as easy as pinning the rebels down on the beach with cannon and commencing a wholesale slaughter.

One by one, Washington's troops have been pulled from the front lines, with orders to march in absolute silence. They have not been told where they are going, only that they are pulling back to a more advantageous position. No talking or even coughing is allowed. Wagon wheels are wrapped in cloth to ensure quiet, and officers have been ordered to issue commands in face-to-face whispers. Should the British learn of Washington's withdrawal, they will surely attack in force. As the last two days of fighting have shown, superior numbers and better-trained soldiers would allow the British Army to destroy the Americans. The war would be over, Washington would be hanged, and independence would be forever lost. So, it is imperative that this retreat be flawless.

As the beach below Washington becomes choked with men, soldiers can no longer make their way down to the boats. A line forms, leading up the steps, and onto the ridge. By now, Washington's army knows its destination. The men are eager to reach Manhattan. Many are already planning to quit the war and return home, a thought that seemed impossible just hours ago, when the rebels were on the verge of total annihilation.

The backup of soldiers waiting to set foot on the beach grows to a hundred yards long, then to a quarter mile. Panic sweeps through the ranks. After forty-eight hours of utter devastation at the hands of Gen. William Howe's army, fighting in mud and water up to their knees, and seeing friends and fellow soldiers run through by British bayonets, the Continental soldiers see this retreat as salvation. But the idea of being so close to safety only to have the British once again find them tests the limits of their fear.

Washington notices with alarm that the soldiers on the beach are no longer following orders. Despite the foul weather and stiff currents, one group of men has boarded a boat and is preparing to shove off before the general has given the command to do so. Furious, George Washington races down the stairs and pushes his way through the throng. He bends down and grabs a large rock with two hands, then draws up to his full height and lifts the heavy stone over his head.

"Damn you!" he shouts at the soldiers crowding into the skiff. His voice cuts through the utterly quiet night. All eyes turn to watch.

"Leave this boat instantly or I will sink it to hell," he roars, threating to hurl the rock through the wooden hull.

The threat works; the anarchy is over. The soldiers immediately do as they are told. Order settles through the ranks.

At last, the rain stops. The wind dies. A protective camouflage of fog blankets the East River, which soon turns smooth as glass.

Now it is time to go.

The first wave of rowboats shoves off for the one-mile journey to Manhattan. Like the wagons, the oars are covered in cloth to muffle the sound. Most boats are so overloaded that the water is just two or three inches below the gunwales — but they are afloat. And thanks to a group of Massachusetts soldiers who labored as fishermen before the war, the boats are helmed by very capable watermen.

The time is 11:00 p.m.

Sunrise is 5:24 a.m.

The most important six hours in America's short history are about to take place.

A defeated George Washington vows to be the last man out.

The hour of 5:24 a.m. comes and goes. But though the dawn has arrived, Washington's retreat continues. A fog so dense that one soldier complains he can "scarcely discern a man at six yards' distance" makes it possible for the rescue flotilla to continue its back-and-forth between Brooklyn and Manhattan. But the general knows that time is running out. As he maintains his vigil at the ferry landing, he knows that soon the British will realize the rebels have fled.

It is now 7:00 a.m. Washington steps onto the last, heavy-laden rowboat. His entire army is safely across. The only items left behind are a few cannon too heavy to pull through the mud.

George Washington is the last man to leave.

Halfway across the East River, he turns and watches with relief as the first astonished units of British soldiers arrive at the ferry landing. The fog now lifting, the enemy sees the general clearly — but can do nothing.

George Washington is safe — for now.

9

London, England
October 31, 1776
Noon

King George is savoring victory.

More than three thousand miles from New York, the thirty-eight-year-old monarch sits enthroned in the British House of Peers, just moments away from delivering his opening address to Parliament. The ceiling is vaulted, making for unreliable acoustics, and the great walls are covered in tapestries celebrating the defeat of the Spanish Armada more than one century ago. Arrayed before the throne are the leaders of England, many sitting on padded benches known as woolsacks. Those men belonging to the House of Lords wear scarlet wool robes trimmed in white miniver fur, while members of the House of Commons stand in the back of this great room with its vaulted ceiling with the nonlegislative spectators, dressed without ceremony. The members receive no salary for their time in Parliament, and must rely on a second profession to make a living.*

It has been more than four months since King George last addressed this distinguished body as part of the annual Closing of Parliament, delivering a speech in which he took great pains to focus his attention on the war in America.

"We are engaged in a great national cause, the prosecution of which must be inevitably be attended with many difficulties and much expense," he stated on May 23. As is usual in Parliament, his voice was drowned out by dissenters shouting their opinions. "I will still entertain a hope that my rebellious subjects may be awakened to a sense of their errors, and that, by a voluntary return to their duty, they will justify me in bringing about the favorite wish of my heart, the restoration of harmony and reestablishment of order in every part of my dominion.

"But," the king then sternly warned, "if a due submission should not be obtained from such motives and such dispositions on

*Members of the House of Commons did not begin receiving a salary until 1911.

their part, I trust that I shall be able, under the blessing of Providence, to effectuate it by a full exertion of the great force with which you have entrusted me."

That final threat troubles many in Parliament's minority Whig Party. They believe in reconciliation, not extermination. To some, however, the Whig argument borders on treason, implying as they believe it does that the troubles in America were brought on *by* King George himself and his punitive treatment of the colonists.

Moments before the summer recess was officially convened, outspoken Whig politician David Hartley introduced a motion that Parliament should not recess at all, for fear that a lengthy summer break would allow the king to pursue his war policies without parliamentary oversight.*

Hartley's motion was immediately rejected — though not for reasons that had anything to do with politics. June through September finds London at its humid, fetid worst, and many politicians wanted out. Heat accentuates the body odor of the unwashed poor. Lice infestations are rampant. There is no

*Hartley was a good friend of Benjamin Franklin, whom he met and socialized with during Franklin's tenure in London.

such thing as public sanitation, so residents simply empty chamber pots onto the streets, allowing the aroma of fecal matter to mingle with the stench of rotting garbage, scraps of offal thrown away by the local butchers, and the carcasses of dead cats, dogs, and horses.

In addition, the common man in London often quenches his thirst by drinking from the murky brown waters of the River Thames — which also serves as the city's raw sewage and factory waste dump. Thus, each year, London is plagued by an epidemic of dysentery and diarrhea. Many citizens, seeking to avoid these maladies, prefer to douse their thirst with copious amounts of cheap gin.*

*Gin has been often wrongly identified as a British invention. The liquor was first distilled in Holland, and became popular in England only when Dutch-born William of Orange sat on the British throne in the late seventeenth century. At one point in the eighteenth century, an estimated eight thousand vendors sold cheap and often lethal doses of high-proof liquor on the streets of London. Soon, the government outlawed the gin street vendors. But through the years, gin and tonic became one of the world's most popular cocktails. That happened because, around the world, British subjects dissolved antimalarial

■ ■ ■ ■

Prior to the summer recess, Parliament was united in the belief that the colonies must remain British. Yet members were torn over how to make this possible. The Tory majority loyal to the king believed war to be the only answer. In their opinion, prisoners of war should be shipped to the British colony in India and the rebel leadership hanged to prevent further uprisings.

But the Whig minority insisted that the American colonists were still British citizens. Thus, they were in favor of giving in to the colonists' demands for parliamentary representation and rescinding some of the punitive Coercive Acts.

On July 8, a casually transmitted line of information from Gen. William Howe to King George changed the political landscape: "I am informed that the Continental Congress have declared the United Colonies free and independent states."

King George and the vast majority of Parliament were outraged. There would be no reconciliation.

---

quinine tablets into carbonated water and then mixed this "tonic water" with gin to hide the taste.

Then, in mid-August, the entire Declaration of Independence was published in the newspaper the *London Chronicle*. Public reaction was swift and angry, with many British citizens viewing the document as nothing more than a clever justification for treason.

A typical comment came from Ambrose Serle, the civilian secretary to Adm. Richard Howe, an elder brother of Gen. William Howe. He wrote that the Declaration proclaims the "villainy and madness of these deluded people."*

Most public opinion centered on the two opening paragraphs, which justify independence and introduce the unique notion that free men should be accorded "the pursuit of happiness" — an absurd concept to

*General Howe and his elder brother Richard were authorized by King George to broker peace with the colonists. On September 11, 1776, the two met with John Adams, Benjamin Franklin, and Edward Rutledge, in what has since been labeled the Staten Island Peace Conference. The sticking point, of course, was the Declaration of Independence. General Howe demanded that the colonists rescind the document before peace talks moved forward. The colonial representatives refused.

Britain's impoverished masses, a group numbering roughly three-fourths of the island's population, most of whom can neither read nor comment on the Declaration. Almost all of them are doomed to a life of misery and want, thanks to a social structure that prevents upward mobility from one class to another. Seeking to keep wealth and power for themselves, the British upper class makes quality education a constant for their children, yet none is provided for the working man, who can ill afford to pay tuition.*

To King George, the Declaration is a personal affront. By far the document's lengthiest passage consists of eighteen blistering accusations against the king's character and policies. The words chosen by Thomas Jefferson are deliberately provocative, designed to publicly humiliate a monarch who revels in the fantasy that his colonial subjects universally adore him.

*The first census in the British Isles took place in 1801, with the combined population of England, Scotland, Ireland, and Wales numbering 15.7 million people. The population for Great Britain during the American Revolution can only be estimated, but it is believed nearly 1.0 million called London home.

Now, as the Declaration begins to make its way around Europe, Jefferson's disrespect raises questions about how King George will fight back.

While the war is certainly preoccupying George, he is also harboring a secret. His mental health is in decline. The king has become prone to long, disjointed discussions with members of his royal court, veering uncontrollably and without warning from one topic to another. The same can be seen in his writing, where sometimes single sentences ramble on for a full page. George now has trouble sleeping, and his vision is beginning to blur. So far, neither the king nor any of his advisers sees these symptoms as anything more than duress — there is the stress of the colonial war, along with Queen Charlotte having brought their eleventh child into the world six months ago.

George's reputation as a learned and passionate husband, father, and ruler guarantees that his behavior will go unquestioned — until it becomes too late. Very soon, the king's descent into madness will begin in earnest. Behavior that is now merely eccentric will be replaced by violent, manic episodes and, ultimately, confinement to a straitjacket.*

But on this last day in October, as the king formally opens Parliament, he is the very image of a regal monarch. For two long months, he has kept his emotions in check, refraining from a public response to the Declaration of Independence.

But soon, he will parry the words of Thomas Jefferson. With any luck, British troops will capture Jefferson and the other backers of the Declaration before the year ends. When that happens, the king will personally see to it that the tall Virginian hangs.

No one insults the king of England.

*The disease (which researchers believe was caused by a blend of hereditary porphyria and the arsenic used not only to powder his ceremonial wigs but also to treat his mental health) reached its peak in 1789, when thanksgiving services for his recovery were held at St. Paul's Cathedral in London. It went into remission for many years, but never fully disappeared. More episodes of manic, incoherent behavior between 1801 and 1810 resulted in his being removed from the throne. His son, the Prince of Wales, George Augustus Frederick, succeeded him as George IV. George III spent the last ten years of his life suffering from blindness, rheumatism, and dementia.

■ ■ ■ ■

King George uses the power of optics to appear as authoritative as possible, sitting before Parliament in his ermine robes, wearing a heavy crown of gold, pearls, and diamonds. "My Lords, and Gentlemen," he states, by way of greeting. His voice is loud and his delivery polished. Today, much more than on most days, he feels his full power as monarch.*

"Nothing could have afforded me so much satisfaction; as to have been able to inform you, at the opening of this session, that the troubles which have so long distracted my colonies in North America were at an end; and that my unhappy people, recovered from their delusion; had delivered themselves from the oppression of their leaders, and returned to their duty."

The king pauses, knowing that his words

*George III's robes were made by Ede and Ravenscroft, a London shop then owned by Martha and William Shudall. The shop had held the royal warrant for robe making since 1694. It is still in business, on Chancery Lane in London, currently serving as robe maker and tailor to Queen Elizabeth II, the Prince of Wales, and the Duke of Edinburgh.

will go down in history. The British Empire is larger than the Roman Empire of two thousand years ago. A group of rabble-rousers cannot and will not be allowed to form its own nation.

The king's demeanor is bolstered by news from America. As almost every legislator in this room knows, the war has been nothing short of a spectacular success. British forces now control not just Long Island but, having crossed over into Manhattan, all of New York City. In the north, Canada is now safely in British hands.

Much of this is due to inept rebel leadership, particularly George Washington. While General Howe can do no wrong for the British, Washington's army stumbles from one humiliating defeat to another. The British military leadership refuses to even acknowledge Washington as having military rank, because they don't recognize the government that granted it to him. Thus, they even refuse to state his rank in their written requests for surrender. Rather than "General," Howe refers to Washington by the title of "Esquire."

But the king must be careful. The denunciations made in the Declaration by Thomas Jefferson are so personal that he must not even acknowledge them, lest he appear vulnerable in the face of criticism. So, he goes to the heart of the matter. He intends to warn not only the rebels but also the powers of France and Spain that the American threat cannot be tolerated.

"If their treason be suffered to take root, much mischief must grow from it, to the safety of my loyal colonies, to the commerce of my kingdoms, and indeed to the present system of all Europe.

"No people ever enjoyed more happiness, or lived under a milder government, than those now revolted provinces."

Finally, putting his own spin on Thomas Jefferson's "life, liberty and the pursuit of happiness," the king concludes on a paternal note.

"My desire is to restore to them the blessings of law and liberty, equally enjoyed by every British subject, which they have fatally and desperately exchanged for the calamities of war."

Parliament erupts in shouts and applause.

The king is pleased.

Soon, his tormentors will die by the rope — as they should.

10

Thomas Jefferson is anxious.

Almost four thousand miles from London, the author of the Declaration of Independence lies in bed with his wife, Martha. Outside the many-paned bedroom windows of this borrowed home, the moon is dark. Almost five years into their marriage, Thomas and Martha's passion for each other still burns hot. The grief surrounding her midsummer miscarriage still lingers, but the lovers have wasted no time in conceiving a new child, who, if born without incident, will be a sibling to their four-year-old, Patsy.

Martha Jefferson is due to deliver sometime in May. She is a small woman, little more than five feet tall, a lithe brunette with hazel eyes whose petite features stand in sharp contrast to Jefferson's towering stature. Once again, she has begun to add the prodigious curves of her typical pregnancy, not knowing that the added weight and her chronic diabetes play a part in the silent killing of her unborn children.*

The other matter dominating Jefferson's thoughts is the struggle for independence. Abandoning the Congress to be with Martha was just the first step in the Virginian removing himself from the grind of national politics. Jefferson and his fifteen-year-old mulatto slave, Bob, rode away from Philadelphia the first week of September, making the 268-mile journey home to Martha at

*Thomas and Martha Jefferson had no idea she was afflicted with diabetes. In fact, it was only in the twentieth century that historians began to believe, based upon her recorded symptoms, that Mrs. Jefferson was diabetic. Children born to diabetic mothers often come into the world with low blood sugar or jaundice, or they are stillborn. The use of insulin as a successful treatment for diabetes was begun in the early 1900s. It's worth noting, however, that some scholars believe malaria may have been the cause of Martha's miscarriages.

Monticello. The mountaintop home is their refuge, a simple two-story dwelling offering endless views of the thick forests and peaks of the American frontier.

Jefferson's journey was not easy. The roads were unpaved and rutted, there were many rivers and streams to ford, and there were few places to stop for proper lodging. Indeed, after the first fifty miles of travel, Jefferson entered the wilderness and thick primeval forests.

But the journey was uneventful, and on September 9, 1776, at roughly the same moment Congress declared that the thirteen colonies would henceforth be named "the United States of America," he stepped through the front door of Monticello.

Within weeks, however, Jefferson realized he could not separate himself from the cause of independence. So, he and the pregnant Martha boarded a carriage and traveled east all the way across Virginia to the capital city of Williamsburg, where Jefferson assumed his seat in the state's House of Delegates.*

That is why the Jeffersons have now taken

*Formed in 1619, this body was the first elected legislature in America. Originally known as the House of Burgesses, it was dubbed the House of

up residence at the home of longtime friend George Wythe. But once more, Jefferson is confronted with a dilemma. Earlier this fall, the president of the Second Continental Congress, John Hancock, requested that the Virginian return to the revolution — imploring him to sail immediately for France with Benjamin Franklin. Their goal would be to convince French king Louis XVI to assist in the American war effort. Franklin accepted the assignment immediately — indeed, he is now somewhere in the middle of the Atlantic, two weeks into his voyage to France.

Not so Jefferson. On October 11, after three agonizing days of indecision, he again chose Martha over his nation. He would not join Franklin in Paris. The introverted Virginian could not imagine subjecting a pregnant Martha to the rigors of an Atlantic crossing during this storm-tossed time of year; nor could he envision making the journey without her.

Jefferson's decision angered his fellow Virginian Richard Henry Lee, who chastised him for putting his personal life before his country. Lee compared Jefferson's marital commitment to that of being a British slave

---

Delegates in 1776. Its last act as the "House of Burgesses" was to vote in favor of independence.

— should the war be lost.

"I heard with much regret that you had declined both the voyage, and your seat in Congress," Lee wrote. "No man feels more deeply than I do, the love of, and the loss of, private enjoyments; but let attention to these be universal, and we are gone, beyond redemption lost in the deep perdition of slavery."

Jefferson never responded.

But while the Virginian may seem indifferent to the cause of independence, making no effort to join a militia or otherwise take up arms for liberty, his ongoing intellectual attacks on King George have broadened the scope of the American rebellion.

"I saw, too," Jefferson will write years from now, justifying why he turned down the appointment to France, "that the laboring oar was really at home, where much was to be done."

Jefferson is a popular figure in the assembly, promoting his own idealistic views on how best to expand liberty. He has begun by altering Virginia's laws to reflect the new reality of its being a state, not a colony. Freedom of religion has been expanded, the Church of England has been disestablished as the one true theology, and the right of primogeniture, a feudal tradition that gives firstborn sons power of inheritance to the exclusion of others, is soon to be abolished.

In this way, Thomas Jefferson fights the British monarchy — by destroying its traditions. The battle Jefferson wages is one for lasting change — he wants few remnants of the English imposition. It is a cause that does not yet bear this title but that will soon be remembered as a Revolutionary War.*

Jefferson believes that all of Virginia's existing laws must be rewritten or completely thrown out. His mind works frantically, as does his writing hand. Jefferson puts his prodigious thoughts on paper each day, organizing the various issues facing Virginia, and America, into a wide-ranging collection of essays: "Notes on Religion," "Notes on Heresy," and, just this morning, "Notes Concerning the Bill for the Removal of the Seat of Government in Virginia."

It seems there is nothing the fervent mind of Thomas Jefferson cannot imagine. But as he sleeps next to his beloved wife on this dark autumn night, not knowing if the baby

*Among the first known uses of the word *revolution* to describe political change was the Glorious Revolution in 1689, which saw England's King James II removed from the throne.

growing inside her womb will live to see its first birthday, Jefferson also believes that *he* might not live to see his unborn child's first year.*

As a signer of the Declaration of Independence and known member of the Second Continental Congress, Thomas Jefferson is a marked man. Already, the British Navy has attacked the coasts of South Carolina and Virginia. The ships have since sailed north to support General Howe in his fight against George Washington at New York, but it is inevitable that they will soon return to Virginia and bring the fight to Jefferson's front door.

When that day comes — and it will — Thomas Jefferson will be forced to run for his life.

Revolution comes with a cost.

But there is no turning back. In the morning, Jefferson will rise at dawn, as always. He will soak his feet in cold water and

---

*Thomas Jefferson's first and only male child will come into the world on May 28, 1777. He was never given a name, though some sources claim the boy was called either Peter, after Jefferson's father, or Thomas. The baby boy lived just seventeen days, most likely dying of fevers associated with influenza and diarrhea.

record the temperature outside his window, just as he does every day. He will dress; eat a simple breakfast of coffee, cold ham, and bread; and say good-bye to Martha before making his way across the Palace Green to the state legislature.

In this routine, the introverted Jefferson manages his emotions.

Ironically, taking the assignment in Paris would have guaranteed his personal safety. He would have had nothing to fear in the court of Louis XVI.

But Jefferson has no stomach for the puffery and debauchery of royal living.

He prefers the simple things in life: love, routine, and the intellectual work of defining true liberty. For now, his life is calm.

But not for much longer.

11

Benjamin Franklin is retching.

His hands grip the aft wooden railing of the USS *Reprisal*. A thirteen-striped American flag snaps high above Franklin's head.* Franklin is bent at the waist, facing down into the turbulent Atlantic Ocean as his upset stomach almost overwhelms him.

The *Reprisal* is a small ship, currently buffeted by nonstop waves and wind. The vessel is astonishingly compact, measuring just one hundred feet long and thirty feet at the

*There is no official American flag at this point. George Washington marched into battle flying a standard of thirteen red and white stripes set against a field of blue featuring the X-shaped cross of St. Andrew. The *Reprisal*'s thirteen stripes are displayed against a field of yellow.

227

beam. Despite this, she boasts a crew of more than one hundred men, plus Franklin and his two grandsons. On both sides of the *Reprisal,* an armament of cannon, eighteen in all, lines the main deck, facing out to sea. The *Reprisal* is built for speed, not comfort, and right now Benjamin Franklin is experiencing this firsthand.

It has been a difficult journey for the seventy-year-old Franklin. After almost thirty days at sea, his body is plagued by psoriasis, gout, and pustules. His intestinal discomfort is not caused by seasickness, for that is one malady to which Franklin's weathered physique seems impervious. Instead, it is the steady diet of salt beef that is convulsing his stomach on this November morning. It is his deepest desire to get off this warship as soon as humanly possible.

"I was badly accommodated," the Doctor will write of the crossing, "in a miserable vessel, improper for those northern seas, was badly fed, so that on my arrival I scarce had the strength to stand."

Despite his misery, Benjamin Franklin knows that his presence on the *Reprisal* is vital. He is America's greatest celebrity. His lengthy list of accomplishments in science and at the highest levels of government have made his name synonymous with the cause of freedom — and also guarantee that he will be quite a prize should the British capture the *Reprisal.* His show trial and ultimate hanging in the Tower of London would be a dagger in the heart of the American cause. Already, British cruisers have harassed the *Reprisal* on a number of occasions during Franklin's voyage, but the nimble brig has managed to slip away each time.

The *Reprisal,* too, is a proud symbol of America. Her captain is forty-one-year-old Lambert Wickes, whose ancestors were among the first settlers of Maryland's Eastern Shore. Once known as the *Molly,* the rechristened *Reprisal* now carries a name promising vengeance for enemy transgressions. She is the first vessel in America's new yet growing naval arsenal to carry such a blatantly aggressive name, so it is appropriate that she now become the first American vessel to sail into European waters.

Life aboard the small ship is challenging, even in good weather. Franklin and his grandsons, seventeen-year-old William (whose father now rots in prison at the Doctor's behest) and seven-year-old Benjamin, must sleep belowdecks, in a space with little ventilation or even enough room for

Benjamin Franklin on his way to France aboard the Reprisal

them to stretch out in comfort. There is no privacy. Scores of men surround them, and the small cabin in which they sleep is barely the size of a large closet. Meals are taken with the captain, in his larger cabin, or in the communal mess area belowdecks with the men. But as Benjamin Franklin knows very well, no matter where the location, the food is abysmal.

Though a relatively small ship, the *Reprisal* enjoys a large crew, consisting of a captain, lieutenants (meant to serve "in lieu" of the captain, should the situation arise), coopers, carpenters, a doctor, ship's boys, and sailors. Officers wear breeches, waistcoats, and long-sleeved jackets, while the rest of the crew attire themselves in shirts and short, loose pants known as slops. Officers wear buckled shoes, but many sailors prefer to go barefoot, for greater ease in climbing the rigging. Only the most senior officers and esteemed passengers such as Franklin are allowed a cabin and private restroom facilities. The remainder of the men sleep in hammocks suspended just below the main deck. The rotating system of standing watch means that half the crew is on duty while the rest sleep. The term *head,* in reference to a toilet, comes from the special board extending from the "beak head" of the ship (the pointed bow) out over the ocean for passengers to use as a communal toilet. The wind and waves dispatch any odor or mess.

Right now, Captain Wickes is extremely concerned. He hurries to find Franklin, eventually locating the Doctor near the two towering masts of the main deck. Wickes has been ordered to take Franklin directly to France and not engage in any hostilities en route. But just a few days out of Quiberon Bay, off the Breton coast, lookouts have spotted two English merchant vessels. In the eight months since taking command of the *Reprisal,* Wickes has shown a singular talent for bedeviling the British Navy, particularly during early action in the Caribbean. Now he is eager to strike another blow.

In this, Captain Wickes seeks a personal act of reprisal: his brother, Richard, was killed by a British cannonball in heavy fighting off the coast of New Jersey five months ago. Wickes was an eyewitness to that death.

But orders are orders. Wickes cannot attack unless his higher-ranking passenger gives permission. Now, with the coast of France almost within sight, Captain Wickes approaches the miserable Franklin and requests permission to attack the two British merchant ships.

The suffering Franklin does not hesitate. The attack is ordered.

The British merchant ships are headed back to ports in England and Ireland — one to Hull, the other to Cork. They are brigantines, speedy two-masted vessels not much different in construction than a brig. Captain Wickes captures them without a fight, and both ships, and their full cargo of goods from French ports, are taken as prizes.*

*Capturing the two vessels was a form of piracy known as privateering. Though the British had

232

■ ■ ■ ■

Less than a week later, Benjamin Franklin is ferried ashore. Franklin has no idea how long he will be in Europe, or if he will ever return to America. He has accepted the

---

engaged in such maritime theft since the days of Sir Francis Drake, two hundred years earlier, they expressed diplomatic outrage at the *Reprisal*'s success. The *Reprisal,* however, was not a privateer, but a Continental Navy vessel. The British were outraged by its victories because they did not recognize the legitimacy of the U.S. Congress and therefore its navy. It is not known how Wickes managed to capture the ships. A warning shot across the bow from the *Reprisal*'s cannon, along with the common knowledge among sailors that quick surrender was more likely to result in lenient treatment of prisoners, would have been valid reasons for the British seamen to give up. A "prize crew" would then board the captured vessels and sail them back into a French port, there to be sold. The victorious captain and his crew received percentages of the total. As for the prisoners taken, some were given the option of switching sides to sail with the Americans, while others were held in the hope of arranging a future prisoner swap with the British.

position as commissioner to France with the full knowledge that his nation desperately needs a European ally. It is a duty Franklin does not take lightly. He plans to start by requesting "clothing and arms for twenty-five thousand men, with a suitable quantity of ammunition, and one hundred field pieces."

But bullets are not enough. The Americans need an active ally, one that will recognize them as a sovereign nation, and then send money, soldiers, and warships to help fight for the cause of independence.

Despite his advanced years, there is no better man to argue the patriot cause than Benjamin Franklin. Securing a French alliance will not be easy. The wily genius will have to seduce the French monarchy and allay its fears that the American rebellion will fail. The French are hesitant to anger the British if there is little hope of colonial success.

Franklin is aware that the French long to regain a toehold in America, one they lost in the French and Indian War. Through the careful use of diplomatic finesse, he hopes to leverage that desire in America's favor.

As Benjamin Franklin nears the French coast aboard a small ferry, he is the object of scrutiny. The French royal court would be happy to see the hated British destroyed. But George Washington's crushing defeat at Brooklyn and his subsequent three months of retreat have cast a pall on Franklin's visit. There is serious doubt in the court of Louis XVI about whether the Americans have the ability to wage effective war.

Dr. Franklin needs to dispel that doubt.

And of course, George Washington needs to start winning.

General Washington has never crossed the Atlantic. Nor has Thomas Jefferson.

Given a choice, few choose to make the journey at all.*

Benjamin Franklin has sailed the passage

*Other than merchants and sailors, the transatlantic journey was most frequently undertaken by the poor and hopeful, fleeing the poverty of Europe to make a new life in America. Many paid for the voyage by selling themselves and their children into years of indentured servitude. More than a few died en route, from shipboard diseases, and their bodies were immediately thrown overboard. However, death was not always a reason for not paying one's way: if a passenger perished more than halfway across the Atlantic, his remaining relatives were still personally liable for the fare.

seven times.

When the Doctor accepted the invitation to be commissioner to France, he did so with the full knowledge that he would undergo a punishing two-month ordeal at sea just to reach French shores. Also, there would be a very good chance his ship would sink. Yet, he went anyway.

It was an act of courage. As one passenger wrote of the transatlantic crossing,

[D]uring the voyage there is on board these ships terrible misery, stench, fumes, horror, vomiting, many kinds of seasickness, fever, dysentery, headache, heat, constipation, boils, scurvy, cancer, mouth rot, and the like, all of which come from old and sharply-salted food and meat, also from very bad and foul water, so that many die miserably.

Add to this want of provisions, hunger, thirst, frost, heat, dampness, anxiety, want, afflictions and lamentations, together with other trouble, as e.g., the lice abound so frightfully, especially on sick people, that they can be scraped off the body. The misery reaches a climax when a gale rages for two or three nights and days, so that every one believes that the ship will go to the bottom with all human beings on

Franklin in his famous cap

board. In such a visitation the people cry and pray most piteously.

But deprivation is nothing new to Benjamin Franklin. Earlier in 1776, he made his horrific journey to Canada and back, braving deep snows and numbing cold to further the cause of American independence. His lone souvenir from that arduous mission was a marten fur cap, which proved useful in warming his bald head.

Now it is the end of this grueling journey from America to France, a passage so emotionally and physically draining that almost a decade later Franklin will still

237

remember it vividly as the trip that "almost demolished me."

The fur cap has come in handy during the many bitter cold days and nights on deck. It is fast becoming Franklin's trademark — indeed, it will soon become the talk of Paris, igniting a fashion craze all its own.

But on this windy late afternoon, Franklin is a long way from Paris. He and his grandsons step off the small fishing boat and onto the streets of a fishing village named Auray.* Franklin and the boys are just happy to be on land, and quickly send for a carriage so that they can continue their journey to the French capital.

Benjamin Franklin is a man with little to lose. His wife is dead, his daughter-in-law is dying from "accumulated distress," and his illegitimate son is in prison.† His adopted

---

*Franklin stepped ashore at the harbor of St. Goustin, which is today considered the "old part" of Auray. His arrival is still commemorated with a plaque, a local dock, and a public school named in his honor.

†In a letter to his father seeking leniency, William Franklin describes his forty-nine-year-old wife's fragile condition as being a chronic though unknown illness: "She is naturally of an exceeding weak constitution, and for several years past has

hometown, Philadelphia, has grown to a city of thirty thousand people, most of whom want Benjamin Franklin to do something for them. So, now, in a new country, the Doctor sees many possibilities.

Franklin's only emotional anchors are his grandsons, William Temple Franklin and Benjamin Franklin Bache. By taking them to France, the Doctor hopes to protect them from the dangers of war, while simultaneously providing them with a traditional European education. Or, as he wrote to his son William prior to the trip, "This is the time of life in which you are to lay the foundations of your future improvement."

Benjamin Franklin still grieves the heartbreaking loss of his once-beloved son William to the royalist cause. And each day, he lives with the knowledge that he has condemned his boy to a hideous life in prison. But now, in France, far away from the chaos of the American Revolution, he hopes that his grandsons will prosper. It is common knowledge that the British would gladly kidnap the relatives of the rebel leadership and hold them hostage.

France is Benjamin Franklin's new life.

---

needed my constant care and tenderness to keep her in tolerable health."

The young grandsons, Temple and Benny, as he calls them, are now the only family that matters.

For his part, *Reprisal* captain Lambert Wickes is happy to see Franklin and his grandsons go. Soon, Wickes will sell the cargo he has acquired from the two British merchant ships, and the *Reprisal* will resume terrorizing any English vessels she encounters.*

Wickes is a daring captain and will now prowl the English Channel in search of confrontation.

Meanwhile, on French soil, Benjamin Franklin is being watched. British spies will soon inform London that he has succeeded in his journey. Although he is an object of derision in England, Franklin, King George knows, is a threat. He must not succeed in convincing the French to join the

*Captain Wickes and the *Reprisal* spent the next eleven months harassing shipping around the British Isles, capturing many vessels and delivering them to ports in France. On October 1, 1777, while sailing back to America, the USS *Reprisal* sank in the high seas off the coast of Newfoundland. Captain Wickes and almost the entire crew drowned. Only the cook survived to tell the tale.

American fight.

But Benjamin Franklin has already succeeded, simply by arriving in Paris. His presence is proof that the Americans are willing to take their message of independence globally — and perhaps also to start a new world war in the process. This is a threat that the British take most seriously.

The killing of England now begins in earnest.

Yet, despite Franklin's new age of diplomacy, nothing happens.

America, and George Washington, stand alone, powerless.

12

Upper Makefield Township, Pennsylvania
December 15, 1776
1:00 P.M.

George Washington is desperate.

"These are the times that try men's souls," pamphlet writer Thomas Paine will soon write, summing up Washington's seemingly hopeless situation.*

Now, a lone horseman gallops up the lane

*Paine, who also wrote *Common Sense,* published *The American Crisis* on December 19, 1776, perhaps the darkest hour in the short history of America. It read, "These are the times that try men's souls; the summer soldier and the sunshine patriot will, in this crisis, shrink from the service of his country; but he that stands it now, deserves the love and thanks of man and woman. Tyranny, like hell, is not easily conquered; yet we have this consolation with us, that the harder the conflict, the more glorious the triumph."

to the general's headquarters in a Pennsylvania farmhouse.* On this freezing morning, Washington is glad for the warmth provided by a stone fireplace taller than a man. Through the three large bay windows facing the main road, he can see that the rider's boots and coats are slick with mud, the obvious result of a hard, cold gallop over winter roads. It is Sunday morning, normally a time of ease, but today fear and anxiety grip General Washington. These "express riders" seldom bring good news, so the mere sight of the messenger chills

*The house belonged to William Keith, who purchased the 230-acre site in 1761. Many of his neighbors were Quakers who followed their religious principles and treated the war of rebellion with pacifist indifference, but the Scots-Irish Keith was a prominent Presbyterian and a rebel sympathizer. When he learned that the rebels were nearby, he offered the home to George Washington, who used it as his headquarters from December 14 to 24, 1776. Legend has it that one of Washington's top spies, John Honeyman, whom the British believed to be a Loyalist, was secretly sequestered in a small stone house on the Keith property in order to pass along news of Hessian troop movements in Trenton without being seen. The house still stands.

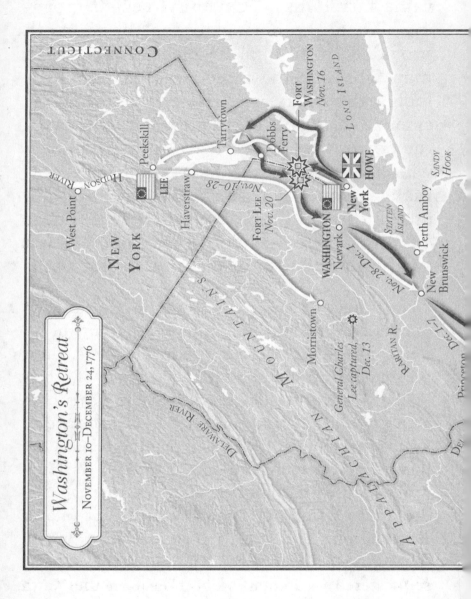

CONNECTICUT

FORT
WASHINGTON
Nov. 16

LONG ISLAND

Peekskill

Tarrytown

Dobbs
Ferry

Nov. 10–28

HOWE

LEE

West Point

HUDSON RIVER

Haverstraw

FORT LEE
Nov. 20

New
York

STATEN
ISLAND

SANDY
HOOK

NEW
YORK

WASHINGTON

Newark

Nov. 28–Dec. 1

Perth Amboy

New
Brunswick

Dec. 1–7

MOUNTAINS

Morristown

RARITAN R.

General Charles
Lee captured,
Dec. 13

APPALACHIAN

DELAWARE RIVER

DEL

Princeton

Washington's Retreat
NOVEMBER 10–DECEMBER 24, 1776

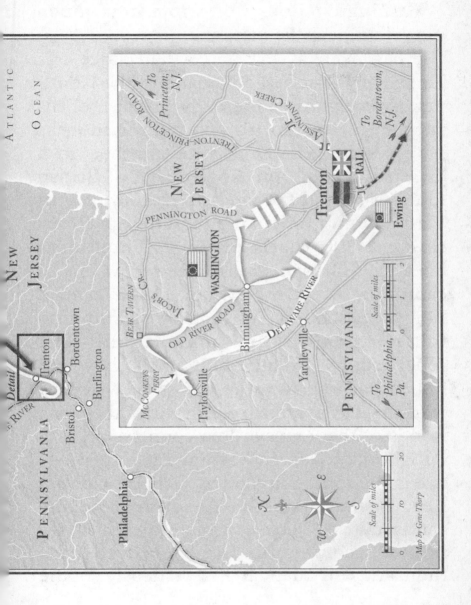

ATLANTIC

OCEAN

NEW JERSEY

NEW JERSEY

To Princeton, N.J.

TRENTON-PRINCETON ROAD

ASSUNPINK CREEK

PENNINGTON ROAD

RALL

Trenton

To Bordentown, N.J.

WASHINGTON

Ewing

BEAR TAVERN

Jacob's Cr.

OLD RIVER ROAD

Birmingham

DELAWARE RIVER

Scale of miles

0   1   2

McCONKEY'S FERRY

Taylorsville

Yardleyville

PENNSYLVANIA

To Philadelphia, Pa.

PENNSYLVANIA

NEW JERSEY

Bordentown

Trenton

Burlington

Bristol

Detail

RIVER

Philadelphia

N

W   E

S

Scale of miles

0   10   20

Map by Gene Thorp

the colonial leader.

Washington does not know how much more bad news he can take.

It has been a year and a half since His Excellency assumed command of the Continental Army. After the early promise of his success in Boston, the past three months have seen one setback after another. In a disastrous battle on November 16, British forces captured the vital stronghold of Fort Washington, overlooking the Hudson River, taking 2,800 rebels prisoner. Three days later, the British crossed the Hudson to capture a second waterfront citadel, named Fort Lee, sending Washington's army into full retreat to escape annihilation.* The rebel troops did not halt until they had pulled back all the way across New Jersey, over the Delaware River, and into the thick woods of the Pennsylvania countryside.

Right now, George Washington desperately needs his top commander, General Charles Lee, to march his army south from the center of New Jersey to reunite with Washington's command. Lee claims to have thousands of men at his disposal, so the

*Fort Washington is now the Washington Heights section of Manhattan. Fort Lee is now a riverfront town in New Jersey.

combined numbers of their troops might be enough for the rebels to launch a surprise offensive into British lines.

After the disastrous New York campaign, such thinking is foolhardy, but Washington believes that now is the time for daring — this despite the fact that his own command is smaller than Lee's. Alarmingly, hundreds of Washington's troops are deserting, returning to their homes rather than endure another freezing night in a makeshift camp, and sure death at the hands of the approaching British.

Throughout the colonies, it is becoming a common belief that the war is lost. Just two weeks ago, on November 30, the British offered a complete pardon to all colonists who would pledge their "peaceable obedience" and complete allegiance to the king. Thousands of citizens are coming forth to take this pledge, putting Washington and the Continental Army in the dangerous role of possibly being the enemy to their own countrymen.

But George Washington refuses to give up. He has no definitive reconnaissance, but he believes that his longtime adversary, General William Howe, stands poised on the opposite side of the Delaware River, ready to invade Pennsylvania. Washington has taken the extraordinary step of destroying boats on the New Jersey side of the river for sixty miles up and down the Delaware, but still he fears that Howe will find a way to cross. A heavy freeze has just set in, with the promise of a hard storm from the northeast soon to bring snow and frigid temperatures. Should the Delaware harden to ice, as it is does each winter, Howe will simply march his men and cannon across the frozen surface.

Then comes good news.

American troops under General Lee are on the march, headed toward Washington. When Lee arrives — today, it is hoped — the colonial forces will be doubled. Indeed, an optimistic Washington is even pondering a surprise offensive when that reunion takes place.

"We have three thousand men here at present," Lee wrote to Washington just days ago, once again finding a way to slow down his march. "But they are so ill-shod that we have been obliged to halt these two days for lack of shoes."

Washington is impatient for Lee's arrival, but just as aware that blending the two commands will bring headaches. The British-born Lee considers himself superior to Washington, and often ignores orders. Over the last week, Washington has repeatedly pleaded for Lee to make haste for his headquarters, but the general has not listened, and has complained about Washington in letters to other American leaders.

As of five days ago, their forces were just fifty miles apart. Just yesterday, Washington sent a messenger to Lee: "I have so frequently mentioned our situation, and the necessity of your aid, that it is painful to me to add a word upon the subject. Let me once more request and entreat you to march immediately."

Now, with the sun already fading in the early afternoon, the lone rider dismounts. Shaking off the cold, he tethers his horse and marches up the steps and into the farmhouse, where he hands a missive to a member of Washington's staff. The message is then hand-delivered to Washington, who is sitting inside.

The news could not be worse.

Two days earlier, General Charles Lee is sitting down to breakfast at ten o'clock in the morning. It is Friday the thirteenth, and the tavern in which he has spent the night smells of last night's spilled beer and unwashed patrons. A dozen men stand guard outside to protect Lee. Nineteen-year-old major James Wilkinson, an aide to American general Horatio Gates, stands near the window, waiting impatiently for Lee to complete a letter to Wilkinson's superior so that the young man might return with it to Gates's headquarters. The general is on the march now from the Hudson River Valley south to Washington's location.*

But the widow White's tavern is three long miles away from his army. Lee left his troops last night in search of paid female companionship, which he found at the tavern. The weather has turned brutally cold, with snow flurries and frost covering the ground at night. So even as Lee's soldiers, many barefoot and ill, huddle close to their campfires to keep from freezing to death, their leader has slept in a warm bed. He has

*Although very young, Maj. James Wilkinson had already served under Nathanael Greene and Benedict Arnold. He fell out with Arnold when the commander demanded that Wilkinson shoot his horse in the midst of his retreat from Canada. Wilkinson did as ordered but felt Arnold to be unnecessarily cruel. Wilkinson would later become infamous for acts of treason against the American government during the Louisiana Purchase. Theodore Roosevelt would later say of him, "In all our history, there is no more despicable character."

enjoyed the hot meals, fine Madeira wine, and other pleasures of this small roadside inn. And rather than rise at dawn to resume his march toward Washington, he slept until Wilkinson roused him at 8:00 a.m.

Although refreshed, Lee is in a foul mood, having just spent an hour lambasting an ineffective group of cavalry officers from Connecticut who showed up for their meeting in dress uniform and ceremonial wigs, a situation the crusty Lee found foolish under the circumstances. A half-written letter to his confidant, American general Horatio Gates, lies on the table before him. Lee's white shirt is open at the neck, wrinkled and yellowing. The general wears slippers but not a hat, and instead of his uniform jacket, he is covered with a thick "blanket coat" to keep warm.

In his letter to Gates — also not a fan of George Washington — Lee labels His Excellency as "damnable deficient."

"He has thrown me into a situation where I have my choice of difficulties," Lee tells Gates. "If I stay in this province, I risk myself and army; and if I do not stay, the province is lost."

Suddenly, Major Wilkinson cries out in surprise. "Here, sir, are the British cavalry."

"Where?" Lee demands, hastily signing

251

the letter.

"Around the house," Wilkinson replies in terror, witnessing for himself that a group of British soldiers has quickly charged up the lane and surrounded the tavern.

"Where is the guard?" Lee demands. "Damn the guard. Why don't they open fire?"

But two of the guards are already dead. The rest are running for their lives.

The British cavalry opens fire on the tavern "through every window and every door," in the words of one of their junior officers, an impudent twenty-two-year-old dragoon from Liverpool named Banastre Tarleton. The British commander, Lt. Col. William Harcourt, has ordered his men to "cut up as many of the [American] guard as they could."*

The widow White, fearful that her tavern will be destroyed, runs to the door and screams to the British that Lee is inside.

*The precise term for Tarleton's rank was that of "cornet," a junior grade that corresponded to the naval rank of ensign. It was utilized strictly by cavalry officers. The British Army abolished this term during military reforms in 1871, renaming the rank "second lieutenant." The British and American navies still use the rank of ensign.

Harcourt immediately orders his men to cease fire, wanting to capture Lee alive. "If the general does not surrender in five minutes, I will set fire to the house," he informs the widow. "I give my solemn oath."

Two minutes later, not even taking the time to get properly dressed, General Charles Lee gives himself up.

A cowering Wilkinson, who has found a place to evade capture, bears witness. "Lee, mounted on my horse, which stood ready at the door, was hurried off in triumph, bareheaded, in his slippers and blanket coat, his collar open, and his shirt very much soiled from several days' use."

A month later, when word of Lee's capture reaches London, bells will be rung in joyful celebration. The Hessians in America will celebrate as well, believing Lee "the only rebel general we have cause to fear."

It is the news of Lee's capture that General Washington receives at 1:00 p.m. on December 15. Almost immediately, a thoroughly disheartened Washington takes quill to paper to put his fears into words.

"The game," Washington admits to his younger brother back home in Virginia, "is pretty near up."*

Word of Lee's capture is immediately messaged to Gen. William Howe. Believing that the rebel army is now shattered, and knowing that winter would make roads impassable and encampment unhealthy, he quartered small garrisons in a number of towns in New Jersey along the main route from New York to Philadelphia, then removed his own headquarters to New York City. There, Howe's blond, blue-eyed mistress from Boston, Elizabeth Loring, awaits him; and he is eager to return to her. Saturday morning, one day after Lee's capture and a day before Washington gets the news, General Howe saddles his horse for the trip to New York. He is accompanied by his top general, Charles Cornwallis, who plans to sail home to England to be with his ill wife until

*John Augustine Washington was forty years old and living on his family's plantation, Bushfield, at the time of his brother's letter in 1776. During the war, John Washington served on his county's Committee of Safety, which sought to undermine any Loyalist activity. He died of unknown causes in 1787, and is buried with his wife in an unmarked grave. Their son, Bushrod, went on to become a U.S. Supreme Court justice.

hostilities resume in the spring.

But George Washington knows nothing of these movements. New Jersey is so rife with Loyalists that his spy network is unable to send him reliable reconnaissance. So, rather than settle into a winter camp of his own, he maintains his defensive stance, believing that his army is all that prevents the British from capturing Philadelphia. Congress is also convinced of this and has already fled the city to conduct business in Baltimore.

When Washington finally receives word of Howe's departure from the battlefield, he doesn't accept it. Instead, reflecting on the stealthy British tactics used on Long Island, Washington thinks Howe's retreat is a ruse — he knows that a Hessian force numbering almost fifteen hundred men still remains on the opposite side of the Delaware, defending the city of Trenton.

Even when the remnants of Lee's army, now numbering just two thousand men, finally arrive to join his force, Washington frets. The terms of the Continental Army's enlistment contracts stipulate that every single soldier will be free to return to his home as of January 1, 1777. With the war going badly, there will be no reason for his troops to risk their lives by reenlisting. In effect, George Washington is just two weeks away from having no army at all.

He must, therefore, find a way to keep the rebellion alive. He knows he must accomplish a "brilliant stroke [to] rouse the spirits of our people, which are quite sunk by our misfortunes."

Throughout the United States of America, and in London and Paris, the thoughts of men, women, and children now turn to Christmas. It will be a time to set the war aside, if only for a day, to celebrate goodwill, hope, and love.

But General Washington is not of that mind-set. As the days until Christmas count down, he hatches a bold plan.

Instead of goodwill, hope, and love, George Washington foresees a Christmas full of carnage, mayhem, and brutal death.

The battle password to be used by the Continental Army consists of three short words that summarize not just Washington's state of mind but the very future of the nation: "Victory or Death."

On Christmas night, a hard winter gale lashes George Washington as he steps into the black Durham boat that will carry him across the Delaware River. It is just past midnight, and Washington's plan is to launch a surprise attack on Trenton, ferrying his entire army across the swift and wide waterway in the dead of night, then marching ten miles to the Hessian lines. Spies have already informed the enemy of Washington's plans, but the attack is so far-fetched that the Hessian commander, Col. Johann Rall, is making no plans to oppose the crossing.

"Let them come," he has responded to the spy. As usual, Rall is drinking and playing cards as he assesses the situation. "We will go at them with the bayonet."

Unlike in Brooklyn, where men fought to get into the boats in their eagerness to retreat, Washington's soldiers now wait patiently for their turn to climb aboard the large vessel and begin their assault. Many stand by campfires, burning every available piece of wood to keep warm. "When I turned my face to the fire, my back would be freezing," one soldier would write. "By turning round and round I kept myself from perishing."

The Delaware River is filled with jagged chunks of ice carried along by a raging current. Under normal conditions, that hazard would be difficult enough. But "a perfect hurricane" also now blows, stinging the men's faces with snow, sleet, and rain. The soldiers will stand in the flat-bottomed boats, squeezed tightly together as they are rowed across by the same Massachusetts seamen who saved them after the debacle in Brooklyn. Normally used to carry ore, these high-sided boats are strong enough to hold forty men per load — indeed, artillery pieces and horses will also make the crossing. But should one of the Durhams strike ice or otherwise be tipped by the abominable conditions, every man aboard will perish. The water is simply too cold and too fast to attempt a rescue.

Washington is among the first to cross. He stands in the pointed bow of the boat throughout the journey, his black cape pulled tightly around his shoulders. When the boat reaches the other side, he sits down on a frozen beehive to supervise the unloading of his men. The Continental Army is crossing in three different locations up and down the river, with his group at McKonkey's Ferry, north of Trenton.

By 3:00 a.m., it is done. There has been no loss of life so far, but Washington has no way of knowing that the other two crossing attempts at other points on the river have failed. Because of the harsh weather and increasing ice floes, only Washington's portion of the three-pronged attack could establish itself on the banks of the river.

The storm grows in intensity, yet Washington pushes his men forward, desperate to ensure the element of surprise so vital to a successful attack. The road to Trenton is pitch-black, and the pace no more than a frozen shuffle. Some of the men see their way by lighting slow-burning lengths of rope designed to be used as cannon fuses. Most wrap rags around their shoes for additional warmth, while many men have no shoes at all — the rags are their only protection from the winter cold.

Throughout, Washington rides tall in the saddle, his unmistakable height and profile looming at the side of the men when they least expect it. "For God's sake, keep with your officers," he encourages those men who slow down or stop. Soldiers who stop will most likely fall asleep and die before they can awaken. In fact, two rebels freeze to death on the march.

Washington himself almost slips off the road when his horse loses its footing on the icy lane and appears about to roll down a steep embankment. Quickly, the general grabs the animal's mane and twists its neck hard, forcing the horse back onto the road and maintaining his own balance and that of his horse.

The general is tense and uncharacteristically angry. There can be no mistakes tonight. A lesser commander would have remained behind, leading the action from the safety of a warm farmhouse. Yet Washington knows that his men are watching. The future of America hangs on the leadership skills he now must display in the dark and cold.

The weather is causing other problems, rendering many of the muskets unusable. The warfare, then, will pit American bayonets against those bayonets used so ruthlessly by the Hessians on Long Island. But even then, the rebels will be at a disadvantage — for every five now-useless muskets, the Americans possess just one bayonet. Those men without a blade must make do with gun butts or fists.

First light arrives shortly after 7:00 a.m.

Sunrise is ten minutes later.

Still, the rebel soldiers remain undetected. Their movements obscured by the thick snow, the colonial fighters march quietly toward Trenton. It is a small city of just a few taverns, shops, a church, and about seventy homes. It did contain a large permanent barracks building constructed by the British in the 1760s, making it one of the few places in New Jersey suitable for a winter garrison.

The Americans have been on their feet for the entire night. They have not slept at all, and despite carrying three days' rations, they have little food or drink left. Yet, a new burst of energy surges as the men come upon Trenton. Washington calmly orders the attack, telling his 2,400 troops to race quickly into town before the Hessians can respond to any alarms.

Reaching the outskirts of Trenton, Washington orders the artillery to fire, formally ending the surprise. As shells rain down on the town, the rebels race through the streets, thrusting their bayonets into the surprised Hessians, whose training ensures a calm professionalism under fire. The two forces, in fact, are a study in military bearing — exhausted, undernourished, poorly armed rebels versus polished and efficient German mercenary warriors. The Hessians are fond of donning fierce peaked copper helmets in battle. Those able to do so, grow fierce black mustaches.

There will later be rumors that the Hessians were drunk or hungover that day, from too much Christmas cheer, but eyewitnesses will state that is not the case. Career soldiers who have spent their whole lives training for this moment, the Hessians have seen the rebels on the battlefield before and do not respect or fear them. The Americans are simply a nuisance, nothing more, and the Hessians' plan is repeatedly to run them through with their seventeen-inch-long bayonets.

At first, the battle goes well for Washington's troops. His men enter the city before those in the Germans garrison can rouse themselves from their holiday beds. Six American cannon fire down King and Queen Streets, their barrels strafing any living being who crosses those thoroughfares. The Hessians call upon their military training and instinctively form into two lines, but the instant they fire upon the rebels and attempt to reload, the Americans swarm their position, coming hard at the Hessians with bayonets, hunting knives, musket butts, and fists.

Other American soldiers, seeking the momentary warmth of a fireplace, use the attack as an excuse to break into homes currently occupied by Hessians. They flush the Germans into alleys and side streets, where still more Americans pounce upon them. Blood stains the snow as soldiers are speared and left to die where they fall.

The Hessian soldiers first registered for military life at the age of seven. For most, their actual service began at the age of sixteen. They have trained under one of the most rigorous systems of discipline in the military world. A simple violation of rules results in thirty lashes, while something more severe, such as leaving one's post, results in hanging. The penalties are so harsh that even family members can be punished if a Hessian soldier misbehaves. Most of all, the Hessians' commitment to physical conditioning and drill is rigorous and ongoing, all in an attempt to produce not just the best soldier possible, but a mercenary force beyond compare.

There is no reason to believe that the impoverished and barely trained American Army stands a chance against such fighting men.

Yet, that is just what is now happening.

As the hostilities turn to hand-to-hand combat, the men smell one another's stale breaths, body odors, tobacco, and last night's alcohol. They scream guttural warnings and commands in different languages, not understanding one another's words but sensing the meaning. It is kill or be killed, with neither side having time to fire or reload a weapon. In the end, it will not be military prowess that turns the tide, but desperation.

The Hessians begin to flee.

The Princeton Road, which represents the primary path to escape, is quickly blocked by Washington's force. Another avenue of flight is the Assunpink Creek, south of town, but the bridge from one side to the other is now in American hands. Two Hessian gun crews attempt to stem the rebel advance, but they are thwarted as well: Americans capture their position and quickly turn their guns on the Germans.

For the Hessians, so comfortable with precision and drill, the scene of confusion is like a vision of hell. Finally, the Hessian commander, Colonel Rall, who ate a long Christmas dinner at the Green Tree Tavern and then drank well into the night, assembles himself and climbs into the saddle. Rall now knows he was foolish to ignore warnings that the American attack was coming. Rall, the son of an army officer, became an officer cadet himself at the age of fourteen and has spent his entire life in the military. Throughout his thirty-six-year career, Rall has defeated opponents on battlefields in Europe, Asia, and America. He is far more experienced in battle than George Washington. Rall believes that he can rout the rebels if he can personally rally his troops. Thus, the charismatic German commander hastily coordinates a charge into the American lines. From a nearby hill, George Washington watches the battle. His view is often blocked by the snow and smoke, so he cannot tell whether Rall is succeeding.

He is not.

Colonel Rall is soon shot twice in the abdomen. Mortally wounded, he falls from his mount and is evacuated to a nearby home, where he dies a few hours later. Found in his waistcoat is the warning passed to him earlier in the night from Loyalist spies.

The Hessians continue to sprint out of the city, racing through snow and frigid streams to the safety of the thick woods and orchards on Trenton's outskirts. A few hundred escape. Those who remain are soon surrounded by the Americans and taken prisoner. The stunned Germans look on as the rebels plunder their storehouses, steal their wagons, and cart off hundreds of pounds of vital supplies, ammunition, and cannon. Frightened Hessian grenadiers, attempting to endear themselves to their captors, offer up their brass-fronted helmets as souvenirs.

Leaving his observation post, Washington now rides into Trenton to assess the victory.

He plans to raise morale and encourage reenlistment by giving each of his soldiers a cash payout for his bravery, based upon the value of the plundered material.

He wastes no time. Forty-five minutes after the battle begins, it is over. He then orders his soldiers to return, with their prisoners and the new cache of weaponry, to McKonkey's Ferry and once again to cross the Delaware to avoid any counterattack by the remaining British and German forces in the area.

The return journey is even more perilous than the initial crossing. The logistics of transporting the Hessian prisoners, captured artillery guns, and looted food stores require several trips back and forth through the icy waters for the weary boatmen. The flatboats are half-flooded from rain and snow, subjecting soldiers and prisoners alike to the onset of frostbite as they stand up to their knees in freezing water. Ice floes dotting the river's surface have become more numerous and now stick to the boats, joining with the current to force some of the vessels downriver. The most effective way of freeing a boat from the ice is for the passengers to jump up and down repeatedly — which they do, taking great care not to fall overboard.

As more and more of the riverbanks freeze

over, it becomes impossible for some boats to reach the shore. Soldiers from both sides must step out and walk on the ice, many times breaking through and falling into the bitterly cold water.

But most men make it, exhausted and battered, into Pennsylvania. Waiting for them is General Washington, who is analyzing the amazing victory. Twenty-one Hessians are now dead, and 918 Germans are being held prisoner. Soon, these mercenaries will be turned over to the Pennsylvania militia, to ensure they do not fall back into British hands.

In addition, six brass Hessian cannon, one thousand stands of arms, fifteen prized Hessian battle flags, and forty horses have been brought back to Pennsylvania.*

Incredibly, only four American soldiers were wounded in the fight.† None was killed.

*A "stand of arms" consists of a musket, cartridge box, bayonet, and belt. However, most frequently, it was just a musket and bayonet.

†Among those wounded is an eighteen-year-old college dropout named James Monroe. A bullet shot through his chest severed an artery. Monroe would recover and go on to become the fifth president of the United States. In the famous

Seeking to memorialize his victory, an exhausted George Washington turns to Major Wilkinson and says, "[T]his is a glorious day for our country."

But he knows it is far more than that. The victory at Trenton saved the entire rebellion from a ghastly defeat.

Of that, there is no doubt.

---

painting *Washington Crossing the Delaware,* by Emanuel Leutze, Monroe is depicted as standing behind the general holding the American flag. This is historically inaccurate.

13

Assunpink Creek
Outside Trenton, New Jersey
January 2, 1777
3:00 P.M.

For George Washington, there is no rest.

Just seven days after his stunning victory at Trenton, the general once again looks out over that besieged city. Rain falls on the colonial positions as early six thousand rebel soldiers prepare themselves for another battle. Washington has led his men across the frozen Delaware yet again, seeking to hold on to the momentum gained in last week's stunning victory. Morale is high among the colonial troops, despite rampant dysentery and a shortage of shoes.* Sensing victory, many men have reenlisted, and a

*Other than their amazing victory at Trenton, one other key reason for high morale was a ten-dollar bonus for reenlistment, which Washington paid in

new complement of untrained militia has joined Washington's veteran corps. His army has once again made the treacherous journey across the frozen river — the general believes that controlling Trenton and the nearby city of Princeton might make it possible to push the British completely out of New Jersey.

---

cash to each man on New Year's Day. Most soldiers made just six dollars a month, so this was a large amount of money. This moment marked a change in the constitution of the Continental Army that had been under discussion by Congress for months. Americans were once opposed to the idea of a standing army, preferring small militias of citizen-soldiers and short enlistments. That changed late in 1776. The Congress began to see that only a trained fighting force would defeat the British. The standard enlistment was changed from a few months to either three years or the length of the war. Early in 1777, Congress also approved Washington's request for greater numbers of artillery, infantry, and even cavalry, which had been in short supply on the American side until then. "A regular army and the most masterly discipline," insisted John Adams, who had once opposed such a force. "Without these we cannot reasonably hope to be a powerful, prosperous, or a free people."

However, Trenton is indefensible. Washington has seen this for himself. So, rather than take up positions in the heart of town and suffer the same fate as Colonel Rall and his Hessian garrison, Washington is setting a trap for the British, who he believes will counterattack shortly.

The general's army holds the high ground overlooking Trenton. The steep banks of the Assunpink Creek lie before them, the ice-choked Delaware flows to the left, and a thick swamp adds protection to the right. Washington's cannon are sighted on King and Queen Streets and on the vital bridge spanning the creek.

Washington's infantrymen have dug in behind protective earthworks, their bodies shielded from musket fire and grape. There is no attempt to hide their presence — tents have been positioned, and campfire smoke curls into the sky. This is the battle George Washington wants, in the location he has chosen.

Spies have alerted His Excellency to the advance of English commander Charles Cornwallis. The lieutenant general's winter leave was abruptly canceled due to the recent colonial victories. Instead of sailing home to see his wife, Cornwallis celebrated his thirty-eighth birthday on New Year's

Eve, then the next morning galloped fifty miles from New York to Princeton. There, he immediately assumed command of the eight-thousand-man British and Hessian garrison.

Cornwallis believes that speed is vital to combat, so he does not delay in marching on Trenton. This morning, after leaving a small force behind to hold Princeton, his army began a ten-mile trip. The trek has been neither quick nor easy: thick mud has slowed the twenty-eight cannon and the supply wagons. American snipers, shooting from the cover of snowy woods, have further hindered the British advance.

But now, as the winter sky grows dark, Cornwallis finally reaches the outskirts of Trenton. His men and horses are filthy, the red clay of the muddy road from Princeton coating man and beast alike.

George Washington hears the unmistakable sound of an approaching army — whinnying horses, creaking caisson wheels, the bawl of commands. Soon after, he sees the first columns of redcoats. It is a much larger force than he anticipated. He quickly realizes that not only is the Continental Army outnumbered, but the British and Hessian lines are comprised entirely of professional soldiers while Washington's army is overwhelmingly inexperienced. Many of his soldiers were making their livings as shopkeepers and farmers just a week ago.

Washington knows he is in trouble. Such a large army can easily surround his men and slowly tighten the noose. The rebel position, which just moments ago seemed ideal, now feels tenuous.

Quickly, George Washington strategizes a new, bold plan.

Moments later, the first wave of British troops opens fire.

The differences between George Washington and Charles Cornwallis could not be greater. Washington was raised as a middle-class Virginia planter. His fortune was earned through marriage, ambition, and a knack for achieving great success through hard work. Indeed, from farming to diplomacy to leading men into combat, Washington excels at all. That's why the Second Continental Congress named him commander in chief, and, even after the horrific setbacks in New York just a few months ago, his men continue to fight hard for him.

Washington is meticulous in his paperwork and correspondence, a fussy trait that seems at odds with his physical appearance. The general's rugged stature also conceals his two ongoing sources of pain: his wife Martha's inability to bear a child and the terrible anguish that comes from his deteriorating teeth.

Right now, the situation with Martha cannot be helped. Their eighteenth wedding anniversary is just days away, but the general long ago sent her back to Mount Vernon to be away from the fighting. Despite the physical distance, theirs is a devoted and affectionate partnership. And as a man of honor and deep integrity, Washington realizes that straying from the marital bed can only undermine his moral stature as a leader of men.

"I retain an unalterable affection for you, which neither time nor distance can change," he wrote to Martha earlier in the war, signing the letter "Your Entire George Washington."*

Washington's other cause of personal pain is not so easily hidden: he has almost no teeth. The general blames a childhood habit of cracking walnuts with his molars for the

---

*Martha will save her husband's letters for the rest of her life, though, in an effort to keep their love life private, she will one day burn all but two of them.

dentures he now wears. The false teeth are made of hippopotamus ivory held in his mouth by strands of gold wire affixed to his few remaining real teeth. Thus, Washington smiles little, and lives with the constant pain of inflamed gums from the ill-fitting dentures. He grumbles about the way the fake teeth make his lips puff outward, and he is obsessed with all manner of dental gadgetry — spending a regular portion of his income on teeth scrapers, tooth powder, dental files, and medication to ease the pain.

His stoic countenance has added to the heroic stature in which his soldiers view him. In his refusal to smile or unduly celebrate, they see a brave and humble leader.

There is no such adulation of Lt. Gen. Charles Cornwallis. Six years younger than Washington, Cornwallis is an outstanding officer, having shown his prowess at the Battle of New York and the British victory at Fort Washington.

Yet, Cornwallis also has the unfortunate task of taking orders from Gen. William Howe. The wealthy and educated Cornwallis, who has spent his entire adult life fighting Britain's wars around the world, considers Howe a timid playboy. Cornwallis favors a strategy of rapid assaults designed

Lt. Gen Charles Cornwallis

to surprise and ultimately crush an opponent. He chafes at Howe's preference for more patient, methodical plans of attack.

Yet, as Howe's subordinate, the chubby Cornwallis has no choice but to carry out his commands. The rank and file will follow him into battle just as they would any other British general, for that is their duty. Cornwallis is not the sort to ride into the thick of the fray aboard a white charger, risking his life in the manner of George Washington. Instead, the British general stays to the rear of the action, issuing commands as information comes in from his frontline officers.

Like Washington, Cornwallis is happily

married. He and his wife have a son and daughter, now safely ensconced at their family estate in Kent. There was a time when Cornwallis was uncomfortable fighting the American rebels, for he voted in favor of their cause while serving in the House of Lords. But while he admires and considers George Washington an "old fox" for his ability to use deception, the British commander is also keen to crush the rebels and go home.

With the sun quickly sinking, the British charge the bridge over Assunpink Creek — three times trying to penetrate Washington's lines, and three times being pushed back by colonial cannon. "We let them come on some ways," American sergeant Joseph White will remember. "Then by a signal given, we all fired together."

The last volley is deadly canister shot — clusters of iron spheres twice the size of musket balls flying through the air at lethal speed, making a terrible squeaking noise — designed to wound large numbers of opponents with each single cannon blast.

"The bridge looked red as blood, with their killed and wounded and their red coats," Sergeant White will recall of the carnage.

Indeed, British losses are significant, with dozens of dead and wounded.

As the sun finally sets and the sky over the New Jersey countryside turns pitch-black, the British leadership debates its next move. Attacking in the dark brings a host of tactical problems, but they are aware of Washington's tendency to use the dead of night to his advantage.

"If Washington is the general I take him to be," warns General Cornwallis's quartermaster, Sir William Erskine, "his army will not be there by morning."

But another general, James Grant, disagrees, arguing that Washington's only avenue of escape is by crossing the Delaware yet again. He reminds Cornwallis that Washington has no boats nearby to make that flight possible.

Cornwallis knows he has the manpower to encircle Washington's entire army right now and, perhaps, end the war. He is equally aware, however, that his soldiers are exhausted. The British regulars' long march from Princeton, carrying their requisite sixty-pound load of weaponry and clothing, has taken the edge off his men. A hot meal and a night of sleep seem prudent.

Convinced that Washington is trapped, Cornwallis orders a halt to the attack. He confidently tells the council of war, "We'll go over and bag him in the morning."

The British will attack at first light with a frontal assault while simultaneously crossing the Assunpink on the right side of the rebel lines in a pincer movement.

The battle will be bloody, of that Cornwallis is sure. An entrenched foe is not defeated without great loss of life. The American artillery commanders have improved enormously since the war began, and will surely order their men to fire point-blank rounds into the advancing redcoat columns, as they did earlier today.

Setting up camp on the same hill where Washington observed the Battle of Trenton one week earlier, Cornwallis and the British build their campfires and stare across to the other side of the city, where it is clear from the many fires blazing that the Americans are doing the same. They can hear the sound of pickaxes and shovels working through the night as Washington's men continue digging fortifications for tomorrow's battle.

Tonight, Lt. Gen. Charles Cornwallis sleeps well, believing that victory is all but assured.

Come morning, Cornwallis arises and is

stunned: Washington and his army are gone.

In fact, well before noon, after a silent nightlong march down a seldom-used back road unknown to the British, Gen. George Washington attacked and destroyed the small redcoat force occupying Princeton and captured the town. Among the heroes is a young artillery captain named Alexander Hamilton, whom Washington soon plans to promote.

Once Princeton is secure, the Continental Army is immediately on the move, heading north toward Morristown, thirty-seven miles away, a position separated from the British garrison in New York by a protective ridgeline called the Short Hills.

Cornwallis realizes that Washington has outsmarted him. He is now racing to New Brunswick, New Jersey, to protect British supplies and money there.

In this way, the war of rebellion continues, and Cornwallis's dreams of returning to England are dashed.

The battle for Princeton was brief but intense. The American forces were led by Gen. Hugh Mercer. The fifty-year-old Scot is a physician and soldier who fought on the losing side during the Jacobite Rising in Scotland of 1745–46, then smuggled himself into America to escape persecution from the British. He settled down in Pennsylvania and began a private medical practice, only to take up arms alongside George Washington in the French and Indian War. Mercer is known for his bravery and his stubborn refusal to die, as evidenced by his one-hundred-mile solo march through thick forest to safety after being wounded in battle against Shawnee warriors in 1756.

It is sunrise on January 3, 1777, as General Mercer leads the Continental Army's advance column toward Princeton. A sudden freeze iced the roads after midnight, allowing the Americans to slip away from Trenton and march on Princeton without the thick mud that exhausted the redcoats less than twenty-four hours earlier. The wheels of the cannon are wrapped in cloth to dampen the sound. Once again, as in Brooklyn, the order has been spread that the men must not speak or even cough so as to maintain silence during the escape. Some Americans actually fall asleep on their feet during the ten-mile journey through the darkness, yet somehow the colonials manage to shuffle forward in unison. The rags covering the freezing feet of the shoeless are drenched in blood.

It is the job of General Mercer and his

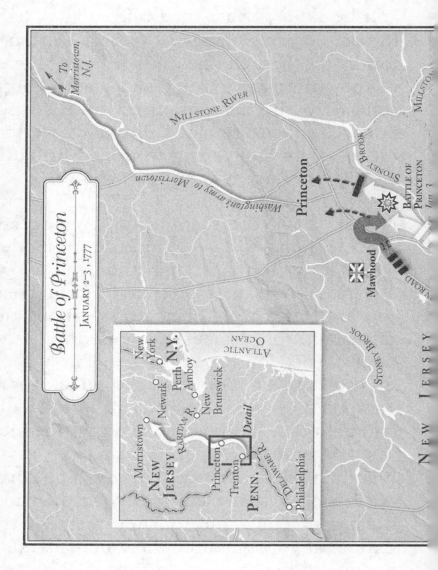

Battle of Princeton
JANUARY 2–3, 1777

To Morristown, N.J.

MILLSTONE RIVER

Washington's army to Morristown

Princeton

STONEY BROOK

BATTLE OF PRINCETON

Mawhood

ROAD

NEW JERSEY

STONEY BROOK

MILLSTON

New York
N.Y.
Newark
Perth Amboy
New Brunswick
ATLANTIC OCEAN
Morristown
NEW JERSEY
RARITAN R.
Detail
Princeton
Trenton
PENN.
DELAWARE R.
Philadelphia

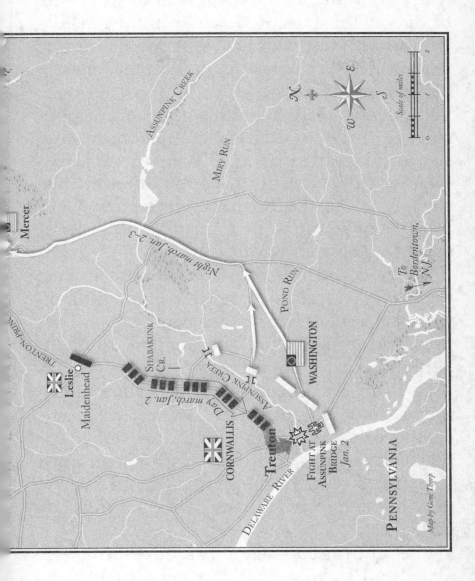

Map by Gene Thorp

PENNSYLVANIA

Assunpink Creek

Miry Run

Pond Run

To Bordentown, N.J.

Mercer

Night march, Jan. 2–3

Trenton Princeton

Shabakunk Cr.

Maidenhead

Leslie

Day march, Jan. 2

Assunpink Creek

Washington

Cornwallis

Trenton

Fight at Assunpink Bridge Jan. 2

Delaware River

Scale of miles
0   1   2

N
W   E
S

three hundred fifty men from Delaware, Maryland, and Pennsylvania to destroy the bridge at the Post Road, two miles outside Princeton. This will block Cornwallis's force from a hasty return once it becomes aware of Washington's ruse.

Suddenly, Mercer and his men come upon a large body of British troops marching south to reinforce the Trenton attack. Neither side expects to see the other at this early hour, so the British commander, Col. John Mawhood, at first mistakes Mercer's army for Hessian reinforcements.

"They could not possibly suppose it was our army," Bostonian soldier Henry Knox will later remember. "I believe they were as much astonished as if an army had dropped perpendicularly upon them."

The surprise encounter brings forth confusion and violent death. When, after an early volley, the Americans are slow to reload their muskets, the British sprint into their lines with bayonets drawn. Mercer's gray horse buckles as it is shot by a musket ball.

The courageous general finds himself alone and surrounded by a band of British soldiers. He is wearing an overcoat that covers his uniform and rank insignia. Aware that George Washington wears just such a cloak on the field of battle, the jubilant British believe they have actually captured the American commander in chief.

"Surrender, you damn rebel," the redcoats command.

Mercer will not. Fifty yards away, he can see what happens to rebels who yield. One lieutenant with a broken leg was dragged from beneath the wagon where he was hiding, bludgeoned with a gun butt to the point of near unconsciousness, and then repeatedly bayoneted. Another captured lieutenant, Bartholomew Yates, was stabbed thirteen times and died.

Mercer draws his saber and attacks. The regulars swarm the Scottish immigrant, taunting him as they wait for the moment to pounce. It would be simple merely to shoot him, but they do not wish "General Washington" to enjoy such a hasty demise.

Finally, a swinging gun butt catches Mercer in the head. He collapses. More blows rain down on his skull, leaving the general unconscious. Then the British bayonet him, but still Mercer lives.

Soon afterward, the real George Washington gallops into battle to rally Mercer's men, ultimately turning the tide of the battle in favor of the colonials.

He appears out of nowhere, his presence

encouraging the Americans to press the attack at a time when many are beginning to flee in terror.

Colonel Mawhood's two infantry regiments and his column of light cavalry stand between the Americans and Princeton. Turning back toward Trenton is not an option. Washington gallops through his army, pushing them back to the fight.

"Parade with us, my dear fellows," the American general cries from astride his horse, his voice calm and cool. He fearlessly puts himself in range of British musket fire but behaves as if he were in no danger at all.

"There is but a handful of the enemy and we will have them directly," he shouts.

The rebels respond. They now fall upon the enemy with utter fury. British dead and wounded soon litter the local orchard. Colonel Mawhood and the rest of his terrified men sprint for their lives. Washington gives chase on horseback but then lets them go, ordering his army once again to turn toward Princeton — and victory.

"It was a glorious day. . . . I happened to be in the first and hottest of the fire," Pennsylvania junior officer Joseph Reed will write home to his wife about the sight of Washington seizing command of the battle.

General George Washington

"I would wish to say a few words of the actions respecting that truly great man, General Washington, but it is not in the power of language to convey any just idea of him.

"His greatness is far beyond description. I shall never forget what I felt at Princeton on his account, when I saw him brave all the dangers of the field and his important life hanging as it were by a single hair with a thousand deaths flying around him. Believe me, I thought not of myself. He is surely America's better genius."

Meanwhile, Gen. Hugh Mercer is carried from the field and taken to a farmhouse that has been converted into a field hospital, where his severe wounds are tended to by Dr. Benjamin Rush, coincidentally, a signatory to the Declaration of Independence. Mercer clings to life, his crumpled skull and stab wounds a vivid reminder of the fate that awaits George Washington should he ever fall into British hands.

Nine days after the battle, General Mercer breathes his last.* Washington has already said good-bye to his dear belligerent friend, and is finally settling into winter quarters in Morristown, there to regroup

*Among General Mercer's descendants are legendary composer Johnny Mercer and World War II general George S. Patton.

and drill his army for the summer campaign. The tide of the war has turned, and Washington's victories are celebrated throughout the colonies.

In London, some British are questioning the need to wage war in the colonies.

In Paris, where Benjamin Franklin has now labored for a month to entice the French into helping the rebel cause, the news of Trenton, Princeton, and Morristown is cause for jubilation. The French have long been waiting for a sign that the Americans can actually win this war.

Finally, Washington has provided one.

14

Hôtel de Hambourg
52 rue Jacob, Paris, France
January 19, 1777
Mid-morning

Benjamin Franklin is being watched.

It is Sunday morning here in the small room serving as Franklin's temporary head-quarters. As usual, the Doctor rose at 5:00 a.m. for a leisurely three-hour period of bathing, breakfast, and planning. He shaves himself rather than submit to the "bad breath of a slovenly barber." Franklin will work until noon, then "read or overlook my personal accounts, and dine" for two hours. In the afternoon, it is more work, then on to an evening of socializing before retiring to bed at 10:00 p.m.

The schedule is intentionally selfish. Just two days ago, Franklin celebrated his seventy-first birthday, and this routine helps conserve his energy. The Doctor is guarded, often cloaking himself in mystery even as his cult of celebrity in Paris society grows. The gray marten fur hat he wears at all times to keep his head warm has become so popular that many Parisian women try to emulate its appearance by forming their hair into the same shape, a hairstyle known as the "coiffure à la Franklin." Local merchants are keen to make a profit from the eminent American's mysterious and sudden arrival in their city, much to Franklin's bemusement.

"My picture is everywhere," Franklin writes home to his daughter Sally; "on the lids of snuff boxes, on rings, busts. The numbers sold are incredible. My portrait is a best seller, you have prints, and copies of prints, and copies of copies spread everywhere. Your father's face is now as well known as the man in the moon."*

Here on the rue Jacob, Franklin is assisted by his illegitimate teenage grandson, Tem-

*Thirty-two-year-old Sarah "Sally" Franklin Bache lives in Philadelphia with her husband, Richard, who served as the U.S. postmaster-general. She is the mother of eight children and devotes her time to assisting with the war effort by sewing clothing for the troops.

ple, who now serves as the Doctor's social secretary. Franklin's other grandson, seven-year-old Benny, attends boarding school just outside the city, in Passy, where he will learn to speak French so well that he will nearly forget his English.*

Yet, Franklin's fame does not come without a cost, which is why he now pens a response to a letter from Mrs. Juliana Ritchie, a Philadelphia expatriate in Paris who recently paid him a social call. Franklin's desk is untidy, as it was on the day of her visit, with important papers spilling on top of one another. But it is Mrs. Ritchie's letter he focuses on.

"You are surrounded with spies," her note warned, "who watch your every movement: who you visit, and by whom you are visited. Of the latter there are those who pretend to be friends to the cause of your country but that is a mere pretense."

This is perhaps the most poorly kept secret in Paris — and Franklin is not the only citizen under observation. The French

*On the Left Bank, Passy is well within the city's boundaries now, a short walk from the Eiffel Tower. Also on the Left Bank today, near the Square de Yorktown, is the rue Benjamin Franklin.

capital swarms with undercover agents. It is almost impossible for anyone of social status to go anywhere without his actions being scrutinized and reported.

King Louis XVI, the twenty-two-year-old monarch who has been seated on the throne of France for a mere two years, has thousands of official spies in his employ.* Political factions and organized crime networks throughout the city also use vast armies of snoops.

Benjamin Franklin has been in Paris just a month, but he is already the subject of a police report: "Doctor Franklin, who lately arrived in this country from the English colonies, is very much run after, and feted," the report states in bemused fashion. "He has an agreeable physiognomy. Spectacles always on his eyes, but little hair — a fur cap is always on his head. He wears no

*These figures are based upon an accounting of France's official registers, published by French writer Louis-Pierre Manuel in 1792. In addition to the 6,000 spies in Paris, Manuel reported a figure of 19,300 official spies throughout all of France. Manuel, a French revolutionary who belatedly became a supporter of Louis XVI, was guillotined in Paris one year later for his loyalty to the king.

powder, but a neat air. Linen very white [and] a brown coat makes his dress. His only defense is a stick in his hand."*

Franklin's response to Mrs. Ritchie is intentionally comical — and long overdue. The Paris mail arrives nine times a day, but the Doctor has waited a week to compose his letter. Jokingly, he promises that even if his personal valet "was a spy, as probably he is, I think I should not discharge him for that, if in other respects I liked him."

Franklin's attempt to mollify Mrs. Ritchie is sincere, but he would do well to heed her warning. For one of his closest friends and confidants is, in fact, a British spy — an agent of espionage so talented that his mission will not be publicly revealed for more than a century.

The young man's name is George Ban-

---

*Franklin's physical appearance was considered astonishing in Paris, for he seemed completely indifferent to the rigorous French code of dress, which included mandatory ruffled lace shirts, shoes with elaborate buckles, and white silk stockings. Many men and women often shaved their heads to avoid the constant threat of lice, donning wigs. Franklin's scalp was already mostly bald, but he made no attempt to groom his few remaining strands of hair.

croft, the same good friend and botanist whom Franklin once supported for election to the prestigious Royal Society, and who boldly supported him after the infamous hour of ridicule in the London cockpit in 1774. Believing Bancroft to be a man he can trust, Franklin personally requested that he be hired as secretary to the American delegation in Paris, responsible for handling all manner of diplomacy and sensitive paperwork.*

Big mistake.

Within months, King George III will know the Doctor's every move.

Surrounded by spies, embraced by the temptations of Parisian society, and struggling to communicate in a language he is only now learning, Franklin comes to realize that his task will be neither quick nor simple, and that he may end up living in France for a very long time. Yet, as he takes up residence in a luxurious château on the outskirts of the city, and becomes more acquainted with some of the wealthiest

*The website of the U.S. Central Intelligence Agency makes note of Bancroft, saying, "What a spy he was! Bancroft was the asset that case officers and analysts today dream about."

widows and libertines of Paris, this thought troubles him less and less.

Even as Franklin settles into Paris, though, a wealthy French teenager has decided to sail for America to join the rebellion. Indeed, he is so determined to fight that he spends more than a hundred thousand livres of his own money to purchase a vessel that will take him to the American Revolution.

The teenager's name is Marie-Joseph-Paul-Yves-Roch-Gilbert du Motier, Marquis de Lafayette.

Or, as history will record him, Lafayette.

The wealthy young marquis is well connected in Europe and determined to make his reputation on the battlefields of America. In order to do that, he has to impress Gen. George Washington, who is openly disdainful of European aristocrats. Upon meeting Lafayette in August 1777, Washington is polite but dismissive of his military desires.

This will soon change.

15

Freeman's Farm
Eight miles south of Saratoga, New York
September 19, 1777
3:15 P.M.

America's boldest general attacks.

A crazed Benedict Arnold gallops his horse into the center of the British Army, ignoring the grapeshot flying all around him. Stumps still cover the recently cleared farmland. The brilliant red and gold of autumn frame the thick white musket smoke. The general's left leg still aches from the musket ball that nearly caused its amputation two years ago, just outside Quebec, but Arnold refuses to acknowledge the pain.

"Riding in front of the lines, his eyes flashing, pointing with his sword toward the advancing foe, with a voice that runs clear as a trumpet," one American soldier will

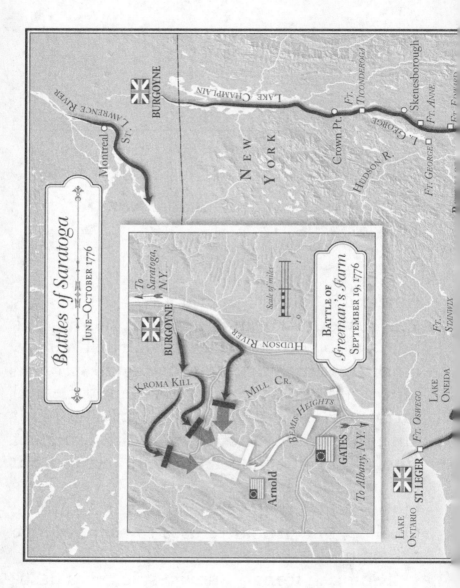

Battles of Saratoga

June–October 1776

Montreal

St. Lawrence River

BURGOYNE

NEW YORK

LAKE CHAMPLAIN

Crown Pt.

Ft. Ticonderoga

Skenesborough

L. George

Hudson R.

Ft. George

Ft. Anne

Ft. Edward

Battle of Freeman's Farm

September 19, 1776

Scale of miles

HUDSON RIVER

To Saratoga, N.Y.

BURGOYNE

KROMA KILL

MILL CR.

BEMIS HEIGHTS

Arnold

GATES

To Albany, N.Y.

Ft. Stanwix

Lake Oneida

Ft. Oswego

Lake Ontario

ST. LEGER

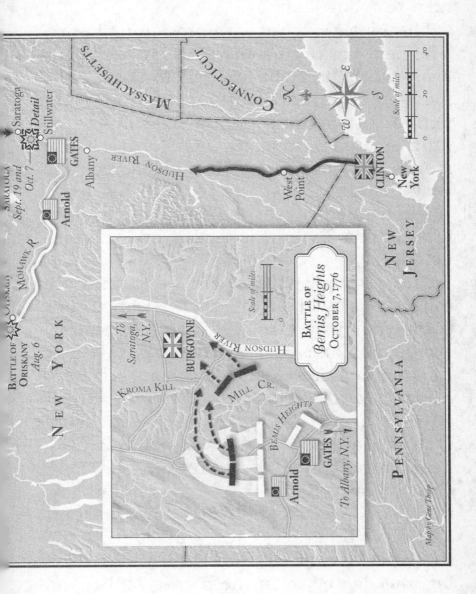

MASSACHUSETTS

CONNECTICUT

SARATOGA
Sept. 19 and
Oct. 7

Saratoga

Detail

Stillwater

GATES

Albany

MOHAWK R.

Arnold

HUDSON RIVER

BATTLE OF
ORISKANY
Aug. 6

NEW YORK

West
Point

CLINTON

New
York

NEW
JERSEY

N
W   E
S

Scale of miles
0   20   40

PENNSYLVANIA

BATTLE OF
Benus Heights
OCTOBER 7, 1776

HUDSON RIVER

To
Saratoga,
N.Y.

BURGOYNE

KROMA KILL

MILL CR.

BEMIS HEIGHTS

GATES

Arnold

To Albany, N.Y.

Scale of miles
0

Map by Gene Thorp

later remember, "[Arnold] called upon the men to follow him."

The battle has raged almost four hours. The fight has been a chess match, with each army wheeling right and left to answer the many charges and feints of its opponent. Periods of intense shooting are followed by long stretches of calm before the battle ignites once again. Arnold, considered "the very genius of war" by one of his men, single-handedly leads the bold American attack. His small force is nimble but outnumbered.

On the north side of the battlefield are nine thousand British and Hessian troops commanded by Gen. "Gentleman Johnny" Burgoyne. The British plan, approved in London by Lord George Germain, secretary of state to the British colonies, is for Burgoyne's army, now marching south from Quebec, to link with the army of Gen. William Howe, marching north from New York City. The two forces will connect in Albany, thirty miles south of Burgoyne's current location. Together, they will control the strategically vital Hudson River Valley, driving a wedge between the patriot hotbeds in New England and the rest of the colonies south of Connecticut.

Nine thousand American soldiers now

stand between Burgoyne and Albany, but the general is unworried. His adversary is Gen. Horatio Gates, the British-born commander of the Continental Army's Northern Department. Gates is an indecisive, risk-averse career soldier fond of digging in and fighting a defensive battle rather than going on the attack.

Indeed, this morning, when American scouts first reported that the British Army was marching toward the rebel positions, Gates did absolutely nothing. Rather than sending men immediately to meet the British, he held them back. Gates himself is holed up in the small shed that constitutes his headquarters, protected by trenches, artillery, and improvised fortifications. There he awaits Burgoyne's army.

But Benedict Arnold is not a man to wait.

A self-proclaimed "coward" as a child, Arnold is now thirty-six, a stocky five-foot-nine military genius with coal-black hair, piercing gray eyes, and a propensity for drunkenness and rage. The Connecticut native can be insecure and even needy in his personal life — yet rare is any man Arnold's equal on the field of battle.

Arnold urges Gates to let him attack.

Gates refuses. He possesses an Englishman's disdain for the sloppy appearance of the rebel soldiers, more impressed by the straight lines of battle and bright red uniforms of the Brits than colonial marksmanship and Indian-style ambush. Also, Gates longs to replace George Washington as the American army's commander in chief, and has quietly lobbied Congress for such a promotion. He cannot afford to make a single mistake.

Arnold does not care about any of that. He simply wants to win the battle. He continues to badger Gates, pleading to lead his soldiers into the field and prevent the British breakthrough.

Finally, Gates agrees, but his decision is not based on battle tactics. Hoping that Benedict Arnold will be defeated, and therefore marginalized, Gates allows him to command a small harassing force comprised of several hundred of Daniel Morgan's sharpshooting rangers and three hundred men from the First New Hampshire Regiment.* Both Morgan and Henry Dearborn

---

*A unit specially formed to harass the British with their marksmanship, Morgan's Riflemen were led by Virginian Daniel Morgan, a backwoodsman who had also served with Washington at Braddock's Defeat. The riflemen used the "long rifle" — also known as the Kentucky rifle or Pennsylva-

of the First fought under Arnold at Quebec, where they were taken captive.* Only recently released in a prisoner exchange, they are now eager to get their revenge on the British.

In allowing the attack, General Gates adds one condition: there will be no reinforcements. Should Arnold and his men get into trouble, they must fight their way out or die. Privately, Gates hopes for the latter.

Arnold, however, likes his chances.

No other American commander has had more success against the British. Even his lone defeat was glorious, a bold midwinter march in 1775 through uncharted Maine wilderness to capture the English fortress at Quebec. Arnold failed in that attempt, but his tactical ambition earned him the nickname "American Hannibal."†

While disciplined under fire, Arnold can

---

nia rifle. Developed for hunting rather than warfare, this weapon had a barrel up to four feet long, allowing for superior range and making it possible to fire at distant targets on the battlefield without the shooter's being exposed to enemy gunfire.

*Henry Dearborn of the First New Hampshire is the namesake of the city of Dearborn, Michigan.

†The nickname, coined by James Warren,

be antagonistic and alienating off the battle-field. As the war finishes its second year and the Continental Army is transforming from a gang of untrained militia to a professional fighting force, the former merchant and smuggler has been regularly passed over for promotion in favor of more politically connected officers. So it is that Benedict Arnold is second in command here at Freeman's Farm, answering to General Gates, who has a deep and abiding hatred for him, desirous that he not receive a shred of glory.

In the words of Lt. Col. James Wilkinson, "General Gates despises a certain pompous little fellow."

Another American officer, Lt. Col. John Brown of Massachusetts, is far more scathing. Brown, who served under Arnold in Quebec, has written a handbill denouncing

---

paymaster-general for the Continental Army, in a letter to Samuel Adams, refers to Hannibal Barca, the Carthaginian general who effected a surprise attack on the Roman Empire by using elephants to cross the Alps in 218 BC during the Second Punic War. One of Benedict Arnold's officers during the Quebec journey was a nineteen-year-old New Jersey native named Aaron Burr, who would later become vice president of the United States and would also kill Alexander Hamilton in a duel.

his former commanding officer. "Money is this man's God," he writes, "and to get enough of it he would sacrifice his country."

As soon as he receives permission to attack, Arnold races his men onto the field, positioning them in forests and ravines where they remain unseen. Morgan's Riflemen, many of whom acquired their prowess with a weapon as backwoods hunters, communicate through turkey calls. They settle into their firing positions just moments before the main column of Burgoyne's army marches into view. With rehearsed precision, each American marksman chooses a target and awaits the command to open fire.

British officers are the first to die. In their clean bright-red uniforms, often accompanied by a sash, they are easy targets. Completely hidden from the redcoats, Morgan's Riflemen inflict death from a distance of almost three hundred yards. The British consider this form of warfare cowardly, but Arnold does not care.

The artillery crews are the next to die, for their cannon can do far more damage than a single soldier with a musket.

To the British, the shots seem to come from every direction. Terrified, the men in Burgoyne's advance unit turn and flee from the hidden attackers. They race back into their own lines — only to encounter more death. In the confusion and the obscuring musket smoke, they are mistaken for Americans and shot down by their own redcoat brethren.

"Come on, brave boys," Arnold cries. "Come on!"

The Americans step from hiding and fearlessly race toward the British line. Arnold leads the way on horseback, exhorting and cheering the rebel force.

"Arnold rushed into the thickest of the fight with his usual recklessness, and at times acted like a madman," Lt. Col. Alexander Scammell of the Third New Hampshire Regiment will recall, adding that the battle was "the hottest fire of cannon and musketry I ever heard in my life."

But General Burgoyne is not easily defeated. His superior numbers allow him to push the rebels back, only to see Arnold lead another charge. Despite his earlier pledge not to allow reinforcements, Arnold's initial success motivates Gates, who reluctantly sends more troops into the fray, swelling the rebel attacking force to three thousand men. Six thousand more Americans remain in reserve, just in case Burgoyne breaks through.

Hour after hour, the battle continues, a back-and-forth drama starring two armies fighting for superiority. The British are desperate, knowing their supplies are low and there is no fortification to protect them. The Americans are determined, well aware that a victory over such a large British force may turn the tide of the war.

One thing is certain: few will doubt the toughness of the American fighting men from this day forward.

The battle of Freeman's Farm — or, the First Battle of Saratoga, as it will become known — ends in darkness. Burgoyne's advance is stopped. The Americans suffer three hundred dead, the British six hundred. Bodies sprawl across the broad pasture, easy prey for the men from both sides who will sneak out in the night to loot the corpses of their earthly belongings.

As for Benedict Arnold, his bravery goes unmentioned when Horatio Gates sends Congress a report of the day's battle. Instead, Gates takes all the credit for preventing the British breakthrough.*

*Gates denied that Arnold was even on the battlefield that afternoon. And even today, despite the many eyewitness accounts in favor of Arnold, there is debate as to whether he was on the front

The insult does not end there: inexplicably, Gen. Horatio Gates relieves Benedict Arnold of his command before the fight is determined.

Yet, Arnold cannot bring himself to go home. There is sure to be another big battle at Saratoga. Though he no longer has any role in Gates's army, he remains in his tent a mile south of the battlefield, spending days and nights pacing restlessly. He refuses to leave, even when Gates issues him a pass that will permit Arnold to travel south to fight under George Washington.

Benedict Arnold longs for the moment when Gates will reconsider and, once again, allow him to wage war. There is no indication that this will happen, but that hope keeps Arnold in Saratoga.

On the British side, Burgoyne is having his own problems. General William Howe is not en route to Albany, nor is his army. Before the campaign even began, the War Office had ordered Howe on a different mission, to take Philadelphia, perhaps believing it could be done quickly enough that he could

---

lines or was held back to coordinate troop movements. The authors of this book believe Arnold led his men into battle.

return to New York to help Burgoyne. But Burgoyne had not been informed of this change, and believed the main army to be in New York City, ready to come to his aid.

So, as George Washington knows, Howe is now in Germantown, Pennsylvania, almost three hundred miles south of General Burgoyne. The date is October 3, two weeks after the First Battle of Saratoga began. News of colonial success has just reached the American commander in chief, General Washington, and he is eager to spread the word to his troops, for tonight is the eve of battle and his army is in need of encouragement. At dusk, the rebels will begin yet another all-night march, hoping to surprise the British with a predawn attack.

"The Commander in Chief has the satisfaction to inform the army," Washington writes from the comfort of the small stone farmhouse now serving as his headquarters. The letter will be circulated and read aloud to all his troops.

"In a capital action, the left wing only of General Gates' army maintained its ground, against the main body of the enemy, commanded by General Burgoyne in person; our troops behaving with the highest spirit and bravery during the whole engagement. . . . In short, every circumstance promises success."

The news from Saratoga could not have come at a better time. For it is not just the Continental Army that requires an infusion of hope, but also General Washington himself. Over the last month, his enemy General Howe has shown himself to be the superior commander, outmaneuvering Washington's troops and defeating them dramatically on two separate occasions.*

The humiliation intensified on September 26, when General Charles Cornwallis marched the British Army into Philadelphia unopposed — Washington was unable to position his troops to stop the British. It is often traditional in wartime for a nation to surrender if its capital falls to the enemy, but Philadelphia is a capital in name only. The new U.S. government fled just days ago. The Congress now does its business in York, Pennsylvania. In addition, many of the city's prominent patriots also departed, choosing a life on the run rather than sure prosecution for treasonous behavior by the British. Even the Liberty Bell, which later became the very symbol of America's freedom, was hastily carted out of

*The Battle of Brandywine on September 11 and Paoli's Massacre on September 20–21.

Philadelphia.*

For every rebel victory, there has been a bumbling defeat. Many in Congress believe that Washington should be relieved of his command.

The news from Saratoga, however, is a true source of elation. If George Washington can defeat Howe the next morning at Ger-

*The "Liberty Bell" was originally cast in England in 1751. Just before the British occupation of Philadelphia, it was removed from the belfry of the Pennsylvania State House and carried by wagon to the Zion German Reformed Church, in what is now Allentown, Pennsylvania. It remained hidden beneath the church floorboards throughout the British occupation of Philadelphia. The story that the bell pealed on July 4, 1776, to announce American independence, is false. The bell *was* rung in 1760 to announce the coronation of King George III. The well-known crack in it occurred sometime in the middle of the nineteenth century. Although legend says the bell was taken out of Philadelphia during the fighting to prevent it from being melted down for munitions, it was more likely simply to ensure it would not be stolen. Musket balls were made of lead, not bell metal. The Liberty Bell could have been recast as a brass cannon, but the British did not produce their artillery pieces in America.

mantown, and if Gates can force Burgoyne to surrender up north, the British Army will be through. The war will be over.

Thus, General Washington gets emotional and delivers a rare poetic speech to his troops:

> This army, the main American Army, will certainly not suffer itself to be outdone by their northern brethren. . . . Let it never be said, that in a day of action, you turned your backs on the foe. Let the enemy no longer triumph. They brand you with ignominious epithets. Will you patiently endure that reproach? Will you suffer the wounds given to your country to go unrevenged? Will you resign your parents, wives, children and friends to be the wretched vassals of a proud, insulting foe — and your own necks to the halter?
>
> General Howe . . . has left us no choice but Conquest or Death. Nothing then remains, but nobly to contend for all that is dear to us. Every motive that can touch the human breast calls us to the most vigorous exertions. Our dearest rights, our dearest friends, and our own lives, honor, glory and even shame, urge us to the fight.
>
> And my fellow soldiers! When an op-

portunity presents, be firm, be brave — show yourselves men, and victory is yours.

Washington's words are for naught. He marches his men sixteen miles from their encampment in southeastern Pennsylvania, splitting them into four columns in order to envelop the British. The distance is far enough that he is sure Howe will think an attack impossible.

The Americans have the numerical advantage: eleven thousand troops to Howe's nine thousand. Portions of Washington's army are able to find the enemy and attack at 5:00 a.m., but thick fog covers Germantown, making it difficult for the four columns to coordinate. One American major general, Adam Stephen, will later be court-martialed for drunkenness. In the end, Washington's troops cannot defeat the British troops and must retreat, marching the sixteen miles back to camp.

Washington's bold gamble to catch Howe sleeping almost paid off. Yet it failed because of poor weather, lack of communication, and the exhaustion brought on by asking thousands of men to march through the night and then fight as if completely rested.

Interestingly, Washington's defeat will soon be the talk of Europe. Leaders such as the Prussian king Frederick the Great are amazed that an army could rebound from previous losses to attempt such a bold attack. "Such a people, under such a leader," Frederick will later be paraphrased as saying, "would survive even greater trials and mischances than the loss of their capital city."

In Paris, where Benjamin Franklin hastens to make much of the successes at Saratoga and the near miss at Germantown, French diplomats are now assured that the American fighting man is every bit the equal of the British. Slowly and cautiously, negotiations proceed to convince French military forces to enter the fray.

Most important, the loss at Germantown does not affect rebel morale. Officers and enlisted men alike marvel at how close they came to defeating the British. Writing to a friend one week after the battle, American general Israel Putnam says, "This action convinced our people that, when they attacked, they can confuse and rout the flower of the British Army."

A footnote to the Germantown fight is the presence of a most unique British officer. His name is Capt. John André, and he will spend the next nine months living inside Benjamin Franklin's British-requisitioned

Philadelphia home. André is twenty-seven years old, speaks three languages fluently, and was recently returned to the British in a prisoner exchange after a year in American captivity.

General Washington and Captain André did not meet on the field of battle at Germantown, but their lives will become inextricably intertwined.

Also, unbeknownst to both men, a third soldier will play a role in the upcoming drama.

His name is Benedict Arnold.

Three days after Germantown, the smell of rum on his breath, General Arnold gallops his horse toward a small band of Hessian defenders. The Second Battle of Saratoga is a rout, and everywhere, the British and Germans sprint for their lives.

Arnold's patience has paid off. At 2:00 p.m., as General Burgoyne attempted once again to break through the American lines to march on Albany, a desperate Horatio Gates finally ordered his best commanding officer to charge the British lines.

"It is late in the day but let me have men and we will have some fun with them before sunset," Arnold proclaimed happily. Then, drinking a large portion of rum to steady

Benedict Arnold

his nerves, the general saddled his horse and galloped into battle.*

Arnold's success was almost immediate,

*Arnold was also known to give his horse a bit of rum before a fight. Many American soldiers drank

with the British fleeing before him and the rebel army taking control of the battlefield.

It is only now, with the battle won, that a line of Hessian regulars fires one last volley before turning to flee. Arnold is hit. He feels the sickening snap of his femur as a Hessian musket ball pierces his thigh and shatters the bone.

The same round of Hessian gunfire strikes Arnold's horse, killing it instantly. The animal collapses and rolls onto its left side, slamming its thousand-pound weight onto Arnold's broken leg. The force snaps the bones again, in several places.

A wave of nausea and adrenaline washes over Benedict Arnold. He is on the verge of passing out, yet continues to call out commands. He even orders that one of the Hessians who fired the shot at him be spared the thrust of a bayonet, for the battle is already won.

This should be the defining moment of Benedict Arnold's military career. His heroism should never be forgotten. The American victory at Saratoga, for which he can rightfully claim ownership, is about to effect a dramatic change in the war.

---

before battle, leading the British soldiers to denounce them as drunkards.

But for the rest of Arnold's life, his left leg will be two inches shorter than the right. The bone will not be set properly during his many months in the hospital, causing the leg to mend in an awkward fashion. Far from seeing himself as an irrepressible force of nature, as he did just moments ago, Benedict Arnold will come to view himself as "crippled." The shattered leg will make him unfit for battlefield command. He will become bitter and resentful, consumed with self-pity.

Thus, a single musket ball will soon put the quest for American freedom in a precarious predicament.

16

House of Lords
London, England
November 18, 1777
12:30 P.M.

King George III is losing control.

"My Lords and Gentlemen," the sovereign begins his annual speech for the opening of Parliament. He speaks from the throne, his body rocking back and forth. The usual crowd of red-clad lords is arrayed before him. Ten massive but frail tapestries depicting Lord Howard of Effingham's victory over the Spanish Armada in 1588 cover the walls. Once a symbol of England's power, the now-deteriorating panels loom over the proceedings with foreboding.*

"The continuance of the rebellion in

*Lord Howard originally commissioned the tapestries to hang in his London home, which they did from 1595 to 1616. Laced with threads of

319

North America demands our most serious attention," the king says, employing the usual rapid-fire patter that many are unable to make out.

This is an understatement. Word is beginning to reach London that all is not well in the colonies. There are reports that General Howe's army is floundering in its attempt to crush George Washington; also, that Burgoyne's advance on Albany has stalled.

This should be a time of joy for King George. Just two weeks ago, Queen Charlotte presented him with their twelfth child. And although he is still given to lengthy and rambling conversations, the king's mental health issues appear to be under control for

---

pure silver and gold, each tapestry was fourteen feet tall and twenty-eight feet wide and cost the equivalent of eighty-seven years' wages for a normal working man. In 1616, Howard sold the tapestries to King James I. They hung in the House of Lords from 1644 to 1834, when they were destroyed by fire. Ironically, his heir, the Earl of Effingham, serving in Parliament during the Revolutionary War, was so opposed to the war in America that he resigned his army commission when his regiment received orders to go there. His denunciation of the war was so public that the Americans named a warship after him.

the moment.

However, the news from America has shaken him. This is the king's third such address since the hostilities began — and will be by far the least well received. Truth be told, the king does not enjoy these ceremonial occasions, which often put him on the defensive. He prefers to meet individually with his ministers in a special room at the palace known as the King's Closet.* Each man must bow three times upon entering the presence of the sovereign, and never turn his back on him. George demands that each minister remain standing at all times, as a further sign of deference. These one-on-one meetings are designed to prevent the alliances against the king's policies that could form if he met his subjects in a larger group setting.

Now, instead of a single minister bowing before him, King George speaks to the hundreds of members of Parliament, all of whom listen with a skeptical ear.

"It is the most pusillanimous speech ever produced," royal observer Horace Walpole

*At the time, there was a King's Closet at both St. James's Palace, in London, and Windsor Castle in Berkshire. Both are considerably more palatial than a simple closet.

scoffs. "Far from announcing the complete conquest of America, which had been promised this campaign, it only talked of hoping for important success."

The arrogance that once defined the British attitude toward waging war in America is slipping away. George is deeply anxious about losing the colonies, but well aware of the growing public hostility regarding the millions of pounds being spent on the war in America.* Now comes word from British spies in Paris that France seems to be willing to join the conflict. This is no longer a civil war, with the rebels seen as unhappy British subjects rising up against king and Parliament. The Americans are now a military nation all their own, soon to have very powerful allies.

The very future of the British Empire is in doubt.

Should French and American troops succeed in pinning down the British Army and Navy in America, the island colonies of

*British newspapers reflected the nation's growing discontent with the war. "We were told that the Americans were cowards," one newspaper will remark of the king's speech. "And now we are told they are so obstinate they will not be conquered."

Great Britain will be undefended. The French are already making plans to invade England, and hope that their Spanish allies will simultaneously invade Ireland, a nation that shares their Catholic faith.

This is not a scenario King George and his prime minister, Lord North, could have foreseen when they began squeezing the Americans for more tax money a decade ago. Indeed, there is a small but growing sentiment in Parliament that the taxation against America ought to be repealed.

"I still hope that the deluded and unhappy multitude will return to their allegiance," the king continues. "And that the remembrance of what they once enjoyed, the regret for what they lost, and the feelings of what they now suffer under the arbitrary tyranny of their leaders will rekindle in their hearts a spirit of loyalty to their sovereign, and a spirit of loyalty to their mother country."

Concluding his speech, King George now stands, per tradition, and leaves the House of Lords so that Parliament might debate without him present. But, already, his critics are deriding his speech as "timid, feeble, and disheartening."

One frail old man rises to define the moment. The words he speaks, uttered in a low whisper but with brilliance and clarity, will stand forever as one of history's greatest testimonials to the character and power of the American citizen, and to the futility of waging war against him.

The speaker is William Pitt the Elder, known as Lord Chatham. At sixty-nine and in failing health, the man who served as prime minister from 1766 to 1768 is now a political pariah. He rarely appears in Parliament these days — but today is a different story. Lord Chatham once helped expand the military might of Great Britain. Now he prefers to limit that power.

"I rise, my Lords, to declare my sentiments on this most solemn and serious subject. . . . I love and honor the English troops. I know their virtues and their valor. I know they can achieve anything except impossibilities." Chatham pauses, measuring the mood of the chamber.

"And I know that the conquest of English America is an impossibility."

The crowd murmurs, but Chatham continues:

My Lords, you can not conquer America. What is your present situation there? We do not know the worst, but we know that in three campaigns we have done nothing and suffered much. Besides the sufferings, perhaps total loss of the Northern force, the best appointed army that ever took the field, commanded by Sir William Howe, has retired from the American lines. . . .

As to conquest, therefore, my Lords, I repeat, it is impossible. You may swell every expense and every effort still more extravagantly, pile and accumulate every assistance you can buy or borrow, traffic and barter with every little pitiful German prince that sells and sends his subjects to the shambles of a foreign prince — your efforts are forever vain and impotent. If I were an American, as I am an Englishman, while a foreign troop was landed in my country, I never would lay down my arms.

Never. Never. Never.

Chatham has just months to live. He does not speak for political gain, but for the sake of England's future.

Voices of opposition ring out in the House chamber, but Chatham ignores them. He knows his words are falling on deaf ears, for he has few allies in Parliament. Still, there is no sense of futility in his message as he draws to a conclusion: "I call upon the spirit and humanity of my country, to vindicate the national character. I invoke the genius of the Constitution. From the tapestry that adorns these walls, the immortal ancestor of this noble Lord frowns with indignation at the disgrace of his country."

Then Lord Chatham sits, exhausted.*

For all the passion in his plea, his appeal goes unheard. The House of Lords votes 97 to 24 to reject the resolution to repeal the colonial taxes and recall the king's army.

Even with the very real threat of a French invasion, Parliament once again chooses to align itself with King George and his continued suppression of American citizens.

It is the evening of December 2, 1777, when the shocking news arrives from America: Gen. John Burgoyne has surrendered 5,895 men at Saratoga and suffered another 1,300 dead.

*For more than a decade, Chatham has spoken in favor of American rebellion. The most memorable speech to Parliament was delivered on January 14, 1766, when he marveled at colonial reaction to the Stamp Act. "I rejoice that America has resisted. Three million of people so dead to all feelings of liberty, as voluntarily to submit to be slaves, would have been fit instruments to make slaves of the rest." Chatham's last speech in the House of Lords will be on April 7, 1778.

"The King went into agonies on hearing this account," Horace Walpole will write. The horrific news soon triggers a minor return of the king's mental illness. George ceases to behave like a sovereign and, much to the embarrassment of all who witness his behavior, instead becomes a giddy madman — "so indecently merry that Lord North endeavored to stop him," Walpole adds.

And while minority voices in Parliament continue to rise up in protest of the war, the "national indignity" of Burgoyne's failure stiffens the resolve of the king and his legislative majority.

The killing of England continues.

17

Hôtel Lautrec
Paris, France
February 6, 1778
Evening

Benjamin Franklin is having his revenge.

Clad in the same suit of soiled Manchester velvet that he wore during his public humiliation in London's cockpit four years ago, the aging diplomat sits down at the desk of French foreign minister Charles Gravier, the Count of Vergennes. Two documents are placed before him: the Treaty of Alliance between France and the United States, and the Treaty of Amity and Commerce. Franklin and Vergennes have labored over the details for a month. Now it is time to sign.

Since Saratoga, Franklin has done his best to be coy about America's deep need for military assistance. The French, however, have aggressively pursued this new military alliance. They fear that the British will seek peace with the rebels, thus preventing the French from regaining territory in North America.

The young French king, Louis XVI, has ordered this new partnership between nations. On January 8, 1778, Vergennes confirmed this through a letter to the French ambassador in Spain: "The supreme decision was taken by the King. He did not take it under the influence of his ministers."

It has been four years since the British Privy Council sought to embarrass Benjamin Franklin. The suit of Manchester velvet he is wearing was brand-new on that day, and the Doctor has not worn it since. This is intentional. Though the jacket and breeches have long since gone out of style, Franklin has saved them especially for the day he might exact "a little revenge."

That day has come.

He dips his quill into an inkwell and then signs his name.

France is now America's war partner.

For Dr. Franklin, the Paris stay has not been all about diplomacy. His social life is the talk of Paris — especially his relations with the opposite sex.

"It is well for my penitent to know that

there are seven grave sins, and of the seven, my dear brother, you commit only one," the lovely Anne-Louise Brillon writes to Franklin one month later. She is just thirty-three, and Franklin is now seventy-two. Their relationship transcends age and circumstance: Brillon is the married mother of two.

In a flirtatious moment, the Doctor has engaged Madame Brillon in a conversation about his soul. Her response is a recounting of the seven deadly sins, of which the seventh is lust.

"All great men are tainted with it: it is called their weakness. . . . You have loved, my dear brother. You have been kind and lovable; you have been loved in return! What is so damnable about that? Go on doing great things and loving pretty women — provided that, pretty and lovable though they may be, you never lose sight of my principle: always love God, America, and *me* above all."

Franklin waits three days to return her letter. On Tuesday, March 10, writing from his new home in Passy, he admits:

I am charmed with the goodness of my spiritual guide, and resign myself implicitly to her conduct, as she promises to lead me to Heaven in a road so delicious, when

330

I could be content to travel thither even in the roughest of all the ways with the pleasure of her company.

I lay fast hold of your promise to absolve me of all sins past, present, and future, on the easy and pleasing condition of loving God, America, and my guide above all things. I am in raptures when I think of being absolved of the future. . . . God forgive me, as often as I see or think of my lovely confessor . . . I am afraid I should never be able to repent of the sin, even if I had the full possession of her.

But Franklin's passion for Madame Brillon will not be consummated. He is allowed to watch her bathe, and has even played a game of chess while she soaked in the tub next to him, but Madame Brillon will forever remain the unrequited object of his desire.

"You are a man and I am a woman," she writes in her response. "There is no great harm in a man having desires and yielding to them. A woman may have desires, but she must not yield."

This is not the end of the relationship between Benjamin Franklin and Madame Brillon, for he delights in the mental stimulation almost as much as the physical. Their rhetoric will continue for the many years he will remain in Paris, even as he surrounds himself with a bevy of other lovers: Madame Helvétius, Madame Le Roy, Mademoiselle Le Vieillard, Madame Chaumont, to name a few.

With the negotiations for France's involvement in the war at an end, Franklin fills his days brokering affairs of the heart. Despite his advanced age and odd habit of wearing his fur hat and a brown puritan smock, the widower has no trouble attracting ladies' attention.

King Louis XVI, who has a growing dislike for Franklin due to the latter's preference for democratic governments over monarchies, even goes so far as to mock the American's philandering ways by presenting one countess who has fallen under Franklin's spell with the gift of a chamber pot, a picture of the Doctor lining the bottom.

"The life of Dr. Franklin was a continual scene of dissipation," the visiting John Adams will write, cataloguing a schedule filled with hangers-on, social calls, dinners, recitals, and liaisons.

John Adams has arrived in Paris on congressional business. At first, he is taken aback by Franklin's debauched lifestyle, but soon he sees a practical side to it.

"This course of life contributed to his pleasure — and I believe to his health and longevity."

Which, of course, the good Doctor would affirm. But while this American patriot absorbs the many pleasures of Paris, other patriots are suffering a terrible ordeal — at a place called Valley Forge.

18

Valley Forge, Pennsylvania
February 16, 1778
Mid-morning

George Washington's army is desperate.

It has been a miserable winter, with rebel troops camped just eighteen miles away from the British Army, which is comfortably housed in Philadelphia. While the English are enjoying the luxuries of a big city, Washington's men are suffering grievously.

"For some days past, there has been little less than a famine in our camp," says Lt. Col. Alexander Hamilton, writing on behalf of George Washington. The bond of trust between the general and his young aide-decamp has grown substantially since Hamilton's arrival on the staff nearly one year ago. Now, rather than dictate letters or take the time to write them himself, Washington

334

George Washington and Alexander Hamilton

very often directs the twenty-three-year-old Hamilton to compose his correspondence, after which Washington simply signs his name.*

This particular letter is a cry for help. The Continental Army is starving. Hamilton's missive, addressed to New York governor George Clinton, is an urgent plea for food.

On the surface, the situation in Washington's headquarters is almost serene. A small

*Hamilton's actual birth year is uncertain. He could be as much as two years younger.

blaze roars in the fireplace of this massive stone cottage. Martha Washington has recently arrived from Mount Vernon, to the general's delight. She joins the slave cook, Hannah Till, and the aging Irish house-keeper, Elizabeth Thompson, in adding a feminine touch to the general's current situation. All around Washington, his staff bustles about, keeping themselves busy, and warm, during this long winter encampment.

Outside the cottage, however, things could not be direr. Row upon row of small log huts fill a broad meadow, tongues of wood smoke curling out of hundreds of makeshift chimneys. Half-dressed men scurry outside to openly relieve themselves, not caring who sees them, and then quickly race back inside to the warmth of their shelters. The average hut is a log cabin with a ceiling height of six and half feet. Each structure is fourteen feet long and sixteen feet wide. The men sleep twelve to a hut, on straw spread across bare dirt floors, inhaling the fireplace smoke filling their dank quarters. There is nothing clean or comforting about these hovels. When a man dies, his body is removed, but it is common for the remaining men to continue sleeping on the same straw — which, in many cases, is infected with lice, maggots, or even smallpox. There is no furniture, and no kitchens.

Even if the huts were equipped with kitchens, there is very little food. The men are supposed to be issued a pound of meat or fish per day, along with flour and peas, but there is frequently not enough to go around. Most often, the soldiers make do with "fire cakes," flour and water mixed together and cooked in a skillet over the fire or on a heated flat rock. If a hut runs out of food before the next allotment, the soldiers starve.

It is a situation that is quickly becoming untenable. The men while away the frigid days playing cards and dice, cooking whatever food they can find, and, in the unlikely event that a libation is made available, drinking. When called upon to perform military duties such as standing guard, many soldiers stick their heads out their hut door and shout the familiar refrain "No bread, no soldier!"

If they were to fight in their present condition, there would be little hope of victory. Their firearms are covered in rust and lack bayonets. Many weapons can't even fire.

And then there is their attire.

The soldiers themselves provide their own clothing. The men from New England seem better prepared for the winter, while soldiers from warmer states such as North Carolina suffer in their thinner garments. The states are supposed to provide clothing for their soldiers, but many have failed to do so. Therefore, even if the temperatures drop close to zero, most of Washington's men do not have overcoats and many do not even have shoes — footwear having rotted away months ago.

Throughout the camp, field hospitals stand amid the rows of huts. They are nine feet high and twenty-five feet long, with a chimney at one end. As in the cabins, the sick sleep on straw. General Washington has issued an order that each hospitalized man be visited daily by a representative from his brigade, but this directive often goes unheeded; the men are afraid of catching a disease. The doctors themselves have no such qualms, treating the ill and also making regular visits to the hovels the soldiers call home. Every Wednesday and Saturday, the physicians make a report of the sick, whether hospitalized or not. This number continues to grow with each passing day.

Sentries stand duty in the freezing rain, clad in blankets, dressing gowns, and any other sort of clothing they can find, their frostbitten feet wrapped in rags. Soldiers have resorted to sharing clothing, offering the few garments they own to the men stepping outside to stand guard. Upon returning to the cabin, the man leaving guard duty will be expected to offer those same rags to the next soldier on duty.

These are the lucky ones: as Hamilton, writing for Washington, recently noted in a letter to Virginia governor Patrick Henry, a quarter of his twelve-thousand-man army is "unfit for duty by reason of their being barefoot and otherwise naked."

Hundreds more are dead already or are dying from starvation, typhus, smallpox, dysentery, and influenza. Almost all suffer from an insidious condition known only as "the itch," brought on by lice infestation. The army's malnourished artillery horses are also perishing at an alarming rate, due to a lack of forage. They are quickly butchered for their meat, and their carcasses, which now litter the frozen ground, left to rot.

Adding to Washington's responsibility are the wives and camp followers who have made their way to Valley Forge. Their role is to offer physical comfort and emotional support, but these women and children must also be fed and housed.*

*Married women were sometimes allowed to sleep

It is in this dismal environment that Washington now signs his letter to Governor Clinton. This is not the first time he has written to an influential official asking for help. With the Congress doing very little to provide for his men, the general has cast a wide net in search of provisions, sending letter after letter in the hope of securing food and clothing.

"A part of the army has been a week, without any kind of flesh," Washington writes, referring to the lack of meat and protein in the daily diet. "Naked and starving as they are, we cannot enough admire the incomparable patience and fidelity of the soldiery, that they have not been . . . excited

---

in huts with their husbands, but most often women and children were kept in separate housing. All were expected to work in order to be afforded a daily ration, with women doing laundry, sewing, and performing nursing duties. Children did sundry chores around camp, with older boys offered the opportunity to enlist once they reached the legal age of sixteen — although many joined up much earlier. There were prostitutes at Valley Forge, too. These women plied their trade discreetly — the punishment for being caught was expulsion from camp.

by their sufferings, to a general mutiny."

It has been two months since the Continental Army retreated into its winter quarters northwest of Philadelphia. Washington himself observed that the British could easily track their location by following the trail of blood in the snow left by the bare, frostbitten feet of his battered force.

The location at this broad field known as Valley Forge is equal parts tactical and political — the rebel forces are close enough to Philadelphia to satisfy those in the Pennsylvania legislature who would prefer Washington fight through the winter, but distant enough to afford his men the rest and succor they require after months of hard combat.*

Valley Forge's location also has its disad-

*Another vital reason for remaining in the region was the location of the forges specific to southeastern Pennsylvania, which has an abundance of ore deposits and was the hub of American iron production. These forges were vital to casting weapons of war, thus the need to protect them from falling into British hands. Originally called the Mount Joy Forge, the furnace closest to Washington's camp soon became known by locals as the "valley forge," due to its location.

vantages. Thousands of civilian refugees who fled Philadelphia before the British took the city now inundate the Pennsylvania countryside, straining its limited resources. Corruption within the American supply system has seen money and supplies diverted away from Washington's army. And many local farmers are actually hiding their stores of grain from the general's foragers, hoping to sell them at a higher profit to the British.

Thus, Washington and his men are hard pressed to find even the most basic stores. Worse, small bands of British soldiers and Pennsylvania Loyalists are conducting guerrilla operations against the foraging parties, a stark reminder that there is no vacation from war.

"Soon I came in sight of the camp," one officer wrote of his first impression of Valley Forge. "My imagination had pictured an army with uniforms, the glitter of arms, standards — in short, military pomp of all sorts. Instead . . . I noticed soldiers wearing cotton nightcaps under their hats, and some having for cloaks or greatcoats coarse woolen blankets. . . . I learned afterwards that these were the officers."

At first, the army lived in tents. Even Washington, knowing the power of example, endured those windswept and bitter December nights in his own blue-and-white shelter. But soon he ordered that trees be felled for the construction of huts, and he offered a ten-dollar reward to the first group of men to build their own. Within weeks, several of what would be almost two thousand log huts covering the fields and meadows appeared.

As if there were not enough to concern the general, a commission from Congress has arrived to observe the army — and Washington. Questions about his leadership abound, and many in Congress wish to see him replaced. Washington is aware of his critics, but he refuses to acknowledge the dissent publicly — knowing that Loyalists and the British would use this as a propaganda wedge to undermine America's growing strength.*

Deprivation, anger, day after day of filthy despair and impending doom — this is life at Valley Forge. Washington still believes that victory is possible, but the successes at Trenton and Princeton are an entire year in the

*Propaganda, often misconstrued as a modern term, is from the Latin for "to propagate." In 1622, Pope Gregory XV established the Sacred Congregation for the Propagation of the Faith, also known as the *Propaganda Fide.* In time, the word *propaganda* was applied to any attempt to spread an ideology.

343

past. In war, twelve months can seem like an eternity. Endurance has carried the Continental Army through three years of battle, but stamina is no longer enough. A new way must be found to survive this winter and win this war.

Washington is deeply private about his religious views, often spending moments in the morning and evening alone, performing a daily devotional with his Bible. But for all that he has prayed in the past, there has never been a time as desperate as now.

"What methods you can take, you will be the best judge of," ends his letter to Governor Clinton, Washington's fear barely concealed beneath the surface, "but if you can devise any means to procure a quantity of cattle or other kind of flesh, for the use of this army, to be at camp in the course of a month, you will render a most essential service to the common cause."

Seven days later, George Washington gets his answer.

It is not a herd of cows or some other source of food, and the relief does not come from Governor Clinton.

Instead, it is Benjamin Franklin who has provided an answer to Washington's prayer.

Lt. Col. Alexander Hamilton realizes that

his leader, George Washington, has almost lost control of the American army.

Hamilton, born illegitimately on the Caribbean island of Nevis, has proven himself an indispensable member of Washington's staff. He is a wiry five foot seven, a competitive and ambitious soldier who has fought since the war began, first in a militia and then in an artillery company. Hamilton's intelligence and courage were quickly noticed, and three generals offered him the all-important position of aide-de-camp. He refused, preferring to fight rather than accept a rear-echelon position. It was only when General Washington offered the same aide-de-camp job that Hamilton accepted.

Alexander Hamilton soon concluded that Washington needed to overhaul the entire command structure of his army. Almost immediately, he wrote a three-thousand-word manifesto emphasizing the need for greater discipline and punishment for wayward soldiers. Washington accepted the criticism because he knew that his army would not hold together much longer. The general also realized that if the nearby British force had any ambition, an attack might seal America's doom.

Alexander Hamilton knows that his commander is a brave man, but Washington's lack of in-depth military knowledge and tactics often leads to his defeat by superior British generals. Sometimes Washington's men fight like a true army, but most often they behave as the individual tradesmen, farmers, and societal castoffs they were before the war began.

Both Hamilton and Washington see catastrophe in the future. "Unless some great and capital change suddenly takes place," Washington writes to Congress, "the army must inevitably be reduced to one or other of these three things — to starve, dissolve, or disperse."

On February 23, 1778, that "great and capital change" arrives.

In the summer of 1777, Benjamin Franklin wrote a letter in Paris recommending a Prussian soldier named Friedrich Wilhelm Ludolf Gerhard Augustin von Steuben for a position in the American army. Baron von Steuben, who prefers to be called "Baron," was referred to Franklin by Claude Louis, Count of Saint-Germain, the French minister of war. As the French slowly became more involved in the American war effort, in defiance of a treaty of neutrality with England, they decided to send a well-trained European officer to America to transform the Continental Army into a fighting force worth their financial backing. Franklin's letter was addressed to the Congress, and word of von Steuben's imminent arrival soon reached Washington at Valley Forge.

So it is that George Washington mounts his favorite horse, Blueskin, and rides several miles outside Valley Forge to meet a man he is not yet convinced can help him. But the respect the general shows by going out to greet von Steuben is deeply felt by the Prussian.

"General Washington came several miles to meet me on the road," von Steuben later writes, "and accompanied me to my quarters, where I found an officer with twenty-five men as a guard of honor. When I declined this, saying I wished to be considered merely as a volunteer, the general answered me in the politest words that the whole army would be glad to stand sentinel for such volunteers."

The Baron is forty-seven and has come to America to rehabilitate his reputation. He would have preferred to remain in Europe to work as a soldier for hire, but allegations of improper relations with male soldiers are proving a detriment to his career chances on the Continent — and are perhaps even threatening his imprisonment. Those same rumors will eventually follow the Baron to America.

At six foot two, von Steuben is George Washington's equal in height, with a slight paunch and a long, aquiline nose. He wears a Prussian general's uniform and a red-jeweled medallion around his neck. The Baron carries the recommendation letter from Benjamin Franklin giving his rank as lieutenant general, but the fact of the matter is that although von Steuben served on the staff of Frederick the Great, he has never risen above the rank of captain. Nevertheless, the Prussian's years of training have prepared him for the challenge of transforming the American army.

Von Steuben's eyes sweep Valley Forge as he enters the camp for the first time. He cannot help but see the lack of discipline, and his senses are assaulted by the odors coming from the mounds of sewage. The Baron is accompanied by his aide, a servant, and his pet greyhound, Azor. He is appalled by the conditions at Valley Forge but knows that they will soon change.

As he settles into his own stone cottage, the thickly muscled, double-chinned, homosexual Prussian officer has only one thought

Baron von Steuben

in mind — to save the U.S. Army.*

For George Washington, the Prussian's arrival presents yet another challenge.

"The General is well, but much worn with

*The difference between Hessians, who are fighting for the British, and Prussians is partly a matter of geography. Hessians took their name from the Hesse-Kassel and Hesse-Hanau regions of what is now central Germany. The Kingdom of Prussia was much larger, at one time stretching across northern Germany from Denmark to what is now the Czech Republic.

fatigue and anxiety," Martha Washington writes to a friend. "I never knew him to be so anxious as now."

In addition to the lack of food, clothing, and shoes, Washington has personnel issues. He already has the French marquis Lafayette spending the winter at Valley Forge. The young officer is showing himself a true believer in the American cause, enduring the cold and hardships without complaint, but there is resentment among some American units about taking orders from a foreigner. Washington does not need another European officer adding to the commotion. Making matters worse, von Steuben barely speaks English and has an obvious bent toward self-importance. In order to keep an eye on him, Washington assigns Lafayette to assist the Baron, who does speak the marquis's language, French.

But Franklin's letter, along with von Steuben's military bearing and lifetime of training within the vaunted Prussian military tradition, leads Washington to be cautiously optimistic. Despite the horrific conditions at Valley Forge, his men have chosen to stay on rather than sneak away in the night, showing their loyalty and love of America by enduring vast hardships. It will all be for naught if the Continental Army does not use the downtime winter affords them to become professional soldiers. Congress has already drafted a resolution calling for an "inspector general, agreeable to the practice of the best European armies," in the hope of raising discipline in the American ranks.

So, Washington, Lafayette, and von Steuben begin their challenge. The fighting will begin anew in three months — maybe sooner. Von Steuben must work quickly to create a revitalized Continental Army. Success means he can stay on, perhaps leading men into battle.

Failure means von Steuben will be sent away.

For his own sake, the Prussian must succeed.

In truth, the Baron is nearly penniless. Middle age has arrived and, with it, the dwindling of personal opportunities. Despite his grand façade, this is the Prussian's last chance.

So begins the transformation of the American army.*

***

*Many of von Steuben's methods of drill and training are still in use today. He is considered by some historians to be the father of the U.S. Army.

Marquis de Lafayette

■ ■ ■ ■

The Baron spends his first few weeks at Valley Forge observing the troops. He takes
long walks around the grounds, scrutinizing

minute details of everyday life. The scene of chaos and disarray is beyond anything he has ever seen in a military encampment.

"Matters had to be remedied, but where to commence was the great difficulty," he would later write.

"With regard to their military discipline, I may safely say no such thing existed. In the first place, there was no regular formation. A so-called regiment was formed of three platoons, another of five, eight, or nine, and the Canadian regiment of twenty-one. The formation of their regiments was as varied as their mode of drill."

Many American officers do not even live at Valley Forge, preferring to sleep in homes miles away. Some have abandoned the war altogether for the winter, traveling home to wait for spring.

Beginning in early March, von Steuben slowly starts making changes. He rises each morning at 3:00, smokes a single pipe, and drinks one cup of coffee while his servant shaves and grooms him. He is in the saddle and riding to the parade ground by first light. Assisted by Hamilton's translations, he communicates his orders to the army. One of the few words of English von Steuben knows is *goddamn,* and he uses it frequently, to great effect. Sometimes he doesn't say anything at all: "When duty was neglected," one officer will write, "the baron's look was quite sufficient."

The appalling lack of sanitation comes to an end. Latrines are dug, but always on a downhill slope outside camp. Until now, the Americans have never practiced such a simple concept. Also, George Washington makes it a whipping offense for a man to relieve himself in public.*

Kitchens are built for communal eating, specifically situated on the opposite side of Valley Forge from the latrines. Great ovens begin preparing loaves of bread to feed the entire army.

Rather than soldiers being housed in random fashion, von Steuben orders them billeted together by company. The companies, in turn, are grouped with their regiments — the regiments with the brigades, and the brigades with the divisions.

---

*The connection between human waste and the spread of deadly diseases such as cholera may seem like common sense, but as late as the Mexican-American War, in the 1840s, American troops were still defecating in the same rivers and streams they used for washing clothes, drinking water, and cooking.

■ ■ ■ ■

Von Steuben realizes it is impossible for one man to train an entire army. He also understands that there might be apprehension about embracing his methods, as he is not an American. He therefore selects one hundred twenty of the best officers and soldiers and places them under his personal command. He sees these soldiers as the battle-hardened leaders within the Continental Army.

"I made this guard my military school. I drilled them myself twice a day. And to remove that English prejudice which some officers entertained, namely, that to drill the recruit was a sergeant's duty and beneath the station of an officer, I often took the musket myself to show the men the manual exercise which I wished to introduce."

Thus begins the drill.

Von Steuben teaches this small group of soldiers to march seventy-five steps per minute, always beginning with the left foot. The "quick step" is one hundred twenty steps per minute.

Only when these men are thoroughly trained does the Baron have them display their new skills to the others. "I paraded them in the presence of all the officers of the army," he will write. "They formed in column, deployed, attacked with the bayonet, changed front, etc. It afforded a new and agreeable sight for the young officers and soldiers.

"Having gained my point, I dispersed my apostles, the inspectors, and my new doctrine was eagerly embraced. I lost no time in extending my operations on a large scale . . . in less than three weeks I executed maneuvers with an entire division in presence of the commander-in-chief."

Von Steuben's core group then returns to the ranks, imparting these newly learned lessons to the men within their regiments. These men, in turn, teach others. In this way, the knowledge of basic drill is spread through Valley Forge.

No longer do the Americans spend all day shivering in their smoke-filled cabins. The day now begins at 6:00 a.m. Eight-man squads of soldiers march in parade, a noncommissioned officer to their right, calling out the cadence. The morning drill continues until 8:00 a.m. An hour later, the training starts again, focusing on the specifics of tactics. There is a meeting of all officers at noon, followed by another two hours of drills at 3:00 p.m. The evening is a time of discussing "theoretic maneuvering" with the command staff.

As March turns to April, the sight of entire companies drilling in lockstep becomes commonplace. The sense of camaraderie is augmented by the work of Martha Washington, who has helped organize the many women in camp into a nursing corps. The elegant twenty-four-year-old wife of Gen. Nathanael Greene has also joined the encampment. Caty Greene speaks fluent French, making the Greene quarters a haven for foreign officers. And whether from America or not, the senior officers meet two or three evenings a week at General Washington's quarters for dinner and coffee.

It is General Greene who emerges as a hero of Valley Forge. In March 1778, Washington appoints him as quartermaster general, in charge of procuring food, clothing, wagons, and horses. It is well known that an army's success depends upon being well supplied. General Washington has been reluctant to rob the local citizens of their horses and grain to supply his army, but there is no longer any choice. Greene's troops scour the countryside for supplies, issuing receipts for all they take. This bounty includes grain, horses, cattle, and wagons.

"Like a pharaoh, I harden my heart," Greene tells Washington, when speaking of the daily sight of sobbing local people watching their favorite horses and livestock being led away. He reminds himself that if the Americans do not "forage the country naked," taking possession of all food and grain within twenty miles of Valley Forge, then the revolution will surely fail.

Finally, George Washington feels some relief. As spring arrives in full blossom, he receives the news of France's entry into the war. He also knows that von Steuben's army is ready to fight. Yet the British are holding back, unwilling to engage the rebels.

On May 6, 1778, Washington sets war aside for a night, ordering a massive feast for the entire officer corps. The return of warm weather and the results of Greene's successful foraging mean that plentiful amounts of game and beef fill the camp. The men have all been provided with clothing, although some grumble that they finally have winter clothes just as summer is about to arrive. George Washington also abandons his stoic demeanor and drinks his fill at the special celebration, ordering Alexander Hamilton to ascend a platform front and center to offer toasts in the general's name.

This rouses the officer corps, who are feeling no pain. Washington, whether concerned about having had too much to drink or embarrassed by his poor dental health, is averse to doing his own speaking on this grand public occasion.

"After a sufficient merriment his Excellency retired," one officer will write, "Desiring the officers to be very attentive to their duty."

The meaning of "duty" becomes clear in the days that follow — the British are on the march. The time has come to leave Valley Forge and put von Steuben's lessons to work on the field of battle.

The winter has transformed the army in more ways than one. There will be no more talk of another general replacing George Washington. In the six months spent at Valley Forge, roughly two thousand men have died, about one-sixth of the entire force. The general has endured the severe weather with his men, so much so that his very presence gives them hope, despite these losses.

"I am content should they remove almost any general except his Excellency," Capt. Ezra Selden of the First Connecticut Regiment writes home. "Even Congress are not aware of the confidence the army places in him."

On June 19, 1778, the Continental Army marches out of Valley Forge, ready, at last, to confront the enemy.

19

Monticello, Virginia
August 1, 1778
Morning

Thomas Jefferson is safe.

The Virginian is now thirty-four and hundreds of miles away from the British threat here at his five-thousand-acre mountain-top refuge. Unlike at Valley Forge, there is no lack of food, clothing, or wine. Monticello's stunning 360-degree views of the American frontier offer the Virginian no sign of conflict. Indeed, it is a time of celebration.

"Our third daughter born," Jefferson records in his "Account Book," adding that the child came into the world this morning at 1:30. Her name is Mary.

The baby appears to be healthy, but whether she will survive the next few weeks and grow to adulthood is unknown. The infant deaths of his daughter and son in 1775 and 1777, respectively, left six-year-old Patsy as Jefferson's sole surviving child. At least for now, she has a new sister.

The Virginian is elated by his new daughter's birth but is also wary, as has become his custom. There is no such thing as easy childrearing in the late eighteenth century.

Closing his Account Book, Jefferson sets off for a morning in the fields. Martha sleeps fitfully in her mahogany bed on this sweltering day, her physical health once again deeply compromised by the act of bringing a baby into the world.

Jefferson leaves her to sleep, knowing that his wife's every need will be attended to by her personal slaves. As he steps out into the morning sunshine, the remainder of the Virginian's vast plantation is a beehive of activity — a place of building, planting, and hard work under a blazing August sun.

The humidity is so thick that Jefferson begins to sweat as he strides toward the South Orchard. At this pivotal time in his life, Jefferson is working with his own bare hands to transform the estate. While his slaves and skilled laborers are in the process of laying ninety thousand bricks to establish three new stone columns to the front of the house, the great thinker is spending the summer with thirty-one-year-old Italian gardener Antonio Giannini, planting hundreds of new apple, cherry, nectarine, walnut, apricot, and peach trees in the orchard on the south slope. This is no random planting, but a strict following of the plan Jefferson prepared during his spare time while serving in the Virginia legislature last year. In all, 312 trees are being added, spaced in rows at deliberate intervals between twenty and forty feet to ensure an eye-pleasing aesthetic. In fact, everywhere Jefferson looks, from the builders carefully troweling mortar to the pens of oxen, chicken, guinea fowl, peacocks, and turkeys, Monticello is vibrant with life.

The main house is atop the small mountain Thomas Jefferson has grown to love. The estate is comprised of four farms: Monticello, Shadwell, Tufton, and Lego. Slaves are quartered in log cabins near the fields. Children start working at the age of ten — sometimes younger — but those who show promise are taught a trade at sixteen. It is in Jefferson's best interests to keep his slaves well fed, in order to ensure optimal productivity during the long days of planting, hoeing, weeding, and harvesting. A typical food allotment for each slave is eight quarts of cornmeal per week, four salted fish, and a half pound of pork or beef. In their time off in the evenings or on Sundays, slaves often supplement this diet through fishing and possum hunting.

It has been ten years since Jefferson leveled the mountaintop to begin the house construction, and seven years since he moved into what is now known as the South Pavilion. As the plantation has grown, Jefferson has increased the slave population. At first, he owned fifty men, women, and children, but now possesses more than one hundred, some working in the house, others in the fields, and others doing sundry manual labor as needed.

Jefferson is known for being a rather lenient slave master, offering cash incentives for hard work and productivity, and allowing his slaves to visit the Sunday market in nearby Charlottesville. He forbids his plantation overseers from using a whip and rarely punishes slaves for anything other than fighting and stealing. However, it is common for these orders to be ignored whenever Jefferson is away on business. In extreme cases, disruptive slaves are simply sold to a faraway plantation as punishment, separated from their families forever.

The Virginian once wrote that "all men are created equal" and has written treatises deriding the institution of slavery, but the truth is that he would no more sell his slaves than turn himself over to the British to be hanged. In Jefferson's lifetime, he will own six hundred slaves, buying and selling men, women, and children to suit the needs and debts of Monticello. It is perfectly legal, and he needs the free manual labor to make his plantation profitable. Setting his slaves free in a bold act of humanity would completely disrupt the fabric of Virginia society.

Jefferson was born in 1743, the same year as Jupiter, one of his personal slaves. At one time, they were fast friends and childhood companions. Despite that friendship, Jefferson considers blacks to be lesser human beings. Three years from now he will write that "blacks . . . are inferior to whites in the endowments of both body and mind."*

One slave family in particular is accorded a loftier status at Monticello. Betty Hemings has borne Jefferson's father-in-law, John Wayles, six children out of wedlock. Betty was herself born of mixed-race parentage, meaning that this forty-one-year-old slave's children, grandchildren, and great-grandchildren will be partially European in ancestry and partially black. Yet, these

*Notes on the State of Virginia, 1781.

mixed-race offspring, despite their fair skin and Roman noses, are all destined to a life of slavery.

The youngest of Betty Hemings's children by John Wayles is named Sally. She was born in 1773, just around the time Wayles died. She is now five years old. As a girl of just fourteen, she will become the personal slave of Mary Jefferson, the newborn infant who has just come into the world. Thanks to Sally's mother's sexual relations with Wayles, Thomas Jefferson's wife, Martha, is a blood relation to Sally Hemings, her half sister.

Even more shocking is that once she comes of age, and for twenty years after that, Sally Hemings will share Master Jefferson's bed as his lover.*

*Jefferson never acknowledged the relationship. It first came to light in 1802, during his first term as president, when political pamphleteer and journalist James T. Callender published a report in a Richmond, Virginia, newspaper alleging that Jefferson "kept, as a concubine one of his slaves"; that "her name is Sally"; and that Jefferson had "several children" by her. Sally Hemings never commented on the subject, and Jefferson had a policy of offering no public response to personal attacks. Some do not believe the story, but after

Thomas Jefferson loves his pleasures, and the fruits of the orchard are for his personal enjoyment, as is the expansion of the main house and the tall rows of hops he grows to brew beer. Not so for the tobacco fields being tilled farther down the mountain, tended to by the largest percentage of his slaves. Tobacco is serious business, providing almost all Thomas Jefferson's income.

There is no profit in being a legislator — indeed, the cost of renting lodgings and purchasing meals while in Williamsburg means that Jefferson loses money while serving. Thus, he depends upon the plantation to stay afloat. Tobacco is Monticello's

---

substantial inquiry and DNA testing, the Thomas Jefferson Foundation, which oversees and maintains Monticello, issued this public statement in 2012: "Today TJF [Thomas Jefferson Foundation] and most historians believe that, years after his wife's death, Thomas Jefferson was the father of the six children of Sally Hemings mentioned in Jefferson's records." A complete copy of the "Report of the Research Committee on Thomas Jefferson and Sally Hemings" can be found at Monticello.org.

cash crop, one upon which Jefferson relies to indulge himself in a life of intellectual rigor. He is intent on expanding his personal library by purchasing as many books as possible. Tobacco is the currency making this happen.

Though Jefferson temporarily removed himself from the Virginia legislature to be with Martha during her pregnancy, he keeps in touch through letters with friends and colleagues. It has been almost two months since the British abandoned Philadelphia, fleeing back to New York for fear that the city will fall into French hands. Jefferson knows that during the British retreat, George Washington's revitalized army successfully battled the redcoats to a standstill at the Battle of Monmouth in New Jersey. Gen. Charles Lee, recently returned to the Americans in a prisoner exchange, was among Washington's commanding generals. Unfortunately, the volatile Lee disobeyed orders, which led to his dismissal and eventual court-martial.

Jefferson believes that the French entering the war means the conflict will soon be over. He is not aware, however, that George Washington is guarding against this false sense of security, and is even calling Jefferson out by name to reengage in the conflict by coming back to Congress. Indeed, Jefferson's withdrawal into private life is becoming common throughout the new states. The fanatical patriotism of 1775 has been replaced by apathy toward the war in many places, and even disdain for American soldiers. Jefferson's Declaration of Independence may have ignited the rebel fire, but the embers are beginning to cool.

As the Virginian begins to work on his plantation this hot day, he has no idea that a confrontation will soon arrive — that the war will find its way to the front door of Monticello. On that day, as the British Army comes for his head, no amount of intellectual idealism or newly planted orchards will help Thomas Jefferson — quite simply, he will flee for his life.

The truth is, Jefferson's very existence, and the welfare of the entire new nation, will be placed in jeopardy by one of the most heinous acts of betrayal in world history.

And unbeknownst to Jefferson — or even George Washington — that act of treason is about to unfold.

20

Philadelphia, Pennsylvania
Christmas Day, 1778
Evening

George Washington is in no mood to celebrate Christmas.

The general has been summoned to Philadelphia by the Congress to explain his battle plans for the coming year. The redcoats are gone — having abandoned the city to consolidate strength in New York, so that a sizable number of troops could be sent to protect valuable islands in the West Indies from French attacks. London is fearful that French forces will soon attack the British stronghold on Manhattan. Therefore, the city must be defended at all costs.

As Washington's army enters its second month of winter camp at nearby Middlebrook, New Jersey, Washington spends Christmas sixty miles away with Martha, at the opulent mansion of Henry Laurens, a South Carolina slave trader and rice grower who has just stepped down as president of the Second Continental Congress.* His presence has greatly excited the crème de la crème of Philadelphia society, and there is no lack of chauffeured carriages off-loading the wealthy and privileged at the mansion's door to pay their respects and drink heartily.

George Washington knows that his army is in capable hands, thanks to the stern presence of General von Steuben. Washington himself supervised the construction of log cabin barracks before undertaking the horseback ride to Philadelphia, so he is also content in the knowledge that his soldiers are not sleeping in the open. This has been the mildest winter in many years, and even though the army supply system is still deeply inefficient, there is now plenty of food and supplies for the American fighting men.

*The slave-trading firm of Austin and Laurens, which Henry Laurens owned with his brother-in-law, George Austin, brought almost eight thousand slaves into America between 1751 and 1761. The sales of these human beings made Laurens one of the richest men in America.

There is also little threat from the British Army. Commander in chief William Howe has been recalled to London, where he will soon be ordered to defend himself against charges that he abandoned Gen. John Burgoyne at Saratoga and thus effected the humiliating British surrender that brought France into the war. Howe's successor is Gen. Henry Clinton, a forty-eight-year-old career officer and member of Parliament who is even more unwilling to fight than Howe — and yet he must now wage war in both the American states and the West Indies, against a French foe as well as the Americans. Thus, the war has settled into a protracted engagement between an occupying force that has no intention of leaving and a rebel army lacking the firepower to evict it.

Washington's only battle this year occurred in June. After all the hardship and training at Valley Forge, the lone chance to display American's newfound military expertise came just ten days after the troops broke camp, on June 28, 1778, at a place known as Monmouth, halfway between Philadelphia and New York City. On a brutally hot and humid summer day, with temperatures reaching one hundred degrees, Washington unleashed five thousand men in a surprise attack on a British column commanded by Lt. Gen. Charles Cornwallis. Although they do not succeed in their attempt to capture the British baggage train, the new military concepts learned under the demanding eye of Baron von Steuben allow them to thwart a vigorous British counterattack.

The fighting raged back and forth until dusk, when both sides held their lines as darkness called a halt to the battle. The finale would have to wait until morning. The cool of the night was a welcome arrival. Scores lay dead on both sides, some bodies completely obliterated by cannon fire. In addition, a total of more than a hundred men perished from heat stroke.

The British troops were not defeated, and were able to resume their march to New York City, where they arrived a few days later. But the Americans had held their own in the sort of pitched battle that had proven disastrous in previous years. Washington's troops have made an impression on Clinton. Already hampered by limited forces, he must pursue a different sort of warfare against his now much more professional foe.

Besides the eight thousand troops sent to the West Indies, British troops were dispatched south by ship to invade Georgia in a tactical gambit to open a new front in the war. Not only will the capture of Savannah put another of America's major ports in British hands, it is believed that much of the southern population is loyal to the Crown and will flock to join the British forces. The move places a large British force in closer proximity to the wealthy English sugar-producing colonies in Barbados and Jamaica, which are now in danger of French naval attack.*

Just one month ago, George Washington allowed himself to dream that the war would finally be over. "I had expectations," the general wrote in a letter to his brother John, "that the enemy were about to evacuate New York and bid adieu to the United States."

That has not happened. But now, on this Christmas Day in Philadelphia, George Washington is struggling to enjoy the comforts of a big city. In the four years since his

*The Anglo-French naval battles in the Caribbean are an oft-overlooked offshoot of the Revolutionary War. During the summer of 1778, the French blockaded Barbados and Jamaica and seized the islands of Dominica and Grenada outright. In addition to their strategic value, Caribbean islands were a source of rum and the lucrative sugar crop.

becoming commander in chief, this is his first yuletide without fear of attack.

Washington sleeps each night with Martha by his side, and feasts on prime rib and succulent pig at lavish dinners that go well into the evening. There are drinks, refined conversation, and the perfumed aroma of beautiful women. Nowhere to be seen or felt is the harsh rigor or personal anxiety of Valley Forge from just one year ago.

Still, the general cannot relax.

Indeed, Washington finds the atmosphere in Philadelphia deeply troubling. All around him, people behave as if victory were a mere formality.

Yet, no matter what citizens believe, Washington knows independence is not assured.

Soon, brutal fighting will erupt again.

As George Washington walks the streets of Philadelphia, he sees the devastation the British inflicted upon it.

He notices that there is an absence of trees, wooden fences, and church pews, thanks to the British reliance on burning Philadelphia's wood supply rather than venturing into rebel territory to fell a tree. The basements of many houses and city alleyways were used as redcoat toilets, and the disgusting work of cleanup is still under way. The British and their Hessian allies were fond of moving into homes and stealing furniture from nearby residences. Now, the returning people of Philadelphia look for their missing belongings and return possessions that do not belong to them. Churchgoers are aghast to find their houses of worship desecrated because the British used them to stable horses.

Not as visible, but far more deeply felt, are the scars borne by the women who remained behind in Philadelphia, young and old, many of them defiled by British soldiers. In some cases, even when the women were loyal to the Crown, it was actual rape. In others, a choice, as British officers and soldiers frequented Philadelphia's many bordellos.*

*Despite the fact that rape and other atrocities were hanging offenses, such acts occurred. An example is the British headquarters notation of March 14, 1778, stating that a Cpl. John Fisher was sentenced to be hanged by the neck until dead for "a rape on the body of Maria Nicolls, a woman child of nine years of age." Very often, however, rape was such a shameful act that women kept it a secret to avoid their own punishment. In the case of Maria Nicolls, whose father was a sergeant in

"Most of the young ladies who were in the city with the enemy and wear the present fashionable dresses have purchased them at the expense of their virtue. It is agreed on all hands that the British officers played the devil with the girls," one resident observes. "The privates, I suppose, were satisfied with the common prostitutes."

As George Washington begins what will become a six-week residence in the city of Benjamin Franklin, Philadelphia's wounds haunt him, for he is a man of great compassion and well remembers what the city looked like before the British occupation.

But he is just as burdened by the "idleness and dissipation" he sees each night in the society parties.

The delegates to Congress returned from their exile in York, Pennsylvania, in June and held their first session in Philadelphia on July 2, 1778. It is not lost on Washington that this meeting coincided with the date just two years ago when the vote for independence was passed, for he has not forgotten the strong character and vision of the men who signed the Declaration.

---

the British Army, she refused to share her story until exacting a promise from her own mother "that if she would not beat her, she would tell."

Some of those delegates remain in Congress, but most new representatives are, to the general's eyes, mediocre. There is no longer a Jefferson, an Adams, a Franklin, or even a John Hancock deliberating deep into the night on the meaning of freedom. The chairs in which those great men once sat have long since been burned as firewood. Eventually, their original meeting place will become known as Independence Hall, but during the British occupation, the building was converted into a hospital for wounded American prisoners. When the enemy departed, it became necessary to scrub blood from the floors and fumigate to eliminate the odors of decomposition and filled bedpans.*

From Christmas until his departure back

*Conditions were so overcrowded that American soldiers awaiting treatment slept on the floor and even the stairs. Those who survived were transferred to the Walnut Street Jail, where they were forced to endure the winter on a starvation diet of rats and shoe leather. The bodies of those who did not survive the hospital were tossed into a pit behind the building, along with the skeletons of dead horses and piles of trash. The aroma of decay was so vile that the returning Congress was initially unable to meet in the State House, and

to his men on February 2, 1779, Washington spends his nights enduring the dreary debauchery of Philadelphia society and his days battling Congress. The delegates have authorized him to "superintend and direct the military operations in all the departments in these States," but they refuse to allocate the hard currency the general needs to pay his soldiers.

Washington considers this Congress "the great impediment."

One of the general's officers, Lt. Col. Ebenezer Huntington of Connecticut, is not as diplomatic. "I despise my countrymen," he writes. "I wish I could say I was not born in America. I once gloried in it but am now ashamed of it. . . . You must immediately fill your regiments and pay your troops in hard monies. They cannot exist as soldiers otherwise. The insults and neglects which the army have met from the country beggars all description . . . and all this for my cowardly countrymen who flinch at the very time their exertions are wanted and hold their purse strings as though they would damn the world rather than part with a dollar to their army."

---

temporarily relocated to the College of Pennsylvania, on Fourth and Arch Streets.

■ ■ ■ ■

While the rebel army is deprived, one soldier is living very well indeed.

Maj. Gen. Benedict Arnold has been appointed by George Washington as military governor of Philadelphia. Arnold, still bitter about his treatment at Saratoga, now lives so lavishly that many wonder if he is stealing. But Washington is not concerned. He is trying to get Arnold back on the battlefield, and granting him the governorship is a way to give the major general's shattered leg and other wounds time to heal.

Arnold's job requires him to keep the peace among Congress, the combative Pennsylvania legislature, and the Loyalists who have remained in the city after their British allies fled. This is not Arnold's ideal posting, but he has come to enjoy it very much.

Prior to the war, Benedict Arnold made his living as a merchant. He is obsessed with making money. So, while he entered Philadelphia in June as a soldier in need of a place to recuperate, he soon began a series of barely legal schemes to fund a lavish lifestyle. The major general regularly issues military passes allowing bearers to travel freely into British-occupied New York. Arnold has invested in merchant vessels and has granted the owner of the ships a special pass to transport goods from Philadelphia to the Eastern Seaboard — an illegal act tantamount to smuggling.* He has also secretly undertaken a plan to purchase and hoard crucial supplies in the city of New York, knowing they will be in high demand once the British are forced out by the French. When necessary, he is unafraid to use Continental Army wagons to haul goods and supplies in an effort to enrich himself.

This intense focus on wealth and social status has begun to transform Arnold. He has taken up residence in the mansion recently occupied by British general William Howe, and is transported around Philadelphia in a luxurious carriage.† He

---

*Rebel military authorities did not want ships roaming the seas for fear of their being captured by the British.

†Arnold's home was known as the Masters-Penn Mansion, and was located at 524–30 Market Street. In addition to housing Howe and then Arnold, it would serve as the Presidential Mansion from 1790 to 1800, home to America's first two presidents until the White House was built in Washington, DC. The main building was demol-

hosts elaborate dinner parties, inviting congressmen, local dignitaries, and even British Loyalists to enjoy fine wine and the best food money can buy. Arnold believes the war will end soon and sees no wrong in dining with the enemy. "I flatter myself that there is a time at hand when our unhappy contests will be at an end, and peace and domestic happiness restored to everyone," he writes.

The recipient of the letter bearing these words is prominent Pennsylvania chief justice Edward Shippen IV. Arnold has fallen deeply in love with Shippen's eighteen-year-old daughter, Peggy. Among the beautiful socialite's prior romances was that with British officer John André, still living in Benjamin Franklin's British-requisitioned Philadelphia house and now serving as chief of staff to Gen. Henry Clinton. André considers Peggy a young woman "of wit, beauty and every accomplishment," referring not just to her looks

---

ished in 1832, but the mansion's former location on what is now Independence Mall led to archaeological efforts to unearth the ruins. These findings, which include the site of George Washington's slave quarters during his time in office, are now an open-air museum.

Peggy Shippen

but also to her worldly knowledge of topics ranging from finance to the proper care and feeding of barnyard animals.

Some of the most powerful men in America will also fall for Peggy's charms. George Washington, who dined at the Shippen home in 1774, when she was just fourteen, will admit to being enchanted by her beauty. And a year from now, after she suffers a fainting spell upon receiving unexpected bad news, the dashing Alexander Hamilton will race to comfort her.

Yet, whether British or American, no man really knows Peggy Shippen.

During the British occupation, the Shippen family, Loyalists all, lived a life of apparent luxury. Nights were spent at the theater, in casinos, and dancing at the refurbished City Tavern. Petite, well read, and high-spirited, Peggy was constantly the center of attention, praised for her poise and stunning good looks. But her father struggled to find the financial resources to adorn his four daughters with the latest European fashions such as silk dresses and two-foot-high wigs.

Many men noticed. "We were all in love with her," one British officer will remember of Peggy. She is blond and gray-eyed, fond of laughter and society parties. On those occasions when events do not go her way, however, she is transformed, making a show of weeping loudly and refusing all food and drink for days on end.

Perhaps Peggy Shippen's most profound trait is the coquette's talent for veiling her opinion. She is not only her father's youngest daughter, but also his personal favorite, sharing his Loyalist views against independence. Peggy and her sisters were banished from Philadelphia society early in the war, when their father was accused of being a

British spy and the family was forced to flee to the countryside. The Shippens moved back to their town house on Society Hill as soon as General Howe captured the city, and chose to remain there once Philadelphia returned to American hands, despite falling on financial hard times. Holding Loyalist beliefs in a patriot citadel means Peggy must always be on her guard. The threat of betrayal and imprisonment is very real, thus Miss Shippen knows to keep her own counsel on matters of politics — and loyalty.*

Right now, the man most beguiled by Peggy is Benedict Arnold, twenty years her senior. Amazingly, after a long parade of potential suitors, she is just as besotted —

---

*The extended Shippen family, for whom Shippensburg, Pennsylvania, is named, was deeply divided on the subject of American independence. Peggy Shippen's uncle was George Washington's director general of military hospitals for the Continental Army at Valley Forge. His brothers-in-law Francis Lightfoot Lee and Richard Henry Lee famously signed the Declaration of Independence, and their cousin Henry "Lighthorse Harry" Lee would not only rise to the rank of general during the Revolutionary War, but would also father Robert E. Lee, the Confederate general of American Civil War fame.

mostly by his power. There is a significant societal divide between the genteel Shippen family and the hardscrabble Arnold, but he is relentless in his determination to wed.

By January 1779, there are just two obstacles to the marriage: Arnold's lack of landholdings and his limp, which makes him look weak and infirm.

Arnold's shattered leg is the talk of Philadelphia society. Socialites are prone to engaging in long dialogues about its chances of a full recovery, and the impact it will have on the relationship. "We have every reason to hope it will be well again," Peggy's brother-in-law observes, "but the leg will be a couple inches shorter than the other and disfigured."

Soon, the governor throws away his crutches and learns to walk with a cane. Then his attention turns to buying a large estate the couple can call home. It matters not that Arnold is over his head in debt and placing himself deeper and deeper into a financial position he cannot legally maintain. His obsession for Peggy obscures all financial concerns.

By the end of January 1779, the two are engaged and Arnold is making plans to leave the military — despite the fact that his position as governor allows his business dealings to flourish. His vision is to purchase a 130,000-acre property in upstate New York where he would become a land baron and powerful presence in civilian life. Arnold knows his young fiancée is impressed by wealth and power, and he aims to please her at all costs.

On February 8, 1779, Benedict Arnold meets George Washington at the general's New Jersey headquarters. The two are cordial, with Arnold writing, "I am treated with great kindness by George Washington and the officers of the army."

If Washington is concerned that one of his top generals is deeply in debt, engaging in questionable enterprises, and making plans to marry a Loyalist who once dated a top British officer, he does not make this known.

Instead, he continues to fervently hope that Benedict Arnold will once again become a driving force on the battlefield. But Washington is miscalculating — for Benedict Arnold is now a man of selfish pursuits.

A very powerful man.

21

Philadelphia, Pennsylvania
May 5, 1779
Afternoon

Treachery is under way.

"If your Excellency thinks me criminal, for Heaven's sake, let me be immediately tried, and if found guilty, executed," Benedict Arnold writes in a feverish script to George Washington. Arnold's financial misdeeds have finally caught up with him, and a court-martial is due to begin at the end of the month. Rather than fight the proceedings, however, Arnold wants to speed them up. He longs to silence his critics, clear his name, and get on with the new life he shares with his young bride.

Arnold has another, far more devious reason for expediting the court-martial.

"They have had three months to look for evidence, and cannot produce one against me," he adds. "I have nothing left but the little reputation I have gained in the army."

It has been three weeks since the widower Arnold wed Peggy Shippen in her family town house on Fourth Street. The ceremony was simple, as befitting the hard times upon which the Shippen family has fallen during the war. Never claiming to be a gentleman, Arnold apparently boasted about his wife's performance in the marital bed the following morning.* Crassly as he might behave, however, Arnold's devotion to his young bride is complete. The couple honeymooned in New Jersey and Pennsylvania, spending long days traveling through the countryside by carriage and nights in the homes of friends.

In those hours on the road, Benedict and Peggy unburdened themselves to each other, forging a bond of love and trust that will last a lifetime and endure countless trials. They spoke of financial stability, discussed the outcome of the war, and Peggy confided her deepest Tory sympathies to her new husband, eager for him to know where her heart truly lay.

*The Marquis de Chastellux, a French general visiting Philadelphia, would be the source of this hearsay.

Benedict Arnold is a man constantly flirting with disaster. Money flows through his hands almost as fast as he can accrue it, and "extravagance" seems to be his personal mandate. Peggy's father, knowing that he could no longer care for his own daughter, stipulated in the marital contract that Arnold purchase a lavish home for her. Arnold did so, but the couple must rent out their palatial new ninety-six-acre estate at Mount Pleasant rather than live in it, because they cannot afford the upkeep.*

The enormous debt hanging over the marriage troubles Peggy, for she knows what it is like to grow up in a family of means only to see a fortune slip away.

Yet she also admires Arnold's ingenuity, and trusts he will find a solution to their financial crisis. Rather than be frustrated by her husband's ruthless ambition, Peggy finds it to be an aphrodisiac.

As Benedict Arnold now writes to George Washington from his bedroom inside the former home of Pennsylvania lieutenant governor Richard Penn, he is adamant that

*Once a country estate, Mount Pleasant now lies within Philadelphia's Fairmount Park district. The home is open to the public for tours.

the date of his court-martial be advanced.★ The dreams and aspirations that he and Peggy discussed during their honeymoon are fresh in his head.

Only through triumph in the court-martial can Arnold return to the war, profiteering, and perhaps something more.

In an elaborate scheme already concocted by Benedict and Peggy Arnold during their honeymoon, he will make contact with her old paramour from the British occupation, the cunning and ruthless Major John André. In a twist of fate, André was appointed deputy adjutant general to the British Army, which included responsibility for gathering intelligence, just two weeks ago. Due to a shortage of replacement troops, the British are intent on winning the war through "procuring, digesting, and communicating intelligence of the motions of the enemy." They have begun making lists of American generals who may be turned to their cause. To many, the "revolution" appears dead, with perhaps fifty thousand conservative Loyalists on the verge of enlisting to support the British.

But the English need a man to lead them.

★Richard Penn was the grandson of William Penn, the founder and namesake of Pennsylvania.

"Unless the refugees and other loyalists are put under the command of a person in whom they confide and to whom they have an attachment, they can answer no valuable purpose," reads one British report.

To his advantage, Benedict Arnold is currently famous in London, as Gen. John Burgoyne stands before Parliament blaming his loss at Saratoga on Arnold's brilliant generalship. Clearly, there is no better time than right now for Arnold to engage the British and test what his services might be worth to them.

Through Major André, General Arnold hopes to share military secrets: troop strength, gun emplacements, and tactical plans. He has already met with Joseph Stansbury, a storekeeper specializing in glass and china who is well trusted in Loyalist circles. Arnold has ordered the thirty-year-old Stansbury to communicate with a network of spies led by William Franklin, the former governor of New Jersey and illegitimate son of Benjamin Franklin.*

*William Franklin was released from jail in 1778 as part of a prisoner exchange with the Americans. Franklin's zeal for the British cause only increased during his incarceration. He set up residence in the Loyalist stronghold of New York upon his

Through this network, Stansbury is to pass along a letter from Arnold indicating his desire to join the British cause — for the right price.

Just to make sure that Stansbury can come and go from the Arnolds' Philadelphia home without being questioned, Arnold is awarding him a large sum of money, to ostensibly renovate the dining room.

Treason is a capital offense, but for a famous general like Arnold, jumping to the winning side in the conflict will undoubtedly spare him from the hangman's noose — and allow him to enjoy a long and happy life with his beloved Peggy.

In return for this betrayal, Benedict Arnold hopes to receive enough money to live comfortably for the rest of his days. The burden of debt under which he now lives will easily be forgotten, as he and Peggy can simply walk away from their creditors and begin a new life in England. Ideally, the British will be so thankful that, in addition to money, the king may offer Arnold a knighthood, making the couple "Sir Bene-

---

release and was soon named president of the Board of Associated Loyalists, a group dedicated to spreading terror by murdering patriots in cold blood.

dict and Lady Arnold."

Of course, Benedict Arnold will assume almost all the risk, while Peggy will share only in the reward.

On May 10, 1779, one hundred miles from Philadelphia, in a house in Lower Manhattan, Joseph Stansbury meets with William Franklin about Arnold's bold offer. Franklin, in turn, introduces Stansbury to Maj. John André.

Again, the timing is ideal, for as a man new to his job, André is seeking a triumph in order to impress his superior officer, Gen. Henry Clinton.

André immediately writes back to Benedict Arnold, outlining the codes and methods of communication that will allow them to transmit information, promising that "any partial but important blow should by his means be struck or aimed, upon the strength of just and pointed information and cooperation, rewards equal at least to what such service can be estimated at, will be given."

Arnold is then given a code name: Monk.*

*The name is an allusion to George Monck, a seventeenth-century English patriot who was

The ingenious plot to destroy American freedom has begun.

instrumental in restoring the monarchy to England in 1660.

22

Off the Coast of Flamborough Head
Yorkshire, England
September 23, 1779
5:00 P.M.

The war has come for England.

As the pale autumn sun sets over the Yorkshire coast, American commodore John
Paul Jones gathers his ship's officers on the
quarterdeck to talk strategy. He is a wiry,
clean-shaven man, standing five foot five
and wearing a blue uniform with gold
epaulets. On the main deck, the unmistakable sound of marine drummers "beating to
quarters" echoes down into the ship's hold.
Every member of the three-hundred-man
American and French crew races to battle
stations in answer to this rat-a-tat command.*

A fight is imminent. Jones's aging flag-

*The most effective method of getting the atten-

ship, the *Bonhomme Richard,* is three miles from land. She sails north, pushed by a light breeze.[†]

The Continental Navy's mission has long been defensive in nature, focused on protecting America's shores. Jones takes a different approach, preferring to capture British vessels and their cargo in English waters, bringing the war home to the enemy.

An English warship approaches from the opposite direction, closing the distance as she tacks into the wind. At first, she appears to be very much like the slow former freighter *Richard,* roughly one hundred fifty feet long and forty feet at the beam. But as the English ship draws closer, it is clear she

---

tion of the entire crew at once was the use of the drum and fife. Armies and navies of the era used drums to broadcast signals. The most urgent was the continuous drumroll that signaled "to arms," the call to form for battle.

†Jones owed much of his success to the patronage of Benjamin Franklin in Paris. Franklin's pseudonymous writings, compiled in *Poor Richard's Almanack,* were translated into French as *Les Maximes du Bonhomme Richard.* Thus, when the French loaned the aging freighter the *Duc de Duras* to the Americans, Jones rechristened it in Franklin's honor upon taking command in February 1779.

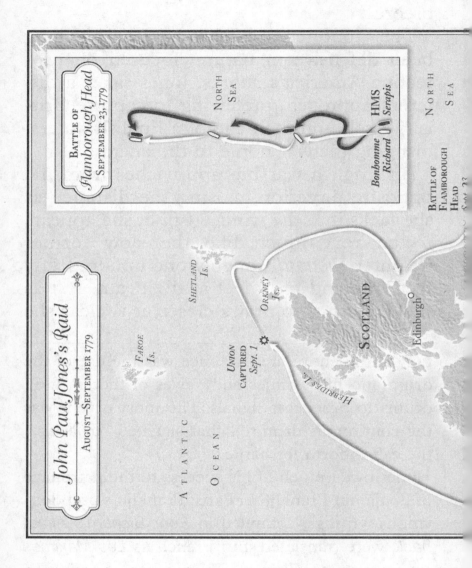

John Paul Jones's Raid
AUGUST–SEPTEMBER 1779

BATTLE OF
Flamborough Head
SEPTEMBER 23, 1779

NORTH
SEA

HMS
Serapis

Bonhomme
Richard

ATLANTIC

OCEAN

FAROE
Is.

SHETLAND
Is.

UNION
CAPTURED
Sept. 1

ORKNEY
Is.

SCOTLAND

Edinburgh

HEBRIDES IS.

NORTH
SEA

BATTLE OF
FLAMBOROUGH
HEAD
Sept. 23

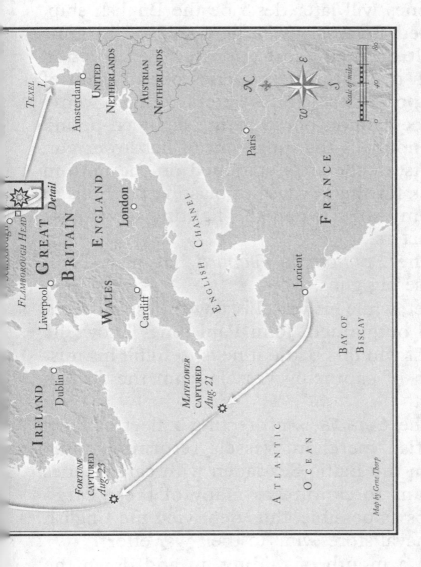

TEXEL I.

Amsterdam

UNITED NETHERLANDS

AUSTRIAN NETHERLANDS

Paris

FRANCE

ENGLISH CHANNEL

London

ENGLAND

GREAT BRITAIN

WALES

Cardiff

Liverpool

FLAMBOROUGH HEAD

Detail

Lorient

BAY OF BISCAY

MAYFLOWER CAPTURED Aug. 21

Dublin

IRELAND

FORTUNE CAPTURED Aug. 23

ATLANTIC OCEAN

Scale of miles

0   40   80

Map by Gene Thorp

is a brand-new vessel gliding nimble and sleek through the waves.

Jones will later describe the English ship, called *Serapis,* as "a new ship of 44 guns built on their most approved construction with two complete batteries one of them of 18-pounders." Jones refers to the twenty fierce cannon bored to fire eighteen-pound cannonballs that poke out of her lower gun ports, deliberately stationed on the bottom deck for the purpose of blasting the hulls of enemy ships when the fighting is at close quarters.

The *Bonhomme Richard* has just six of these big guns.

Yet, while his vessel is slower, less modern, and outgunned, John Paul Jones knows he must win this battle if he is to fulfill his mission of capturing vessels from the British fleet.

The *Serapis* is protecting a fleet of forty British merchant vessels returning home from the Baltic Sea laden with cargo. Jones means to capture as many of these cargo ships as possible, thus depriving the English of naval stores vital to their war effort.

In a month of raiding up and down the English coast, the *Bonhomme Richard* has claimed sixteen such prizes. Jones has become notorious to the British Navy, a daring scoundrel who must be stopped.

Aware of his notoriety, Jones ordered that the *Richard* raise the British flag in an attempt to conceal her true identity, but the masquerade fools no one. In the coastal town of Scarborough, a red pennant has been raised over the castle warning ships at sea that there is a pirate in their midst. Local militia line the shore, hoping to repel any American vessel attempting to make landfall.

This is more than mere precaution, for Jones has plundered the English countryside twice in the last year.*

Defeating the *Serapis,* if that is possible, will require cunning, able seamanship, and a level of daring for which Jones has become well known. Thirty-two and Scottish by birth, John Paul (his birth name) first went to sea at the age of thirteen, sailing with the British merchant fleet. During a 1770 voyage, he flogged a ship's carpenter so viciously that the man died. Upon being

*Jones's continued triumphs stands in marked contrast to that of the French and Spanish, whose attempt to invade England was called off in the summer of 1779 due to storms, poor communication, sickness, lack of supplies, and overall inept planning.

John Paul Jones

granted bail after a short time in a Scottish prison, Paul set sail for the West Indies. He successfully thwarted a mutiny by killing a sailor with his sword in self-defense, but feared the Admiralty courts would see it differently. He therefore fled to Fredericksburg, Virginia, where he took on the surname "Jones," in honor of local planter Willie Jones, whose family showed him great hospitality. Jones switched his alliance to the American cause at the same time. He has learned his trade well, advancing from ship's boy to the most infamous sailor in the Continental Navy.

"If I have any capacity to render good and acceptable services to the common cause," Jones describes his motivations, sounding very much like George Washington, "no man will step forth with greater cheerfulness and alacrity than myself."

Indeed, John Paul Jones has singlehandedly brought the Revolutionary War to British shores, startling the citizens of this island nation into realizing that the American rebellion has become a direct threat.

The *Serapis* draws within twenty-five yards of the *Richard.* The time is now 6:30 p.m. Onshore, spectators line the tall white cliffs, waiting expectantly for the flash of cannon fire that will signal the start of the engagement.

"The moon was rising, the weather being

clear, the surface of the great deep being perfectly smooth, even as in a millpond," an American midshipman will remember. Snipers hide in the topsails of both ships, muskets cocked. Jones orders his men first to kill the enemy sharpshooters and then to turn their guns on any man scurrying about the *Serapis*'s main deck. If anything, the forty American snipers have a little extra courage, thanks to the double order of grog Jones has hoisted up to them.*

"What ship is that?" Capt. Richard Pearson of the *Serapis* cries out. The vessels are close — "pistol shot," as Jones will describe the range — and the British skipper's voice carries easily in the night. The sight of the British flag on the *Bonhomme Richard* makes Pearson reluctant to fire on her first.

Pearson, forty-eighty, is every bit Jones's equal as a navigator, having fought in several major sea battles and having once

---

*Grog is a mixture of rum and water, named after its inventor, British vice admiral Edward Vernon, who was fond of wearing a suit made of grogram (a coarse fabric woven from silk, mohair, or wool) and went by the nickname "Old Grog." The standard ration was a half pint of rum mixed with a quart of water per day.

piloted a ship through a hurricane. During one engagement, his ribs were shattered by a blast of grapeshot, but he refused to leave his post until the battle was won. But John Paul Jones does not know that. What he does know is that twenty brand-new eighteen-pounders are taking aim at his ship. British gun crews are famous for training relentlessly and striving to load and fire their weapons as quickly as possible. The Americans do not have that option, because of a shortage of powder. As a result, the rebel gunners are far less proficient with their aging French cannon.

Finally, a response comes from the *Richard:* "The *Princess Royal.*"

It is not Jones who does the talking, for his well-known Scottish brogue would give him away. Instead, it is the ship's master, Samuel Stacey, who replies.

"Where from?"

This time there is no answer. Stacey's voice has been no more effective than Jones's might have been, considering that his accent, from Massachusetts, sounds nothing like that of a British sailor.

Pearson is insistent. "Answer immediately, or I shall be under the necessity of firing into you."

Yet, even as he yells across the smooth

seas, Jones orders the British colors struck. The American flag is quickly raised in its place. It is one of many different designs in use by the Continental Army and Navy, but one and all on both vessels recognize the ensign as it instantly reveals the *Bonhomme Richard*'s true colors. In the tops (the "topsails"), a nervous American sniper can't help himself: knowing that battle is near, he squeezes off a round.

Only then does Jones give his response.

"We answered him by firing a whole broadside," Jones will later write to his friend and patron Benjamin Franklin. "The battle being thus begun was continued with unremitting fury."

The Americans may have struck first, but within moments, two of the *Richard*'s aging eighteen-pounders explode from misuse — killing the gun crews. The *Serapis*'s own big guns soon destroy the rest of the Americans' eighteen-pounders, leaving the *Bonhomme Richard* with only a handful of lightweight cannon on the main deck. The moon is now completely risen, a full amber globe shining down on the mangled corpses splayed across the decks and dangling in the rigging, many of them old salts with years of experience at sea, but also among the dead are young boys between the ages of eight and sixteen. Fire rages through the lower deck as saltwater seeps in through the holes blasted by cannon. More than a hundred prisoners captured in previous raids are locked belowdecks; many now scream for their release as the *Richard* takes on water. Also below, men crowd into the office of the ship's surgeon, their faces blackened by burns and their maimed limbs soon to fall victim to the necessities of the bone saw. Scores more sailors and marines are already dead, decapitated by the hot metal of grapeshot, ammunition similar to the canister shot used by the army. *Bonhomme Richard*'s situation is grave.

"Has your ship struck?" Captain Pearson calls out over the screams of the burned and maimed, wanting to know if Jones has lowered his colors in defeat.

At last, the British will have their day with John Paul Jones.

The *Bonhomme Richard* is barely able to maneuver. In fact, she will soon sink to the bottom of the North Sea.

"Surrender be damned," Jones yells back across the water. He is exhausted, having slept just one hour the night before, and quite aware he will not sleep at all this evening.

"I have not yet begun to fight."*

The *Serapis* crashes hard into the *Bonhomme Richard,* fouling her bow into the thick rigging at the rear of the American ship. Thinking quickly, John Paul Jones races up a ladder to the poop deck to rope the two ships together. He succeeds, but the bond is tentative. Calling for a thicker rope, he is subjected to a barrage of swearing from ship's master Stacey, frustrated that the *Richard* is disabled and barely able to maneuver.

"Mr. Stacey, it's no time to be swearing now," Jones says lightly, seeking to calm the veteran sailor. "You may be the next moment in eternity, but let us do our duty."

Thus far in the battle, Captain Pearson has outfoxed Jones. He now orders his vessel to drop anchor, believing that if the *Serapis* stands fast, the disabled *Richard* will simply float away on the current, whereupon the British ship's big guns will fire at will and finish the job.

Pearson has no reason to doubt that this

*The precise wording of Jones's defiance is the subject of much debate. The authors defer to the U.S. Naval Academy's interpretation, which quotes these exact words.

bold gambit will succeed. The *Serapis* is one hundred tons lighter, and thus more mobile. She has a protective copper bottom that allows her to sail faster; she also has the advantage in firepower.

But Jones's ropes are holding. The *Richard* remains bound to the *Serapis.* If anything, the vessels now press closer together. Jones's only chance for victory is to immobilize the enemy ship and send his men onto her decks to engage in hand-to-hand fighting. The Americans throw grappling hooks at the *Serapis,* further tangling the vessels. The fighting becomes savage — to the death.

In a scene of chaos, sailors leap onto enemy decks armed with swords, pistols, pikes, and grenades. The ensuing battle is terrifying and bloody, a free-for-all on the high seas. Some men drown, some lose limbs to the blade of a cutlass. Point-blank pistol shots blow off men's faces.

Jones orders his French Marines to clamber up the *Richard*'s three masts and into the topsails to join the ship's marksmen. One by one, those crew members of the *Serapis* unlucky enough to be roaming her exposed upper deck are raked by gunfire.

Belowdecks, however, the *Serapis*'s domination continues as her gunners unleash devastating broadsides with their big eighteen-pounders. Cannonballs enter one side of the *Richard* and exit the other, until the American ship's gun decks are coated in a thick river of blood.

On board the *Serapis,* the young boys known as "powder monkeys" race back and forth to the magazines, ensuring a constant supply of gunpowder. The gunners know to limit the amount of powder near the cannon, for fear that a spark could ignite an explosion, but as the battle continues for hour after hour, the gun deck becomes littered with powder and cartridges.*

Fire and water, the two terrors of a sailor's existence, soon begin to take their toll. The *Richard* is listing, and no amount of emergency hand-operated pumps can stop the

*In a normal day at sea, the gun deck is the hub of shipboard life, a place where sailors eat their meals and sling their hammocks for their four hours of sleep when not standing watch. The gun ports, just six feet above the waterline, are kept closed at all times. Their closure ensures complete darkness but also keeps out the sea spray that chills the crew. The gun deck is a place for backgammon and, for those few seamen who are literate, reading. It smells worse than a barnyard, as the men will go unwashed throughout the entirety of their voyage.

incoming sea. The concern about fire is so great that fighting is halted for a time when the sails of both ships are ablaze — only to resume again when the flames are extinguished.

Every moment of the action can be seen by the crowds lining the distant shoreline. More than a thousand spectators cheer lustily after each cannon blast by the *Serapis*. They discern the two ships by the color of their topsides — black for the American ship and yellow for the *Serapis*.

"The fire of their cannon, especially the lower battery, which was entirely formed of 18-pounders, was incessant," Jones will write. "My battery of twelve pounders on which I had placed my chief dependence was entirely silenced and abandoned."

The *Richard* has just three cannon remaining — lightweight nine-pound deck guns. When the gunner in command suffers a head wound, Jones personally takes charge of the battery. He helps the gun crew maneuver the cannon from one side of the deck to the other. Remarkably, the commodore is not wounded in any way. Refusing to go below for his own safety, as Pearson has done aboard the *Serapis,* Jones stands at the cannon, ready to fire.

He orders his deck gunners to aim high,

hoping not only to cut through the enemy's rigging, but also to kill the British sharpshooters in the opposing tops. Meanwhile, American and French marksmen continue to rain fire down on the *Serapis*'s main deck. The Americans control the upper decks, and the British below. Once Jones sees that the decks of the *Serapis* are clear, he orders those manning the cannon to switch their aim to its wooden mainmast. Three feet thick and painted bright yellow, it holds the key to disabling the *Serapis*. Should the one-hundred-fifty-foot column topple, the British ship's sails will also fall into the sea.

At 10:00 p.m., four hours into the fight, American sailor William Hamilton lobs a series of grenades, hollow iron spheres filled with gunpowder ignited by a fuse, onto the *Serapis*. The first few grenades explode with little effect. But one lucky toss finds an open hatch. The grenade tumbles straight down to the gun deck, igniting the powder and cartridges surrounding the big guns.

A series of explosions rock the *Serapis*. More than one hundred pounds of gunpowder detonates. Twenty sailors are killed instantly. Dozens more are maimed and severely burned.

"Humanity cannot but recoil from the

prospect of such finished horror and lament that war should be capable of producing such fatal consequences," Jones will later write of the grisly scene.

At 10:30 p.m., the decks of both ships are a scene of "carnage, wreck and ruin," in Jones's words. Captain Pearson strikes his colors. It is an act of utter humiliation, for Pearson had been so intent on not surrendering that he had personally nailed the flag to the rail so that it would become a permanent part of his ship.

"Sir, I have struck," Pearson yells over to Jones. Their ships are still locked together. From Pearson's position high on his quarterdeck, he is just twenty yards from Jones, who is still preparing to direct another cannon shot.

John Paul Jones can clearly see the red British ensign still dangling limply from the taffrail, barely fluttering in the slight nighttime breeze. It has been shredded by the battle but is still a symbol.

"If you have struck, haul down your ensign," the commodore barks at Pearson.

Pearson rips down the flag, its fabric tearing loudly as it separates from the nails holding it in place.

The *Serapis* is boarded.

"Have you struck, sir?" a shocked British

lieutenant asks Pearson.

Pearson admits his surrender, then sends the officer below to order a cease-fire.

Captain Pearson makes the surrender official by offering Jones his sword. Almost three hundred men have died tonight; both sides have suffered equally. The losses are all the more staggering for the sight of corpses littering both decks. The deaths are not neat bullet holes or single stab wounds, but appear to be the work of a butcher — faces blackened by the soot of battle and the smoke of fire, arms and legs chopped away by canister. The bodies of these fallen men will soon be unceremoniously dumped over the side.

Disturbing as the sight may be, there is a formality among opponents that must be observed. John Paul Jones ends the hostilities on a civil note, asking Captain Pearson to join him for a glass of wine in what remains of his cabin.*

*Captain Pearson will be taken as a prisoner of war. Initially gracious, he will become angry and restive during his captivity. Upon his return to England months after the battle, he will be hailed as a hero for preventing the loss of the convoy and will eventually be knighted.

414

The danger is not past, however. The *Bonhomme Richard* bobs listlessly just off the English coast, easy pickings for other British warships. The crowds on the shore know that the *Serapis* has lost the battle, so it is only a matter of time before Jones is confronted by another British vessel. Jones desperately tries to save the *Richard,* but she begins to sink lower and lower into the North Sea. Her gun ports are soon breached by the waves. Cutting the ropes, Jones reluctantly orders all hands transferred to the *Serapis,* prisoners included. She no longer has a mast, so as the *Richard* finally settles below the waves, John Paul Jones orders his crew to rig makeshift sails, and the *Serapis* sets sail. For ten long days, she travels east, evading British patrols. Finally, Jones maneuvers her toward the safety of the Dutch port of Texel.

Benjamin Franklin responds to a letter from John Paul Jones, written upon the commodore's arriving safely in Texel. "For some days," Franklin writes on October 10, 1779, "scarce any thing was talked of at Paris and Versailles but your cool conduct and persevering bravery during that terrible conflict."

In London, George III has no public response to the embarrassment John Paul Jones has caused Great Britain. But in Parliament, the antiwar voices grow more vocal and numerous by the day.

The king has no intention of losing the war to the Americans. In fact, he and his war council are set to release a new weapon — but this one is not made of steel. It is a human being named Banastre Tarleton.

23

Lt. Col. Banastre Tarleton does not trust his horse.

The proud commander of the British Legion canters silently through the swamps of South Carolina astride an inferior beast. The officer is twenty-five and brown haired, his strong jaw and aquiline nose just a shade too large for his narrow face. Tarleton's own mount, and those of his men, did not survive the rough sea passage from New York City to Charlotte, South Carolina, four months ago. So, he now rides into battle on a stolen horse, in total darkness, unsure of whether his new mount will spook at the sound of gunfire.

The moon is waxing, but a thick tree canopy allows Tarleton's six hundred fifty

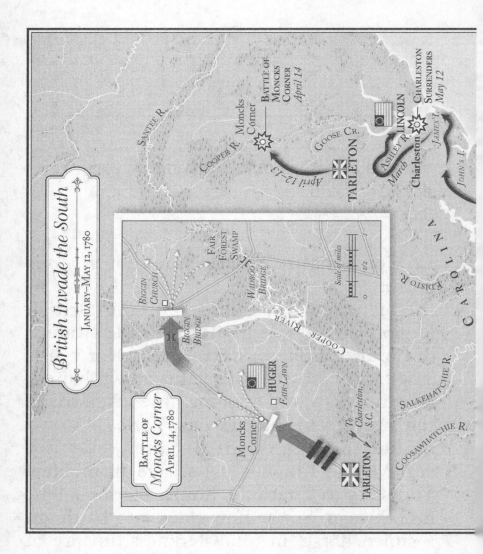

British Invade the South
JANUARY–MAY 12, 1780

SANTEE R.

COOPER R.   Moncks
Corner

BATTLE OF
MONCKS
CORNER
April 14

GOOSE CR.

TARLETON
April 12–13

ASHLEY R.   LINCOLN

CHARLESTON
SURRENDERS
May 12

March

Charleston

JAMES I.

JOHN'S I.

CAROLINA

EDISTO R.

SALKEHATCHIE R.

COOSAWHATCHIE R.

BATTLE OF
Moncks Corner
APRIL 14, 1780

FAIR
FOREST
SWAMP

BIGGIN
CHURCH

BIGGIN
BRIDGE

WADBOO
BRIDGE

Scale of miles

0   1/2   1

Moncks
Corner

COOPER RIVER

HUGER
FAIR-LAWN

To
Charleston,
S.C.

TARLETON

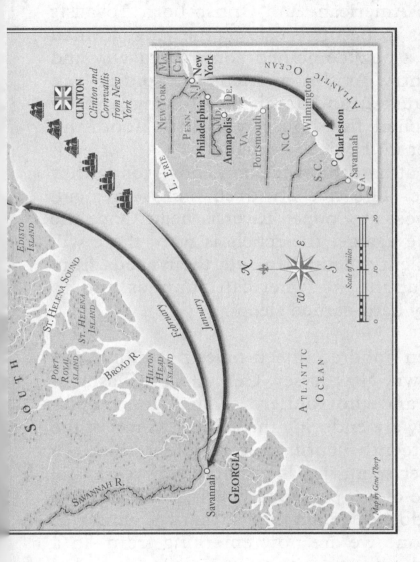

CLINTON

Clinton and Cornwallis from New York

SOUTH

Edisto Island

St. Helena Sound

St. Helena Island

Port Royal Island

Broad R.

Hilton Head Island

February

January

Savannah R.

GEORGIA

Savannah

ATLANTIC OCEAN

N

W   E

S

Scale of miles

0   10   20

Map by Gene Thorp

ATLANTIC OCEAN

L. Erie

NEW YORK

PENN.

Philadelphia

MD.

Annapolis

DE.

VA.

Portsmouth

N.C.

Wilmington

S.C.

Charleston

Savannah

GA.

New York

N.J.

CT.

MA.

men to travel undetected. Tarleton's men enlisted in America, and the ranks include both American- and British-born Loyalists eager to be of service to the king, formed into a new combined corps of cavalry and infantry. At this moment the soldiers are exhausted and famished, having already marched five hours with little food and water in the dead of night.

That hardship will soon end — or so they hope. The five-hundred-man American outpost at Cooper River is near. Once the battle against the rebels is won, there will be plenty of time to sate their needs from the abundant American supplies and to enjoy hard-earned sleep.

Seven hundred fifteen miles north, in Morristown, New Jersey, Gen. George Washington and the soldiers of the Continental Army are enduring the coldest winter of the eighteenth century, even colder than the winter spent in Valley Forge two years ago. "The oldest people now living in this country do not remember so hard a winter as the one we are now emerging from. In a word, the severity of the frost exceeded anything of the kind that had ever been experienced in this climate before," Washington recently wrote.

In all, twenty-eight snowstorms will ravage this winter encampment, with one particularly devastating January blizzard leaving behind snowdrifts taller than the six-foot-two Washington.

The haphazard log huts of Valley Forge have been replaced here in Morristown by neat rows of housing for officers and enlisted men. But appearances are deceiving. Food and clothing are once again in short supply, morale is at a low, and desertion is rampant. Of those who remain in camp, some are more likely to mutiny than reenlist. Indeed, a New Year's Day insurrection by soldiers from Pennsylvania led to the shooting death of a young captain. One week later, when spies informed British commander in chief Henry Clinton of the incident, he boldly sent a messenger to Middletown, offering cash to those men on the American side willing to defect and fight for the English.

The soldiers from Pennsylvania refused, a fact that did not prevent Lt. Col. Alexander Hamilton from writing to a fellow officer about the sad state of American independence: "Our countrymen have all the folly of the ass and all the passiveness of the sheep in their compositions. They are determined not to be free and they can neither be frightened, discouraged nor persuaded to change their resolution."

This is by far the lowest point in the war for Washington and his army. For Hamilton, however, the Morristown encampment is a boon. His social life has taken on new meaning — he is quite fond of dancing, parties, and the pursuit of the fairer sex.

It is common for local society to visit Morristown for an occasional evening of dancing and making merry. It was on one such occasion, in February, that Alexander Hamilton met and fell in love with a brunette named Elizabeth Schuyler, the twenty-two-year-old daughter of Gen. Philip Schuyler. The twenty-three-year-old Hamilton is utterly smitten, and for the first time in years, he has turned his intense focus from the war. The man who still believes that "a soldier should have no other wife than the service" now finds room in his life for affairs of the heart. In the words of Lt. Col. Tench Tilghman, his roommate at Morristown and another of General Washington's bright young aides, "Hamilton is a gone man."

Writing to his good friend Lt. Col. John Laurens (son of Henry Laurens), who is now among the men battling to save the city of Charleston, Hamilton describes Elizabeth in typically precise detail: "She is a good-hearted girl who I am sure will never play the termagant;* though not a genius she has good sense enough to be agreeable, and though not a beauty, she has fine black eyes — is rather handsome and has every other requisite of the exterior to make a lover happy. And believe me, I am lover in earnest, though I do not speak of the perfections of my mistress in the enthusiasm of chivalry."

Hamilton's letters to Elizabeth, whom he calls Eliza, are more romantic. "I have told you and I told you truly that I love you too much. You engross my thoughts too entirely to allow me to think anything else. . . . I meet you in every dream and when I wake I cannot close my eyes again for ruminating on your sweetness."

The turn in Hamilton's romantic life has begun to strain his relationship with George Washington. After almost three years of serving side by side, each has seen the other at his best and worst. Hamilton now longs not just for the favors of Elizabeth, but also to command men in battle — an honor Washington has already bestowed upon Hamilton's good friend Laurens, who is just twenty-five, and also on the Frenchman La-

*An archaic word meaning a "harsh woman."

fayette, a man two years younger than Hamilton and who has been commanding American troops in battle for years. Elizabeth, in fact, has saved Hamilton from the deep despair that enveloped him when Laurens was ordered south to join the fighting.

All-consuming and all-important, the war has come to define Washington, Hamilton, and Lafayette in ways that none of them could have imagined when hostilities broke out five years ago. More and more Americans are growing tired of the fighting and openly long for reconciliation with England, yet these driven three will not relent until the war is won.

The British, meanwhile, gleefully exult in the belief that the American collapse is imminent.

"So very contemptible is the rebel force now in all parts and so vast is our superiority everywhere," Lord George Germain will write to British commander in chief, Gen. Henry Clinton. "No resistance on their part shall be apprehended that can materially obstruct the progress of the King's arms in the speedy suppression of the rebellion."

That suppression is no longer focused on the battlefields of New Jersey, Pennsylvania, and New York. Other than minor skirmishes, there has been no fighting between the armies of George Washington and Henry Clinton since Monmouth, almost twenty months ago.

Capturing New York City and taking control of the North has always been General Washington's objective, but now he spends his time in a defensive position rather than attacking. The hub of the rebel strategy has moved to the fort at West Point, fifty miles up the Hudson River from New York City.*

While Washington waits in New Jersey, General Clinton and his troops are heading south, leaving behind a skeleton defensive

*Washington meant to attack New York in a joint land-and-sea invasion as early as July 8, 1778, after the battle at Monmouth. However, he was forced to remain in a defensive stance outside the city for a number of reasons, including the reluctance of the French fleet to sail into New York Harbor to engage the British Navy. The British have superiority in troop strength, and the rebel force is further compromised due to a lack of pay, clothing, food, and an all-around national fatigue over the war. The British officers' decision to focus their strategy on the south further weakened the size of Washington's fighting force when it became necessary to shift men from the North to the southern theater.

force of British regulars, Loyalists, and Hessian mercenaries to fend off Washington's troops, should they decide to move. With the vital southern port of Savannah now in British hands, General Clinton sets his sights on the crown jewel of Charleston, the most important seaport south of Annapolis.

Only when Charleston is captured will Clinton return to the comfort of New York City, there to serve out the war.

The British plan is simple: regain possession of the colonies one at a time by taking advantage of the large number of Loyalists in the South. Soon, the British Army in the South will reunite with their army in the North, in a great pincer-like movement, crushing Washington and his forces once and for all.

To the west the Americans are hemmed in by the Indian nations allied to the British who, throughout the war, have conducted raids along the frontier forests of New York and Pennsylvania and the settlements in the new territory of Kentucky.

While the French were once considered America's saviors, thus far they have been no help at all. Their navy sails for home at the first sign of a storm rather than fight, and without a naval presence, there is no way Washington can stop Clinton and his redcoats from sailing up and down the coastline or making landfall to attack wherever they like.

This is now Britain's war to win — and George Washington knows it.

Their first step is to capture Charleston.

By April 14, the British Army and Navy have almost surrounded the century-old port. The loss of Charleston would be catastrophic, the largest American defeat thus far in the war. Thousands of American soldiers would be taken prisoner should Charleston fall. Hundreds of precious cannon and muskets would be lost. The Americans are outnumbered almost three to one, and George Washington has been able to send only a few thousand troops to aid the Southern Army under the command of Gen. Benjamin Lincoln.

In truth, the British and Americans both believe that the looming battle is already lost. There is little chance for a rebel victory.

The lone glimmer of American hope is that Charleston is not completely surrounded. American wagons use a single narrow dirt road to ferry food, ammunition, weapons, and outside communications into the embattled port. The precious artery me-

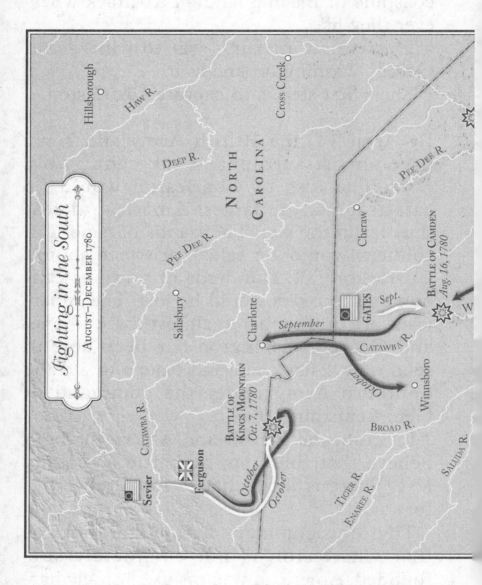

Fighting in the South
August–December 1780

Hillsborough

Haw R.

Deep R.

Cross Creek

Pee Dee R.

North Carolina

Cheraw

Battle of Camden
Aug. 16, 1780

Pee Dee R.

W

Salisbury

Charlotte

September

GATES

Sept.

Catawba R.

Catawba R.

October

Winnsboro

Battle of Kings Mountain
Oct. 7, 1780

Broad R.

Sevier

Ferguson

October

October

Tiger R.

Saluda R.

Enaree R.

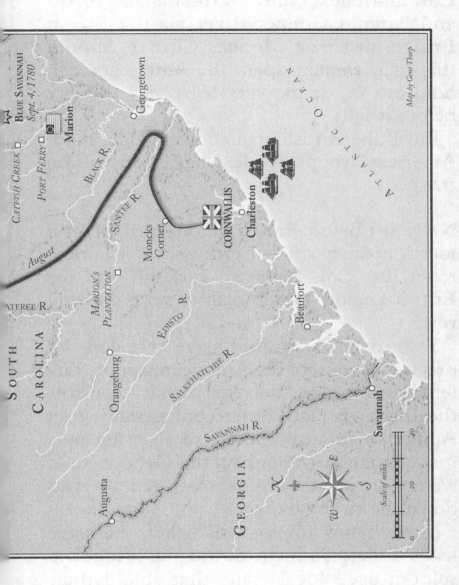
Map by Gene Thorp

anders from Charleston out into the South Carolina backcountry, crossing the broad and languid Cooper River via the Biggin Bridge, just past Moncks Corner. Should this road remain open, the Americans can hold out or, at the very least, flee the city before it falls.

But if the British gain control of the road, American troops inside Charleston will be trapped.

Now, just before 3:00 a.m. on April 14, at a location thirty miles northwest of Charlestown, Lt. Col. Banastre Tarleton and his British Legion march forth to seize the vital road.

Yesterday, a captured slave revealed the precise location of the American troops. Tarleton knows that the rebel cavalry controls the Biggin Bridge. But reconnaissance says American infantry units are sleeping in a meetinghouse overlooking the Cooper River waterfront, with others scattered up and down the river's banks.

In exchange for a small bribe, the slave leads Tarleton's men toward the bridge via seldom-used local trails that shield their presence. Thick forests and blackwater rivers, home to venomous copperheads and cottonmouths, hem in the path on both sides, making this corridor very dangerous indeed.

The night air is damp but not cold. As the British draw closer, Tarleton listens for the telltale signs of an ambush — the click of a musket being cocked, the inadvertent whine of a cannon wheel in need of grease, cracking branches betraying soldiers taking up positions in a thicket.

But he hears nothing. To his surprise, there is no evidence of a cavalry patrol guarding the road.

Though raised the son of a slave-trading politician in industrial Liverpool, Tarleton is used to the sounds of war. An officer in a regiment that remained in Great Britain, he volunteered to serve in this war and has been a part of the British fighting machine in America since almost the beginning of hostilities. As a twenty-one-year-old cornet he participated in the capture of American general Charles Lee in December 1776. His good conduct on this raid advanced Tarleton's career immeasurably. Promoted to brigade major, and now lieutenant colonel in command of his own newly formed regiment, Tarleton has fought in almost every theater of the war.

Thus far in those many days of fighting, Banastre Tarleton has not shown a proclivity for evil. His weaknesses are gambling and women, vices common to many soldiers. Neither presents a problem on the battlefield. Indeed, these shortcomings were easily overlooked one year ago, when Gen. Henry Clinton gave Tarleton command of the Royal Brigade.

But on this night, something changes in Lieutenant Colonel Tarleton. He will no longer feel the need to behave like an officer and a gentleman.

"At three o'clock in the morning, the advanced guard of dragoons and mounted infantry . . . approached the American post," as Tarleton will describe the raid. "A watch word was immediately communicated to the officers and soldiers, which was immediately followed by an order to charge the enemy's grand guard on the main road. . . . The order was executed with the greatest promptitude and success. The Americans were completely surprised."

The flustered cavalry commanders, George Washington's distant cousin William among them, are so astonished that they flee into the swamp, running rather than taking their chances fighting the British.

By Tarleton's estimation, well over a hundred prime Carolina horses are captured, allowing him to personally select the mount that best suits his needs. The British force also seizes food, weapons, and clothing while routing the Americans.

Tarleton's troops charge into the meetinghouse with bayonets fixed, oblivious to the sounds of rebel soldiers wishing to surrender. The slaughter is horrifying. The soldiers stab to death Americans who put up no resistance. One French officer, the major chevalier Pierre-François Vernier, is slashed behind the ear by a saber and then repeatedly cut — "mangled in the most shocking manner," in the words of one Loyalist eyewitness. The abuse continues right up to the moment of Vernier's death. In all, fifteen Americans enlisted men and five officers are killed. Hundreds more flee into the night, leaving the British in complete control of Biggin Bridge.

Adding to the carnage, Tarleton allows his soldiers to abuse the female camp followers, who are now undefended. In the wake of the fighting, two dragoons on a foraging mission travel from Moncks Corner to Fair-Lawn, a local plantation. The owner is Lady Jane Colleton, a widow and prominent Loyalist whose husband died three years ago. Despite her Loyalist stance, Tarleton's soldiers attempt to rape her, but she fights them off, only to be slashed by a sword.

Another woman is not so lucky. Thirty-six-year-old Ann Fayssoux begs Tarleton's men to "take her life and not to violate her person."

Mrs. Fayssoux's pleas are ignored. She is attacked with a sword, strangled, and finally raped. She survives, but is never the same.

For the next four weeks, Banastre Tarleton and his Loyalists lay siege to the surrounding countryside, sealing the road out of Charleston in the process. The fierce band roams the South Carolina countryside, seeking out and destroying any remaining rebel resistance. On May 6, Tarleton obliterates the remnants of the American cavalry at Lenud's Ferry, a crossing point on the Santee River. Men on horseback are crucial in the South, where villages are farther apart than in the North, making the loss of enormous consequence to the rebels. Now that he is in control, Tarleton's scorched-earth policy quickly becomes the talk of the South. General Clinton will write to Tarleton, "I wish you would get three legions and divide yourself into three parts. We can do no good without you."

It has now become a hopeless situation for the Americans trapped inside Charleston. George Washington had ordered Gen.

Benjamin Lincoln to retreat once the city became indefensible. Lincoln instead took pity on the city's civilian population, whose leadership pleaded that Continental troops remain there to protect them. Now more than 5,000 American soldiers and sailors are surrounded by a British army and navy numbering 13,500. Making matters even worse, some ungrateful citizens of Charleston have pledged to burn any American boats that might be used to evacuate Lincoln's troops by sea.

On May 12, after forty days and nights under siege, Charleston falls. The defeat is a stunning blow, giving the British complete control of Georgia and South Carolina.

More than five thousand officers and enlisted men are taken prisoner, the most Continental soldiers to surrender so far in the war.*

Three signers of the Declaration of Independence, Thomas Heyward, Edward Rut-

*Members of local militias were not taken prisoner, but instead allowed to return to their homes in exchange for not taking up arms against the British again. General Lincoln was held for a few months and then exchanged in a prisoner swap. The American Congress launched an investigation into his behavior, but it was never concluded.

ledge, and Arthur Middleton, are arrested and held in a dungeon at the city's Exchange. Fearing that they would somehow maintain contact with rebel elements still roaming the Carolina backcountry, all three will soon be transferred to a prison in faraway Saint Augustine, Florida.

More than a thousand of the captured American soldiers will spend the next year in Charleston Harbor, suffering in aging ships that have been stripped of all nautical accoutrement and transformed into floating prisons. Conditions will be horrid inside these hellholes, which reek of filth and teem with vermin. In time, many of these men will become walking skeletons, for there is little food. Disease will rampage through the confined air of the packed holds, and men will die from tuberculosis, typhus, cholera, and smallpox.

One American prisoner will describe life aboard a British prison ship: "At sundown we were ordered down between the decks to the number of nearly three hundred of us. The best lodging I could procure this night was on a chest, almost suffocated with the heat and stench. I expected to die before morning, but human nature can bear more than one would at first suppose. The want of bedding and the loss of all my clothes rendered me wretched indeed."

An estimated five hundred prisoners will break under the cruelty and accept a British offer to join their ranks. These men will be sent to serve on the tropical island of Jamaica, to prevent their once again joining the rebel cause.

Yet, even in the midst of this suffering, there is compassion. A woman named Elizabeth Hutchinson Jackson makes it a point to visit the incarcerated Americans, nursing those suffering from cholera. She is just forty-three but so haggard from years of struggle and the loss of a husband and two sons that a friend describes her as "a fair haired, very conservative old Irish lady."*

Jackson well knows the name "Banastre Tarleton," for the British Legion rode into her town shortly after the fall of Charleston and surprised the local militia, massacring more than one hundred rebel soldiers, many of whom were trying to surrender. A new

---

*Elizabeth Jackson's husband died in a logging accident at the age of twenty-nine. The tragedy occurred just weeks before the birth of his youngest son and namesake. His other two sons, Hugh and Robert, died as soldiers during the Revolutionary War at the respective ages of sixteen and seventeen.

term was coined that day, *Tarleton's quarter,* which means no quarter at all.

On that terrible day, Jackson tended the dying in a local Presbyterian church and also watched as her thirteen-year-old son became so enraged by the slaughter that he begged to join the fight. Eventually, the Continental Army took him on as a scout and messenger.

Shortly thereafter, the boy was taken captive by Tarleton's men. A British lieutenant slashed him across the face with a saber for refusing to clean mud from his boots and then sent him to a backcountry prison camp. It was Elizabeth who personally brokered her son's release, but not before he almost died of starvation and smallpox.

Now, attempting to alleviate the suffering of those incarcerated in Charleston Harbor is a Herculean task for Jackson, one made all the more difficult by the British insistence on viewing the captives as terrorists and adding to their misery with daily doses of mental and physical torture.

Inevitably, Jackson, an immigrant from Carrickfergus, Ireland, succumbs to cholera. At a time when so many are dying, her passing is a footnote and her place of burial forever lost to history.

But while Elizabeth Hutchinson Jackson

can no longer help the cause of freedom, the rescue of her son from a British prison will have an enduring legacy.

For, his name is Andrew Jackson.

And one day, during the War of 1812, he will get his revenge on the British, at the Battle of New Orleans, after which he will become the seventh president of the United States.

24

Port Ferry, South Carolina
September 4, 1780
5:00 A.M.

The Swamp Fox is being hunted.

It is a little before dawn when Col. Francis Marion orders his fifty-two-man fighting force to break camp. Word reached him just yesterday that a column of Loyalist militia is approaching. Colonel Marion normally prefers the surprise of an ambush, but this morning he feels the need to press the attack. Thus, his soldiers ride through the black gum trees and scrub oaks of this sand hill region along the Pee Dee River. They are farmers, Huguenots, teenagers — all mostly dressed in rags. To distinguish them from the enemy, Marion has ordered that each man wear a white feather in his cap. Marion himself wears a scarlet vest and a form-fitting leather cap inscribed with the words "Liberty or Death."

But now liberty seems a lost cause. The war in South Carolina is going badly. The land between the main cities has become a dangerous place of marauding mercenaries and militias. August has been particularly sticky and hot, and also a time of acute embarrassment for the Continental Army as the British continue to tighten their stranglehold on the region. Two weeks ago, the rebels suffered another stunning setback in the South when a force commanded by Gen. Horatio Gates, the self-styled hero of Saratoga, was routed by British soldiers under Lt. Gen. Charles Cornwallis.

Gates fled the battlefield at Camden, leaving behind nine hundred killed and wounded. Another thousand men were taken prisoner. None other than Col. Banastre Tarleton and his British Legion led the final, crucial cavalry charge. By nightfall, General Gates had run so fast that he was sixty miles north in Charlotte. His reputation would never recover from this act of cowardice.*

*Gates's military career effectively ended after the slaughter at Camden. He made a number of grave errors during the battle, including placing green recruits against the British Army's toughest

Most rebels didn't have the option of taking flight. As an example to any American who would defy the Crown, Lieutenant General Cornwallis made a public show of hanging a dozen prisoners. This vengeful behavior has now become the norm in the increasingly lawless Carolinas, where the British and their Loyalist allies routinely burn farms and homes, kill a man rather than let him surrender, and encourage religious feuds among Baptists, Presbyterians, French Protestant Huguenots, and Anglicans.

---

infantry and feeding his soldiers a diet heavy in molasses beforehand, causing many to suffer from severe intestinal distress, which limited their ability to fight effectively. The loss of troops, artillery, and the entire baggage train, coupled with Gates's inexplicable decision to retreat almost two hundred miles on horseback, left him in utter disgrace. Congress convened a court-martial, though the general's few remaining supporters ended the inquiry. After that, in 1782, he was asked to join General Washington's staff, but he was never allowed to command men in battle. Gen. Horatio Gates died in Manhattan in 1806. Like many figures of the Revolutionary War, he is buried at Trinity Church in Manhattan. However, the exact location of his grave has been lost to history.

The British success is based largely upon an aggressive campaign. Tarleton's dragoons, the main strike force, most recently defeated a band of eight hundred Continental soldiers led by South Carolina's own Col. Thomas Sumter. Like Gates, "the Carolina Gamecock" Sumter was forced to run for his life — and is currently still in hiding.

In the whole American South, there is now just one senior Continental Army officer left to press the fight against the British.

That man is Col. Francis Marion. Born in 1732, the same year as George Washington, the South Carolinian is a roughneck, and an independent man who owns a plantation and does not want to live under British rule.

At five foot two and weighing only 110 pounds, Marion is a thin, knock-kneed forty-eight-year-old with a hooked nose, a receding hairline that rides well past his forehead, and a prominent limp, thanks to an ankle broken after jumping out of a second-story window during a drinking party. Unmarried and childless, he speaks in the fractured syntax of the Carolina Lowcountry and is known for being hard on his twenty slaves. The British are now targeting Marion's plantation, and are soon to seize his home and human chattel.

The Swamp Fox, Col. Francis Marion

Marion draws on an array of skills for revenge. He possesses a thorough knowledge of the local swamps, knows how to live off the land, and demonstrates superior horsemanship. He is also an expert at guerrilla military tactics, due to his experience repelling frontier raids by bands of Cherokee.

Marion and his men attack by night and retreat deep into the swamps to sleep by day. They change camps on a daily basis, and post patrols at all times, to warn allies of the approaching enemy. News of Marion's success has already spread through America, published in newspapers and celebrated in Congress. "Colonel Marien," reads one report spelling his name wrong, "has surprised a party of enemy near Santee River, escorting one hundred and fifty prisoners of the Maryland Division. He took the party and released the prisoners."*

There is no more wanted man in the state of South Carolina than Francis Marion. He and his volunteers are being hunted in every swamp and tributary up and down the coast.

Further endangering Marion, the fall of Charleston has turned South Carolina into a haven for Loyalists. Fearing British reprisals, throngs of citizens eagerly swear an

*The words come from a letter written by Gen. Horatio Gates to Congress on September 9, 1780. Despite his hasty retreat from Camden, Gates is still in command of the Continental Army's southern division. The words were read aloud in Congress on September 20, 1780.

oath of allegiance to King George. Men throughout the backcountry and Lowcountry rush to join Loyalist militias, isolating Marion and his men in the swamps.

"I have given orders that all of the inhabitants of this province who have subscribed, and have taken part in this revolt, should be punished with the greatest rigor," Cornwallis says by way of proclamation. "I have ordered in the most positive manner that every militia man . . . shall be immediately hanged!"

On September 4, Colonel Marion sends a small advance unit of horsemen ahead to scout. The rebel band has now been riding for two hours, and the sun is turning the day uncomfortably warm and humid.

Meanwhile, the Loyalist force under Maj. Micajah Gainey approaches from the opposite direction. Gainey is not yet thirty, and the owner of a plantation in nearby Catfish Creek. The Tory militia he commands is local, raised from among the farmers and laborers living near his home. He now rides forth in search of Marion, knowing that a victory would surely make him a local hero among the Loyalist population. Traveling a few miles behind Gainey's force of forty-five men is another militia, of two hundred men. The two forces combined outnumber Marion and his rebels five to one. Major Gainey is confident of victory.

Just before 8:00 a.m., Colonel Marion's advance unit comes face-to-face with Major Gainey's scouts. To the surprise of the rebels, the Tory cavalry does not fight. Instead, they turn and gallop away, terrified.

Maj. John James, leading Marion's advance guard, orders a charge. "Come on, my boys! Come on! Here they are," he yells, seeing that the Tories are regrouping after a short gallop. It is a clever ruse on James's part, for he is now so far out in front of his riders that he is actually alone.

Still, it works. The Tories mount up once again and flee. In the fighting that occurs, fifteen escape, including Major Gainey. The other thirty do not, many of them killed.

Francis Marion quickly interrogates the new prisoners. Not only do the captives offer up the information he requires, but many also ask to join his militia — which Marion allows, though keeping the newcomers under close watch.

The colonel soon learns that an enemy force of two hundred men is three miles away — and waiting for him. Among their numbers are members of the British Sixty-

Third Regiment, which also fought in Charleston and Camden. The news confirms that it is the regular army hunting Marion, and not just the local militia.

This time, Marion does not attack. Instead, he orders his men to retreat into the thick pine and scrub of a swampy region known as Blue Savannah.

There they wait in the heat, harassed by flies and mosquitoes. Taking cover in the trees, they conceal themselves among the shrubs and await the fight. Marion did not merely order them to retreat, but also instructed them to race away from the battlefield as if in fear, hoping the enemy would think the day was won.

Marion has set his trap. It is a huge gamble, for defeat by the superior British force would not only slaughter this small guerrilla band, but would also spell the end of hope for many in South Carolina who still believe that independence and democracy can prevail over the might of the world's greatest monarchy.

Soon, the British infantry under the command of Capt. Jesse Barfield marches into Blue Savannah, its men not knowing they are walking into a death trap. Suddenly, Colonel Marion's rebels gallop through the British ranks, wielding makeshift swords made from saw blades and shooting down redcoat and Loyalist alike.

The British break and run, taking shelter in the swamps adjacent to the Pee Dee River, cowering in the thick grass and dark waters. One British soldier is bitten, fatally, by a snake. The remaining men wait until the safety of nightfall to wade back onto dry land, relieved to find that Colonel Marion and his men have called off the search for them. Two Americans are wounded, and two horses shot dead. Otherwise, there have been no casualties among Francis Marion's nimble force.

The British are not so lucky. At least thirty are dead, and many more wounded.

Colonel Marion and his men not only have won the day, but have also captured more than sixty Loyalists. Marion shows respect for his prisoners, knowing that, at war's end, they will once again be his neighbors and countrymen. He also displays restraint by allowing the remaining British to hide in the Little Pee Dee Swamp rather than hunting them down. For this reason, five dozen Loyalists switch allegiance, requesting that they be allowed to join Francis Marion's guerrilla band.

In this way, the insurrection gains ground.

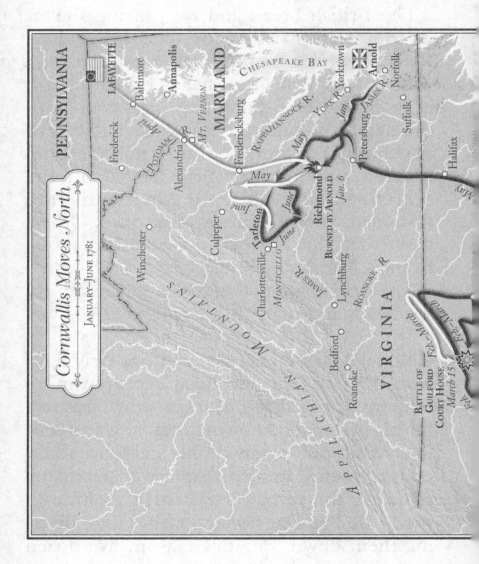

Cornwallis Moves North

JANUARY–JUNE 1781

PENNSYLVANIA

LAFAYETTE

Baltimore

Frederick

Annapolis

MARYLAND

CHESAPEAKE BAY

Mt. Vernon

Alexandria

POTOMAC R.

April

Fredericksburg

RAPPAHANNOCK R.

York R.

Yorktown

Jan.

Arnold

Norfolk

May

Petersburg

JAMES R.

Suffolk

Culpeper

June

June

May

June

Tarleton

Richmond
BURNED BY ARNOLD
Jan. 6

Jan. 6

Lynchburg

Halifax

May

Winchester

Charlottesville

MONTICELLO

June

JAMES R.

Roanoke R.

Bedford

Roanoke

APPALACHIAN MOUNTAINS

VIRGINIA

BATTLE OF
GUILFORD
COURT HOUSE
March 15

Feb.–March

Feb.–March

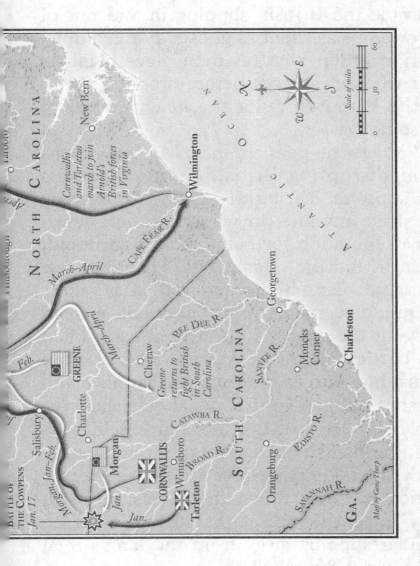

NORTH CAROLINA

SOUTH CAROLINA

GA.

ATLANTIC OCEAN

New Bern

Cornwallis
and Tarleton
march to join
Arnold's
British forces
in Virginia

April

Hillsborough

Cross Creek

March–April

CAPE FEAR R.

Wilmington

March–April

Greene
returns to
fight British
in South
Carolina

PEE DEE R.

Cheraw

Georgetown

SANTEE R.

Moncks
Corner

Charleston

Feb.

GREENE

Charlotte

CATAWBA R.

Salisbury

Morgan, Jan.–Feb.

Morgan

Winnsboro

BROAD R.

CORNWALLIS

Tarleton

Jan.

Jan.

Orangeburg

EDISTO R.

SAVANNAH R.

BATTLE OF
THE COWPENS
Jan. 17

Scale of miles

0   30   60

N E S W

Map by Gene Thorp

And as summer turns to fall, Francis Marion and his ever-growing army will continue to evade the British, slipping in and out of the swamps as silent as ghosts. For example, Marion orders that his men place blankets over wooden bridges before crossing them, all the better to quiet the heavy sound of horse hooves.

Wherever he goes, Francis Marion's focus is on disrupting British communications and supplies, leaving the enemy to think he can strike anytime, anywhere. Marion develops a reputation for being daring and bold, when in fact he is cautious. He takes few risks and plans his forays well in advance. He rarely overwhelms an opponent, instead drawing the enemy into an ambush. When the battles are over, Marion's men often return home to their farms and families and worship publicly in their local churches.

In response to Marion's battlefield success, the British burn plantations and crops. They mistakenly believe that these terror tactics will beat down the rebels. Instead, they have the opposite effect, swinging popular support away from the king's men and toward the rebellion.

By October 7, just one month after the Battle of Blue Savannah, Lieutenant General Cornwallis abandons his plans to invade North Carolina. This is a serious blow to the British Army's southern strategy, but one forced by Marion's growing control over the backcountry of South Carolina. His dominance is reinforced that same day when a thousand Americans defeat a large Loyalist force at a place called Kings Mountain. The fighting is horrifying, as vengeance sweeps through the rebel militias. Loyalist soldiers are shot dead as they try to surrender. Rather than leave the Loyalist commander, a Scottish officer from the British regular army, on the field after he is killed, the Americans allow his excited horse to drag the body through the battlefield and then strip the corpse naked. Even after the fighting is over, the Americans show no mercy — hanging nine Loyalists for treason.

Just one man can be considered Marion's equal in the art of brutal hit-and-run warfare. It is inevitable that Lt. Col. Banastre Tarleton will soon meet Col. Francis Marion on the field of battle. South Carolina has become the hotbed of the Revolutionary War, a place where more battles are fought than in any other state. And it will be Tarleton who will coin the nickname that will follow Francis Marion throughout history. The name is born out of frustration: Swamp Fox.

25

Long Clove Mountain, New York
September 22, 1780
1:00 A.M.

Benedict Arnold's treachery has begun.

Now the commanding general at West Point, he steps out from a thin forest of fir trees and onto the banks of the Hudson River. A rowboat, its oars wrapped in sheepskin to ensure total silence, eases up to the shoreline. Maj. John André, the dashing British officer who once courted Arnold's wife, Peggy Shippen, steps out of the boat. To avoid traveling in disguise, and thus being treated as a spy should he be captured, Major André wears his crimson officer's uniform under a thick blue watch cloak.

The war is now five years old, and it has been sixteen months since Benedict Arnold approached the British about betraying his

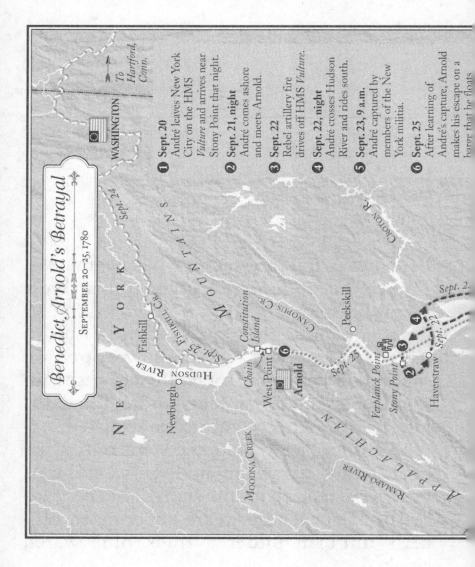

Benedict Arnold's Betrayal

SEPTEMBER 20–25, 1780

1 Sept. 20
André leaves New York City on the HMS *Vulture* and arrives near Stony Point that night.

2 Sept. 21, night
André comes ashore and meets Arnold.

3 Sept. 22
Rebel artillery fire drives off HMS *Vulture*.

4 Sept. 22, night
André crosses Hudson River and rides south.

5 Sept. 23, 9 a.m.
André captured by members of the New York militia.

6 Sept. 25
After learning of André's capture, Arnold makes his escape on a barge that floats

NEW YORK

Fishkill

Newburgh

MOODNA CREEK

HUDSON RIVER

FISHKILL CR.

Sept. 25

Constitution Island

Chain

West Point

Arnold

CANOPUS CR.

MOUNTAINS

Sept. 25

Peekskill

CROTON R.

Verplanck Point

Stony Point

Haverstraw

Sept. 22

Sept. 2.

APPALACHIAN

RAMAPO RIVER

WASHINGTON

To Hartford, Conn.

Sept. 24

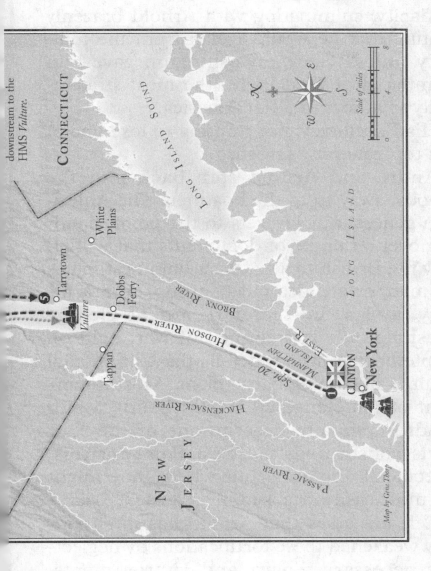

downstream to the
HMS *Vulture*.

CONNECTICUT

LONG ISLAND SOUND

White
Plains

Tarrytown

Dobbs
Ferry

Vulture

Tappan

BRONX RIVER

BRONX RIVER

HUDSON RIVER

HUDSON RIVER

Sept. 20

MANHATTAN
ISLAND

EAST R.

LONG ISLAND

New York

CLINTON

HACKENSACK RIVER

PASSAIC RIVER

NEW
JERSEY

Scale of miles

0   4   8

N
W   E
S

Map by Gene Thorp

country. The drama leading to this moment has consisted of equal parts caution and audacity, culminating with Arnold brazenly stating that he would resign from the military unless George Washington gave him command of West Point, the most strategically vital fort in all of America.

His Excellency, not wanting to lose one of his top generals, agreed.

André and Arnold step back into the woods, away from the boatmen. The American general quickly gets to the point, handing over a bundle of documents that will allow the British to seize West Point: estimates of manpower, location of troops and artillery, and a top-secret record of George Washington's last council of war, held on September 6, which details the Continental Army's upcoming battle plans. Most important of all, Benedict Arnold hands Major André complete descriptions of the four forts constituting the West Point fortress, specifically pointing out where they might be most easily attacked.

Left unsaid is that Arnold has intentionally weakened these fortifications by neglecting necessary repairs and improvements. His troops are scattered across the fort rather than concentrated at the weak spots. Also making an attack easier for the English,

Arnold has ordered a link removed from the heavy chain now strung from one side of the Hudson River to the other to stop British shipping.* Enemy victory will be as easy as sailing up the river and landing troops.

André is impressed. In order to ensure Arnold's treason, he offers a cash payout equal to fifty thousand dollars in gold and a rank of brigadier general in the Royal Army. Arnold is not impressed.

Thirty miles downriver, in New York City, British ships and troops are getting ready to sail upriver. The mission will begin as soon as André returns. The battle plan is designed to hide Arnold's treason: the British will as-

*The "Great Chain" across the Hudson stretched from Constitution Island to West Point. It was six hundred yards long. Each link weighed 114 pounds and measured two feet long. A series of log rafts along the length of the chain provided buoyancy, ensuring that the chain did not sink below the surface, and thus prevented enemy ships from sailing upriver. First installed in 1778, the chain was removed each winter to avoid its destruction by ice. Several links of the Great Chain can still be seen in a monument at the U.S. Military Academy in West Point.

sault West Point and a besieged Arnold will request reinforcements from George Washington, but will surrender before any help can arrive.

However, the ego of Benedict Arnold does not allow him to settle for André's offer. He demands more, suggesting that King George should grant him lands and a noble title if the British are successful.

Major André can make no such promise, and the tense discussion drags into the night. Hours pass. It is crucial for the secrecy of this arrangement that André be rowed back to the *Vulture,* the British sloop anchored downriver, before sunrise. Traveling by ship is the only guarantee that André can safely return to British headquarters, for the overland route is choked with rebel militia who are aggressively looking for the British.

The deal is not done, and André refuses to leave. Intelligence sources have confirmed that George Washington is now on his way to West Point. If the British can synchronize their attack with the general's arrival, the war will most surely end — and André will then be the hero. He must conclude negotiations with Arnold.

When the sun rises on the horizon, it is obvious that André cannot be rowed back to the *Vulture* until night falls once again. He reluctantly makes plans to ride through American lines to spend the day resting at a safe house four miles away. General Arnold has prepared for this eventuality and has brought with him a spare horse for André to ride.

The major well remembers the last instructions of his superior, Sir Henry Clinton, prior to the start of the mission: don't cross American lines, accept no documents from Arnold that could incriminate you if captured, and don't change out of your uniform, or risk being hanged as a spy.

Disobeying the order, André accepts documents from Arnold within moments of their meeting. With daylight now established, André and Arnold ride into American-held territory and toward the town of Haverstraw.

Maj. John André has now disobeyed two of General Clinton's orders. By 10:00 a.m. on September 22, he and General Arnold finally come to terms at a small house in Haverstraw. But André's escape is now in jeopardy. American cannon firing from the shore have laid waste to the *Vulture,* forcing her to withdraw downriver to safety. That leads to more disobedience — as André must now navigate the back roads of the

New York countryside to return to New York City. A pass issued by Arnold will guarantee safe passage for "Mr. John Anderson."

For the ruse to work, however, Major André cannot wear the uniform of an officer of the British Army during his flight. General Arnold offers him a plain set of clothes to wear instead. By the rules of warfare, André is now officially a spy.

About eight hours later, tucking Arnold's documents of betrayal into his boots, Maj. John André sets out for New York City under cover of darkness.

George Washington feels confident.

On the morning of September 23, 1780, he rides out of Hartford, Connecticut, with the Marquis de Lafayette, Alexander Hamilton, and the rest of his staff.* The general has just concluded some very fruitful negotiations with America's French allies, in which he has been promised extensive ships and soldiers at this vital juncture in the war. There is a growing belief that the British can be defeated through a well-coordinated offensive. At the same time, it is acknowl-

*Washington traveled light and fast, his party numbering just a handful of staff plus his bodyguards.

edged that the enemy is far from beaten and could win the war with a few effective moves.

Several scenarios of attack were discussed at the Hartford meetings, all of them incumbent on combining rebel ground troops with French naval might. This is the first-ever meeting between Washington and the Comte de Rochambeau, his French military equal. They are both keen to defeat the British Navy in New York, gain control of the harbor, and then launch an invasion of the city.

The key to the attack is West Point. Thousands of rebel soldiers and large amounts of supplies vital to the war are maintained there. Its fortifications must be powerful enough to repel a British assault. If West Point were taken by the enemy, American and French troops would be unable to invade New York, as British forces would be massed to the north, waiting to launch a counterattack. In all likelihood, the British could then surround the rebels and their French allies, a catastrophe that could spell doom for the American cause.

So it is that General Washington desires a firsthand look at the West Point fortifications, to reassure himself that all is well.

The general and his staff gallop along the

upper road from Hartford to West Point. A chance meeting with a French diplomat in Fishkill, New York, causes Washington a short delay. The Chevalier de la Luzerne is an old friend, an envoy sympathetic to the rebel cause. It was the thirty-nine-year-old Luzerne who loaned his own money to help feed Washington's troops during the harsh winter at Morristown.

So, when Luzerne enthusiastically requests some time with Washington, the general reluctantly delays his trip.

At first light on September 25, Washington and his aides ride hard for West Point. The distance is just twenty-six miles. Washington orders two young officers to ride ahead and instruct Arnold's staff to prepare a meal. Afterward, Washington will take a personal tour of the fortifications with General Arnold.

Washington arrives at Arnold's headquarters, across the Hudson from West Point, at 10:30 a.m. His Excellency is in a rare mood, sensing, after five long years of conflict, that victory is within his grasp. The thought of seeing Arnold once again also fills him with confidence. Despite the many headaches that come with such a tempestuous commander, Washington knows that Arnold is a man who will fight — unlike Gen. Horatio

Gates, whose retreat in South Carolina has actually heightened Arnold's stature.

General Washington steps into the wood-and-stone house serving as Arnold's headquarters. It once belonged to a Loyalist but was confiscated by the Americans. He finds it odd that Arnold has not come outside to greet him personally, but is reassured by the sight of Arnold's wife, Peggy, who is as beautiful and poised as ever. Washington is informed by a young major that General Arnold sends his regrets. He has been called away to West Point temporarily but will soon return.

An hour passes with no sign of Arnold. Washington is then rowed across the Hudson to inspect West Point, and still the fort commander does not show himself.

This initially pleases Washington, just as surely as the natural beauty of the Hudson River Valley and the site of the majestic fortress at West Point. "On the whole, I am glad that General Arnold has gone ahead," Washington comments, "he will give us a salute, and the boom of the cannon will produce a fine effect among these mountains."

But there is no salute.

Washington's irritation grows. He enjoys the occasional show of respect. On this day, reveling in the combined power of the Americans and French at his disposal, he is insulted by Arnold's rude behavior.

His temper increases when Arnold is not there to greet him at the dock. "Is General Arnold not here?" he demands of the officer there.

"No, sir," comes the reply. "He has not been here for two days, nor have I received any word from him."

"This is extraordinary," Washington responds, his curiosity aroused.

After seeing for himself the shocking dissipation and disarray of the West Point defenses, General Washington is rowed back across the Hudson. There is still no sign of Arnold, a mystery now in need of an answer.

"On my return to his quarters he was still absent," Washington will explain to Congress. "In the meantime a packet had arrived from Lt. Col. Jameson, announcing the capture of a John Anderson, who was endeavoring to go into New York with several interesting and important papers, all in the handwriting of General Arnold.

"This was also accompanied with a letter from the prisoner, avowing himself to be Major John Andre, Adjutant-General to the British Army, relating to the manner of his capture and endeavoring to show that he did not come under the description of a spy."

But the question remains: where is Benedict Arnold?

It was at breakfast, just after dawn, at the precise time General Washington and his staff made their journey from Fishkill to West Point, that Benedict Arnold was handed the note that would change his life. He was seated at the table in his home with the two young officers Washington had sent in advance, enjoying his morning meal with them.

Arnold read the note from Lt. Col. John Jameson, taking great care to conceal the growing sense of panic within, for he was most assuredly about to be found out.

In reporting the capture of a British officer by three members of the New York militia, Jameson, a Virginian in command of the outpost in North Castle, New York, was following routine military protocol. The enemy officer was taken into custody and was now being held outside the village of Tarrytown, New York. André had a pass in Benedict Arnold's handwriting, and that was what led Jameson to alert Arnold.

Jameson said he was planning to return André to West Point for questioning.

Arnold continued eating his breakfast as if nothing had happened. Yet his stomach was churning. At the moment, Arnold was the only officer privy to Jameson's note. With Washington just hours away, that would change, for Jameson would surely want to make the commander in chief aware of the British prisoner and the documents in his possession.

Benedict Arnold stuffed Jameson's note into his pocket and finished his meal. Excusing himself by stating that the letter was an urgent summons to his post at West Point, he called for his horse. He then walked upstairs to speak to Peggy, who was dressing for the coming breakfast with George Washington. She was four months away from giving birth to their second child, and their infant son was sleeping in a nearby crib as Arnold hastily explained that he had to run. The most important thing was immediately to reach British lines. He didn't know when or if he and Peggy would ever see each other again. Above all else, Arnold told his wife, she should not let on that she knows a thing, thus putting her own life in danger.

Shocked, Peggy fainted.

Arnold carried her downstairs, asking the young officers to look after his stricken wife. He then galloped his horse down to the

Hudson, where he took a seat in his official barge and asked to be rowed out into the river. To the surprise of the men at the oars, Benedict Arnold was not going to West Point.

Instead, he directed them south, to where the *Vulture,* now out of cannon range, waited patiently for the return of Maj. John André.

"At about 11 a.m. came alongside a rebel boat from West Point," the ship's master of *Vulture* wrote in the log for September 25. "Found it to be General Arnold, who gave himself up."

"Arnold has betrayed me," a devastated George Washington tells the Marquis de Lafayette. "Whom can we trust now?"

The general moves quickly. By evening on September 25, he takes charge of West Point. There is not a moment to waste. Men whom Washington personally considers trustworthy are placed in command; soldiers are immediately stationed at the weakest parts of the fort; and troops whom Arnold sent into the forests to cut wood, thus weakening troop strength, are recalled to battle stations.

Washington then orders that Maj. John André be transferred to West Point for questioning.

Later that day, under a flag of truce, a letter is brought to General Washington.

"On board the *Vulture,* September 25, 1780," reads the heading.

"Sir, the heart which is conscious of its own rectitude cannot attempt to palliate a step which the world may censure as wrong. I have acted from a principle of love to my country. . . . I have no favor to ask for myself. I have too often experienced the ingratitude of my country to attempt it. But from the known humanity of your Excellency, I am induced to ask your protection for Mrs. Arnold from every insult and injury. . . . I beg that she may be permitted to return to her friends in Philadelphia, or to come to me, as she may choose."

The letter concludes: "I have the honor to be with regard and esteem, your Excellency's most obedient humble servant.

"Benedict Arnold."

Peggy Shippen Arnold feigns ignorance of her husband's treason. In fact, when General Washington returns to the Arnold home on the afternoon of September 25, her tactic is to place all blame on George Washington — before dissolving into tears and hysteria.*

*Alexander Hamilton described the scene in a let-

Maj. John André knows he is in mortal danger. He is thirty years old and considers his life to have been "devoted to honorable pursuits, and stained with no action that can give me remorse." But as a military tribunal meets to discuss his fate at the

---

ter to his fiancée, Elizabeth:

I saw an amiable woman frantic with distress for the loss of a husband she tenderly loved — a traitor to his country and to his fame, a disgrace to his connections. It was the most affecting scene I ever was witness to. She for a considerable time entirely lost her senses. The General went up to see her and she upbraided him with being in a plot to murder her child; one moment she raved; another she melted into tears; sometimes she pressed her infant to her bosom and lamented its fate occasioned by the imprudence of its father in a manner that would have pierced insensibility itself. All the sweetness of beauty, all the loveliness of innocence, all the tenderness of a wife and all the fondness of a mother showed themselves in her appearance and conduct. We have every reason to believe she was entirely unacquainted with the plan, and that her first

Continental Army's camp in Tappan, New York, just a few days after his capture, there seems little hope that his life will go on much longer.

In hindsight, André's journey was initially uneventful. General Arnold had assigned him a local Loyalist named Joshua Hett Smith as a guide. It was Smith who provided André with the clothing he wore as a disguise. As the major rode through the New York countryside astride a black horse, in an old purple coat and tattered beaver fur hat, he hardly looked like a British officer. The great cloak thrown over his shoulders hid his appearance even further. The letters from General Arnold were concealed in the soles of his stockings. However, a trained

---

knowledge of it was when Arnold went to tell her he must banish himself from his Country and from her forever. She instantly fell into a convulsion and he left her in that situation.

Peggy was allowed to return to her father's home in Philadelphia. At first she was treated with great sympathy, for few believed she had been in on the plot. However, when the contents of Benedict Arnold's personal letters were studied, there was enough evidence of her role in the conspiracy that authorities demanded that she leave Pennsylvania and be returned to her husband in New York.

John André's deception is discovered.

eye would have noted that the breeches and white-topped boots he wore were more in line with those of a British officer than a backwoods American.

On the morning of September 23, despite knowing that André would soon be entering an area frequented by "cow-boys," local thugs fond of stealing cattle and otherwise harassing the populace, Joshua Hett Smith left André, fearing for his own safety.

So it was that, at nine o'clock that morning, three such "cow-boys" were surprised by André's approach as they played cards alongside the road. John Paulding, David Williams, and Isaac Van Wart were all members of the New York militia. Paulding had just escaped from a British prisoner of war camp, having stolen a Hessian soldier's clothes to facilitate his breakout. He was still wearing the coat when Major André addressed the three men. Even though Paulding had leveled a musket at the approaching traveler, André foolishly said, "Thank God I am once more among friends! I am a British officer out in the country on particular business and hope you will not detain me any longer."

Immediately, Paulding grabbed the bridle of André's horse. "We are Americans," he said. "And you are our prisoner."

Six days later, André now stands in a Dutch church in Tappan, facing the military tribunal that will decide his fate. Among the judges are the Marquis de Lafayette and Baron von Steuben. A letter from General Washington is read aloud, stating the charges and asking for a hasty resolution.

The board listens as André defends himself, admitting every charge against him to be true. It is the agreement of everyone present, Washington included, that André is a gallant young officer. He has shown himself to be honorable and courteous. However, the verdict is clear: André is a spy.

"Agreeably to the laws and usages of nations, it is their opinion he ought to suffer death," a transcriber writes.

General Washington agrees, setting the moment for André's hanging at 5:00 p.m. on October 1.

Major André is shocked, fully expecting to be returned to the British in a prisoner of war exchange. However, it is also common knowledge among officers on both sides that an American of the same elevated status, Nathan Hale, was hanged without ceremony by the British earlier in the war.

But John André does not show his surprise.

"Andre met the result with manly firmness," Alexander Hamilton, who witnessed the trial, will later write of the verdict.

George Washington does not want to hang Major André. He would much prefer to execute Benedict Arnold, but André is the one who was captured. Washington is utterly furious about the betrayal and would love nothing more than to see Arnold stretch a rope — so he offers the British a trade: André for Arnold.

Gen. Henry Clinton has a deep fondness for Major André, and a flurry of letters is exchanged between the generals in which the American concedes to an English request that his hanging be delayed in order that an agreement be reached. But the British finally refuse to exchange Arnold for André.

Knowing the end is near, the major makes a final plea to Washington: he requests death by firing squad rather than hanging.

"Sir, buoyed above the terror of death, by the consciousness of a life devoted to honorable pursuits, I trust that the request I make to your Excellency at this serious period, and which is to soften my last moments, will not be rejected.

"Sympathy towards a soldier will surely induce your Excellency and a military tribunal to adapt the mode of my death to the feeling of a man of honor."

Even after Alexander Hamilton pleads that this is a just alternative, Washington will not be swayed — André must be hanged.

On October 2, 1780, as Benedict Arnold enjoys the safety and luxury of his new life as a British officer in New York City, Maj. John André is led to the gallows just before noon. A length of wood has been laid in the branches of two trees, forming the crosspiece from which André will hang. He wears his British military uniform as he steps up into the back of a wagon, upon which an open pine casket already awaits.

The hangman adjusts the rope around his neck. A white handkerchief is tied around André's head as a blindfold.

"All I request of you, gentlemen, is that while I acknowledge the propriety of my sentence, you will bear me witness that I die like a brave man."

Then, adding his final words, André concludes his short life: "It will be but a momentary pang."

With the flick of a whip, the horse-drawn wagon surges forward, leaving Major André swinging in midair. He is dead within minutes.

26

Richmond, Virginia
January 5, 1781
10:30 P.M.

Benedict Arnold has unleashed hell.

Richmond blazes as the traitor sips whiskey in the City Tavern. Outside, on Richmond's Main Street, flames consume storehouses, foundries, and homes. Arnold, now a brigadier general in the British Army, commands fifteen hundred British redcoats, Hessians, and American Loyalists — many of whom stagger drunkenly through Virginia's new capital. The aroma of bourbon blends with that of wood smoke — from the copious amounts of sour mash, discovered in a warehouse, that Arnold's soldiers are now pouring into Richmond's gutters rather than leaving it behind when they march away in the morning.

Six long years into the revolution, Benedict Arnold has finally brought war to the state his former commander in chief calls home — and he does so with relish.

Yet despite his momentary appearance of ease, Benedict Arnold now lives in constant fear for his life. He wears the red coat with dark blue lapels of a British brigadier general — a permanent reminder that he has truly defected to the British cause. As such, he carries two pistols in his pockets wherever he goes, to avoid capture. Indeed, Arnold is well aware what will happen if the rebels take him alive. In the words of a captured American officer, "They will cut off that shortened leg of yours wounded at Quebec and Saratoga, and bury it with all the honors of war, and then hang the rest of you on a gibbet."

Thus far, the New Year has been a triumph for the traitor. On January 1, his invading fleet of twenty-seven ships bombarded Norfolk, Virginia, from the sea for seven hours, setting the port ablaze and destroying great portions of the city. Immediately afterward, favored by following winds, Arnold's fleet sailed quickly up the James River to attack the capital city of Richmond and its stockpiles of ammunition and supplies so vital to the rebel war effort.

Richmond is a city built of wood, from

the planks covering the muddy streets to the clapboards of St. John's Church, on Indian Hill, where, in 1775, George Washington and Thomas Jefferson listened to Patrick Henry so famously declare, "Give me liberty or give me death." It is Jefferson, the current governor of Virginia, who made a last-minute attempt to save Richmond by hastily forming a volunteer militia. But the two hundred men were no match for Arnold's elite force. The Virginians quickly fled the city, followed soon after by a seething Thomas Jefferson.*

Even as Arnold now feasts in celebration of his dazzling success, he has no idea how narrowly he avoided a public hanging. Less than a month ago, in his fury over Arnold's treason, George Washington concocted a bold plan to kidnap Arnold from his New York town house and smuggle him to New Jersey. A brave rebel soldier named John Champe would perform the deed, first by pretending to desert in emulation of Arnold, then befriending the traitor and offering to

*Jefferson's behavior as a wartime governor will lead to an inquiry into his failure to prepare for the invasion of Richmond. He will be found not guilty.

480

join his newly formed regiment of Loyalist soldiers, the American Legion.

At first, the plan went well. Champe made a great show of deserting to the British side, was embraced by Arnold as a compatriot, and successfully joined the American Legion. Once in position, he was poised to execute Washington's plan and bring the traitor to justice.

But on the very December night in which the trap was to be sprung, Sergeant Major Champe and every other man under Arnold's command were hastily ordered to New York Harbor for a journey south on board transport ships. So, rather than kidnapping Benedict Arnold, Champe spent that evening inside a dank hull, surrounded by enemy soldiers — all of whom would have killed him in an instant if they had known of his true intentions. Three weeks later, as Arnold's fleet arrived off Norfolk, Sergeant Major Champe could only watch helplessly as the British bombarded his home state of Virginia.

In this way, George Washington's elaborate plan to kidnap Benedict Arnold failed. As for John Champe, he is now among the men staggering through the streets of Richmond, his intended role in Arnold's demise not to be discovered until after the war.*

Thomas Jefferson was warned. On December 9, George Washington wrote the Virginia governor about a fleet of British ships laden with soldiers sailing south from New York. Yet Jefferson, now living with his wife in Richmond, failed to act — distracted by the birth of yet another new baby girl, Lucy Elizabeth. As always, Martha Jefferson endured a difficult pregnancy, and is now unable to produce milk for the infant, further concerning the Virginian. His failed last-minute attempt to raise a militia and prevent the destruction of Richmond will forever be a blemish on his record, but the fate of Jefferson's wife and baby are foremost in his mind right now. So great is his disgrace that he puts Virginia in further danger by delaying reports about the British invasion to George Washington, despite knowing that the general has the power to send help immediately.

*John Champe served in the British Army for several months before successfully fleeing back to American lines. He wished to return to combat immediately, but Washington forbade it, knowing that Champe would be immediately executed as a spy if captured by the British.

"Sir," Jefferson apologizes in a letter to Washington on January 10, "it may seem odd considering the important events which have taken place in this state within the course of ten days past, that I should not have transmitted an account of them to your Excellency, but such has been their extraordinary rapidity and such the unremitted exertions they have required from all concerned in government that I do not recollect the portion of time which I could have taken to commit them to paper."

A flustered Jefferson goes on to describe the actions of Arnold's troops in great detail, admitting that the people of Virginia are powerless to stop the British.

Washington responds by ordering the Marquis de Lafayette and twelve hundred troops to Virginia. Lafayette arrives on March 14. The following day, he links up with Baron von Steuben, who has already been sent south by Washington to assist Jefferson's Virginia militia.

In addition to confronting British forces, Lafayette has also been ordered to capture the traitor Arnold. George Washington is consumed by that task. He also remains fixated on invading New York, even though the focus of the war is now shifting to Virginia.

In April, the British warship HMS *Savage* drops anchor in the waters off His Excellency's Mount Vernon home and frees more than a dozen of Washington's slaves. Only the swift intervention of his cousin Lund, the property's caretaker during the six years the general has been away, prevents the estate from being burned to the ground.*

Meanwhile, Thomas Jefferson's personal and professional woes show no sign of ending. At 10:00 a.m. on April 15, young Lucy Elizabeth, just four months old, dies after a brief illness.† Jefferson has coped with death

*Forty-three-year-old Lund Washington went on board the *Savage* carrying a small amount of poultry as a gift to the ship's captain, pleading that Mount Vernon be spared. Later, Lund sent large amounts of livestock to the ship as a gift. George Washington, seeing this as aiding and abetting the enemy, was furious when Lafayette informed him what had happened — yet Lund Washington's actions saved the Mount Vernon estate from being destroyed.

†Thomas Jefferson's records show that he spent £108 for medicine. This translates to more than $18,000 in modern money. The notation was made on April 17, two days after baby Lucy's death, so it is not clear whether the money was for the infant or her ill mother.

on many occasions but is now crushed. The burden of loss is taking a staggering toll. Jefferson's grief is so enormous that he tells friends that "I mean shortly to retire" from politics.

Yet, simply stepping away from the job of governor is not feasible. For, on April 18, just three short days after Lucy's death, Lt. Col. Banastre Tarleton marches north from North Carolina into Virginia to join forces with Benedict Arnold. Jefferson responds by formally moving the Virginia legislature to Charlottesville, the small town just a few miles from his home at Monticello. Some seventy miles from Richmond, Jefferson can take refuge in his mountaintop sanctuary once again.

On May 28, he writes to Washington. The British force in Virginia has now swollen to seven thousand men. The redcoats further south have moved out of the Carolinas and are pushing north to join those already in Virginia. Jefferson's letter states that the war's focus is now the state of Virginia — and that Washington himself should come join the action.

"Were it possible for this circumstance to justify in your Excellency a determination to lend us your personal aid," Jefferson pleads, "it is evident from the universal voice that the presence of their beloved countryman, whose talents have been so long successfully employed in establishing the freedom of kindred states, to whose person they have still flattered themselves they retained some right, and have ever looked up as their dernier resort in distress, that your appearance among them I say would restore full confidence of salvation."

Yet, while the presence of such military leadership as the Marquis de Lafayette, Baron von Steuben, Cornwallis, and Benedict Arnold clearly suggests that the war could be decided in Virginia, Gen. George Washington is still focused on capturing New York City.

Meanwhile, on June 2, British troops capture a messenger carrying a letter from Lafayette to Thomas Jefferson. The missive reveals that the governor and legislature are hiding in distant Charlottesville. Lt. Gen. Charles Cornwallis immediately orders Banastre Tarleton to capture Thomas Jefferson.

And so, Tarleton and his dragooons ride hard for Monticello.

The year 1781 has not been a success for Colonel Tarleton. He failed utterly in his attempts to catch the Swamp Fox in South Carolina. Marion remained one step ahead of him at all times, moving stealthily through the swamps and demanding that his men travel dozens of miles in a single forced journey to evade capture. Cornwallis eventually recalled Tarleton to more traditional military operations before he was able to capture Marion.

On January 17, 1781, at the Battle of Cowpens, Tarleton suffered the first major defeat of his career when he and his men were routed by Continental forces under Brig. Gen. Daniel Morgan, a man who so long ago fought with George Washington at Braddock's Defeat and whose bravery helped secure the victory at Saratoga.

Then, on March 15, Tarleton lost two fingers to a gunshot wound at the Battle of Guilford Courthouse in Greensboro, North Carolina, where an outnumbered British Army defeated the Americans.

Now in Virginia, Tarleton once again undertakes a mission at the order of Cornwallis. On the morning of June 3, one hundred eighty dragoons and seventy mounted infantry gallop out of their camp near Richmond, bound for Charlottesville. They are determined to make the journey in just twenty-four hours — a goal that does not prevent them from stopping to burn a dozen wagons and other Continental Army supplies they encounter along the way.

At ten o'clock that evening, almost halfway through their journey, Tarleton orders three hours' rest for his exhausted troops. The dragoons dismount, water their horses, and enter a tavern to order food and drink.

A patron named Jack Jouett quietly observes the British cavalrymen, suspecting they are headed to Charlottesville and aware that the Virginia legislature is woefully unprotected. He is twenty-six years old, a Charlottesville resident, and a member of the Virginia militia who has signed an oath renouncing any loyalty to King George. Jouett also considers himself one of the best horsemen in western Virginia — a claim that will soon be put to the test. Finishing his drink, he slips outside and mounts his horse, then rides away to alert Governor Jefferson. The moon is full and clear after a long day of rain. Knowing the "byways of the neighborhood," the tall, broad-shouldered Jouett travels all night, remaining off the main roads to avoid capture. The thick woods scratch his face, leaving scars that will remain for the rest of his life.

By 4:30 a.m., a breathless and exhausted Jouett stands before Thomas Jefferson. The Virginian pours him a tall glass of his best Madeira wine as he takes in the news, then orders Jouett to warn the remaining legislators in Charlottesville. Both men know what is at stake, for among these lawmakers are three men who, like Jefferson, signed the Declaration of Independence. All will surely be hanged if captured.*

Jefferson begins his escape by evacuating his wife, their two daughters, and their slaves from Monticello by carriage. He directs them to hide at a nearby farm.

After that, Jefferson eats breakfast, taking time to observe the movement of Tarleton and his men through a telescope. The British troops under Cornwallis are laying waste to the Virginia countryside, burning homes and crops and freeing slaves. This will soon be the fate of his beloved Monticello, of that Jefferson is sure. Even more than the house

*The signers are Jefferson, Thomas Nelson, Benjamin Harrison, and Richard Henry Lee. None of these men will be captured. Though not a signer of the Declaration, Daniel Boone is also among the legislators in Virginia, dressed in the buckskin of a backwoodsman. He will be taken captive by Tarleton but later released after being imprisoned in a coal bin. The reasons for Boone's being let go are a mystery, but there are suggestions that he signed a pledge not to take up arms against the British.

itself, he will miss his collection of books and the years of careful notations he has kept, documenting the weather and all aspects of life here on his mountaintop.

Finally, when the Green Dragoon uniforms begin to encircle Monticello, Jefferson leaves his slaves behind to hide the silver and other valuables, then says a farewell. Just ten minutes before British troops arrive at his door, Jefferson saddles Caractacus, a six-year-old stallion and his favorite horse, then rides down the mountain on trails he knows well, unobserved by Tarleton's men.

Jefferson hides out in a remote house close to where his wife and children are staying. The Virginian will never again actively participate in the war.

Tarleton's men reach Monticello on June 4. Inexplicably, they do not burn the plantation to the ground. Tarleton himself focuses his search on Charlottesville, declining to go to Monticello. Another of Jefferson's farms, Elk Hill, is decimated by a British occupying force. Cornwallis himself uses Jefferson's home as his headquarters, and upon departure, he orders that the Virginian's tobacco and corn crops and his barns be burned. All cows, sheep, hogs, and horses are taken for use by the British Army. The house is spared.

■ ■ ■ ■

Benedict Arnold is also temporarily halted. The British commander Lt. Gen. Charles Cornwallis does not have a high opinion of Arnold and sends him back to New York City. Before he departs, the traitor has a piece of advice for Cornwallis: "Locate your permanent base away from the coast," he informs the British general.

It is a simple suggestion and hardly profound, but Cornwallis ignores it. After all, an officer of the British Crown does not need to heed the advice of an American traitor.

After a long summer of combat, His Excellency the Most Honorable Charles Cornwallis, First Marquis, returns to the Virginia coast in August 1781 and orders his army to set up a permanent base at exactly the place Benedict Arnold warned him about.*

It is a waterfront village called Yorktown.

*Despite his success in Virginia, Benedict Arnold returned to New York City an unpopular man. Many British officers still held him accountable for the death of Major André. Arnold did not help matters by being openly critical of British commander in chief Henry Clinton. In September

491

1781, he was given command of an expedition against the port of New London, Connecticut, just miles from Norwich, the town in which he grew up. In a savage display of brutality, he ordered his troops to set fire to New London. The local fortress, Fort Griswold, was captured in the fighting. The rebel troops surrendered after a day of heavy fighting, but more than one hundred survivors were stripped and massacred.

27

Dobbs Ferry, New York
August 19, 1781
Dawn

George Washington is on the move.

It is a summer Sunday morning as the Continental Army breaks camp and assembles for the march. Three miles to the east, a French army does the same, soon to link up with the Americans. The great day has come: at long last, the combined armies will march away from the fields and valleys they have called home these past two months. The soldiers believe they will soon be fighting in New York City, but that is not the case.

General Washington has long been focused on capturing the city. Just two months ago, British spies intercepted a letter from Washington to the Marquis de Lafayette in Virginia. Lafayette has used his small force

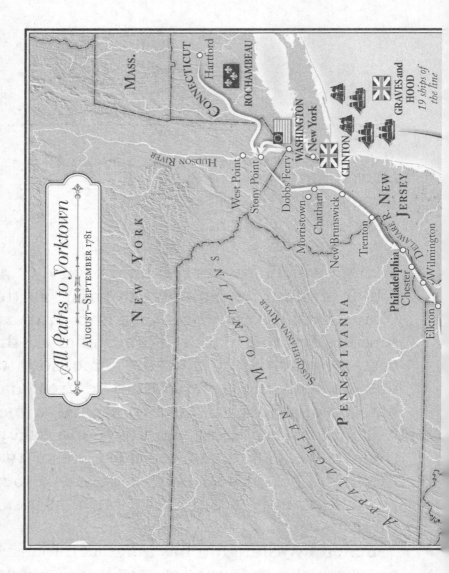

All Paths to Yorktown
AUGUST–SEPTEMBER 1781

MASS.

CONNECTICUT
Hartford

ROCHAMBEAU

NEW YORK

HUDSON RIVER

West Point
Stony Point

Dobbs Ferry

WASHINGTON
New York

CLINTON

GRAVES and
HOOD
19 ships of
the line

NEW
JERSEY

Morristown
Chatham
New-Brunswick

Trenton

APPALACHIAN MOUNTAINS

SUSQUEHANNA RIVER

PENNSYLVANIA

Philadelphia
Chester
Wilmington

Elkton

DELAWARE R.

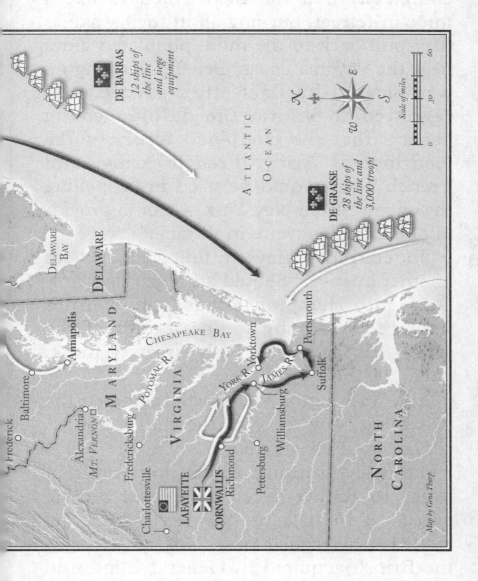

DE BARRAS
12 ships of
the line and siege
equipment

DE GRASSE
28 ships of
the line and
3,000 troops

ATLANTIC OCEAN

N
E
S
W

Scale of miles

0   30   60

DELAWARE BAY

DELAWARE

MARYLAND

Annapolis

CHESAPEAKE BAY

POTOMAC R.

Baltimore

Frederick

Alexandria
MT. VERNON

Fredericksburg

VIRGINIA

YORK R. Yorktown
JAMES R.
Williamsburg
Portsmouth
Suffolk

Charlottesville

LAFAYETTE

CORNWALLIS
Richmond

Petersburg

NORTH CAROLINA

Map by Gene Thorp

well, harassing Lord Cornwallis's army so completely that the British behave like a force in retreat, burning all in their wake as they pull back to the more populated cities near the Virginia coast. General Washington was pleased by Lafayette's success, but regretted to inform the dashing young general that the combined forces of the Continental Army, French Army, and French Navy would be used in "expelling the enemy" from New York — not in providing help for Lafayette in Virginia.

Undeterred, Lafayette followed up with another missive. "Should a French fleet now come into Hampton Roads," the marquis implored, referring to the mouth of the James River, "the British Army, I think, would be ours."

Still, Washington steadfastly clung to the belief that New York was the best option.

That would soon change.

Curiously, Washington did not write that letter to Lafayette in code. Nor did he entrust it to an express rider. Instead, he mailed it by regular post. Not surprisingly, the British acquired it. General Clinton in New York City was so ecstatic about possessing the American plans that he paid the mail thief two hundred guineas as a token of his thanks.* The British Army began preparing for the coming American invasion of New York.

Now, as George Washington watches the majestic might of the combined American and French armies sally forth to do battle, that blunder seems inconsequential. With about twelve thousand troops under his command, Washington has switched his strategy. Much has changed: Alexander Hamilton has finally left Washington's staff and has been assigned to command a battalion of light infantry; Lafayette has pushed Cornwallis all the way back to the Atlantic; and most of all, Washington has just received news that a French fleet of twenty-nine warships carrying three thousand additional marines is sailing north from the West Indies to support the American cause.

There were two stipulations to the French naval assistance. The first was that the ships must leave the American coast no later than October 15 to avoid winter storms.

But it is the second demand that was most consequential. Although Washington is very much the commander in chief of the Continental Army, the French are now the ones making crucial decisions about where the

*Approximately $34,000 in modern currency.

next great battle will be fought.

"There are two places for an offensive against the enemy: the Chesapeake and New York," French general John-Baptiste Rochambeau had written to his naval counterpart, Adm. François Joseph Paul de Grasse. "You will probably prefer Chesapeake Bay, and it is there we think you can render the greatest service."

The suggestion pleased de Grasse, for his decision to sail for America from his home base in the West Indies has left those islands undefended against British naval invasion. Virginia being closer to the West Indies than New York, the admiral opted to follow his colleague's advice.

Accordingly, Washington's entire force now swings south toward Virginia, some five hundred fifty miles away.

"An army is a machine whose motions are directed by its chief," one soldier will write of this day.

The British fully expect George Washington to attack New York City. The notion that he would move his entire army south, leaving New England and West Point naked in the face of a British attack, is so extreme as to be absurd. But Washington is now convinced that by going to Virginia he can trap Cornwallis and the British Army in a snare

— the Continental forces confronting them by land and the French Navy by sea.

"The moment is critical, the opportunity precious, the prospects most happily favorable. I pray that no supineness or want of exertions on our part may prove the means of our disappointment," Washington will write of what lies ahead.*

Lord Cornwallis is equally confident of victory.

From his new base of operations in Yorktown, just thirty miles up the James River, the English commander awaits the arrival of the British fleet. In addition to the marauding services of Banastre Tarleton, who has joined Cornwallis in Yorktown, a task force of nineteen ships with a combined firepower of fourteen hundred guns is now sailing south from New York City to aid Cornwallis's infantry. The firepower should be more than adequate to protect Cornwallis and his seven thousand men, and will continue to show the wisdom of his Virginia strategy. It is here where Cornwallis plans to win the war.

*From a letter to Governor Thomas Sim Lee of Maryland, dated August 27, 1781. *Supineness* is a word for inertia, apathy, or passivity.

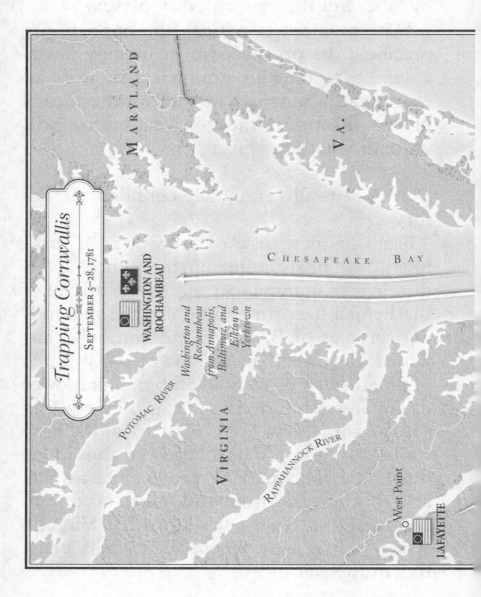

Trapping Cornwallis

SEPTEMBER 5–28, 1781

WASHINGTON AND
ROCHAMBEAU

Washington and
Rochambeau
from Annapolis,
Baltimore, and
Elkton to
Yorktown

MARYLAND

VA.

CHESAPEAKE BAY

POTOMAC RIVER

VIRGINIA

RAPPAHANNOCK RIVER

West Point

LAFAYETTE

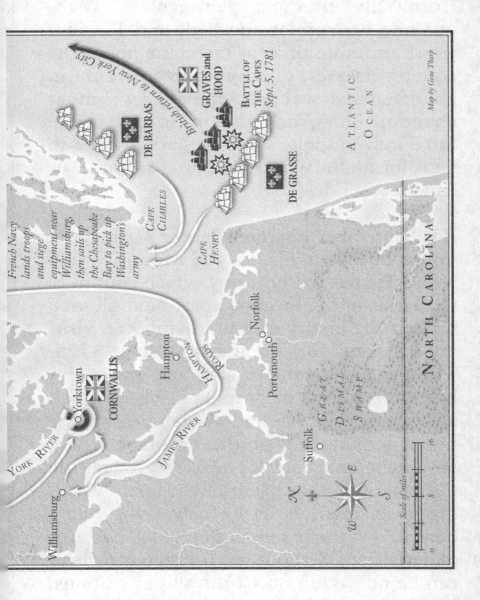

Map by Gene Thorp

"Now, my dear friend, what is our plan?" Cornwallis writes to a fellow general. "Without one we cannot succeed, and I assure you I am quite tired of marching about the country in quest of adventures. If we mean an offensive war in America, we must abandon New York and bring our whole force into Virginia. We then have a stake to fight for and a successful battle will give us America."

It is September 12 when George Washington says good-bye to his beloved Mount Vernon home. He has left his army, which continues to march to the Virginia coast, and allowed himself the luxury of a brief stopover, visiting his home for the first time since 1775. The general means to stay just one night, but the comforts of sleeping in his own bed and seeing Martha, and of standing on the porch looking out at the Potomac River, have kept him here for two. Yet, for all the nostalgia this visit has brought forth, Washington is anxious as he leaves his estate behind — the French fleet *still* has not materialized. Without naval firepower, there can be no assault on Cornwallis's positions.

Impatient and eager, George Washington races to Yorktown. There is no time to waste, for he has less than one month before the

French fleet's October 15 deadline, the date when they will sail away — should they ever arrive at all. The general has no illusions about the future of America's independence — once again, the nation is beggared by apathy; his troops are not being properly fed, clothed, or paid; and as a result, enlistments are tumbling. Yet, as always, George Washington finds a reason to hope.

"We are at the end of our tether," Washington writes to John Laurens, a compatriot of Benjamin Franklin in Paris. "Now or never, our deliverance must come."

28

Williamsburg, Virginia
September 28, 1781
5:00 A.M.

The French have arrived.

The sun is rising as the now combined French and American armies numbering nineteen thousand men begin marching the final twelve miles to the hamlet of Yorktown, where Lord Cornwallis and his army await. It has been a reluctant journey for the Americans. After six years, the war has become frustrating and protracted, with seemingly no end in sight. Traveling hundreds of miles to fight a battle in the south so late in the year is an immense hardship, for it means the troops may winter here, far from their families and homes. Their uniforms are threadbare and Congress is once again short of money, meaning the fighting men do not get paid. If not for French general Rochambeau arranging a loan to ensure their salary three weeks ago, the Continental Army would be fighting without compensation.

The American lines march smartly forward as the day quickly grows warm and humid, each man in step, muskets on shoulders as Baron von Steuben taught them at Valley Forge. But it is not the Prussian who provides their inspiration, nor the sight of their gallant new French compatriots, or even the rumors that the British may finally be on the verge of defeat.

Instead, it is the original soldier in the Continental Army, the general who has led these men since that long-ago winter in Boston. George Washington inspires, cajoles, and commands the respect of one and all. He now inspects the columns astride a tall chestnut horse with a white face and white feet, wearing his uniform of Virginia blue inspired by his time at Braddock's Defeat.

Much has changed about Washington since that massacre in 1754; these last six years as commander in chief have dramatically tested him. The general is just a few months shy of fifty years old but his brown hair has turned gray. Yet the energy is still there. A few weeks ago, Washington sur-

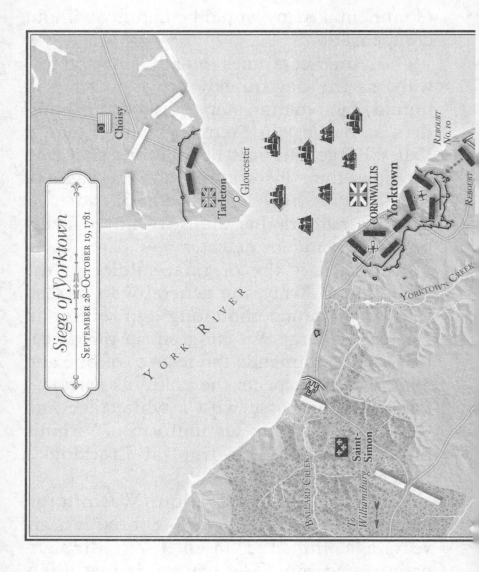

Siege of Yorktown

SEPTEMBER 28–OCTOBER 19, 1781

Choisy

Tarleton

Gloucester

YORK RIVER

CORNWALLIS

Yorktown

REDOUBT No. 10

REDOUBT

YORKTOWN CREEK

BALLARD CREEK

Saint-Simon

To Williamsburg

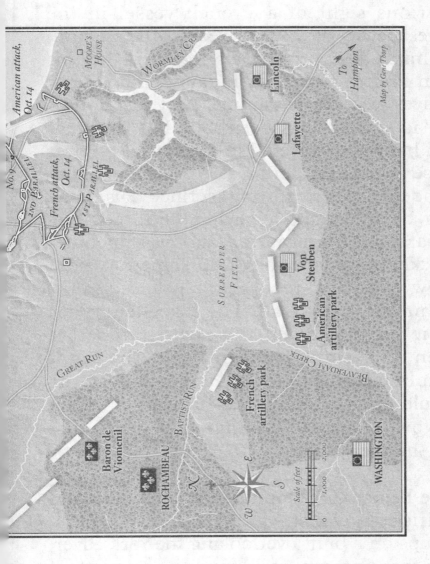

American attack, Oct. 14

MOORE'S HOUSE

WORMLEY CR.

Lincoln

Lafayette

To Hampton

Map by Gene Thorp

No. 9

2ND PARALLEL

French attack, Oct. 14

1ST PARALLEL

Von Steuben

SURRENDER FIELD

American artillery park

GREAT RUN

BAPTIST RUN

French artillery park

BEAVERDAM CREEK

Baron de Viomenil

ROCHAMBEAU

WASHINGTON

N

E

S

W

Scale of feet

0   1,000   2,000

prised even himself, jumping up and down and waving his handkerchief in joy at the glorious sight of a French vessel in the Chesapeake Bay. After weeks of hesitation, Admiral de Grasse finally realized that his own French army was in danger if he didn't deliver his fleet to Virginia. And so, he did.

The struggle has been long but Washington has never wavered in the cause — never once expressed doubt as to whether independence was worth the sacrifice. His home has been attacked, he has endured long separations from Martha, and his sometimes prickly personality has seen some top aides grow weary and request a transfer.

But through it all, His Excellency has believed that given the right number of men, the right location, and the right combination of timing and artillery, he would one day defeat the British.

Now, General Washington believes that day has come.

The British force, numbering nine thousand British, Loyalist, and Hessian soldiers, camps on a bluff overlooking the York River, but that waterway will provide no source of escape. The French fleet now blockades the entire Chesapeake Bay, including the York and James Rivers. It was only yesterday that

Admiral de Grasse finally began delivering on his promise of tactical support. Upon receiving the admiral's missive stating these intentions, General Washington immediately issued orders that the infantry march on Yorktown at first light. It is a landscape the general knows well, for the deepwater port was founded on land that once belonged to a direct ancestor, and Washington visited it several times in his youth.

Now it is Washington's turn to drape the noose. Upon their arrival, the American and French troops will form an offensive perimeter in a semicircle opposite the British lines. With ground forces in front of the enemy and the river at their backs, Washington will then lay siege, pounding the redcoats with artillery until they surrender.

Lord Cornwallis has always had misgivings about Yorktown. "The position is bad," he wrote upon arriving in early August. "I am not easy about my post," he added two days later, quietly making plans to flee back to the Carolinas with his army.

If there was ever a time to escape, however, that moment has passed. Cornwallis's decision to press the war in Virginia is proving to be a grave error. Now he can only pray that help will arrive before he is forced to surrender.

It is almost three weeks since British commander in chief Sir Henry Clinton promised that more soldiers were on the way, stating, "I think the best way to relieve you is to join you as soon as possible, with all the force that can be spared from hence, which is about four thousand men."

"If you cannot relieve me very soon," Cornwallis responded, "you must be prepared to hear the worst."

Day one of the Siege of Yorktown begins with George Washington rising from the ground where he has slept the night beneath a mulberry tree. His army is now one mile from the British lines. The baggage wagon carrying his tent has not yet arrived at the field of battle, so he happily slept in the open. Even when the tent is pitched, he will prefer the smells of Yorktown, the salt air, autumn leaves, and gunpowder, and he will continue sleeping outside on these warm autumn nights. Now that the Americans and French have the British surrounded, the general is eager to begin softening their defenses with artillery fire — but first he must carefully build the fortifications and gun emplacements that will ensure victory.

After a breakfast of soft buckwheat cakes, in deference to his painful mouth, Washington undertakes a personal reconnaissance of the British lines. It is soon clear that the enemy must wage a defensive war, waiting out Washington's offensive from within the confines of the town. Any attempt to break out by attacking into the American lines would be suicide.

The general walks within a few hundred yards of the British forward position, taking note of the location and size of each fortification. Yorktown is a broad plain covered in forest and punctuated by creeks and ravines. Cornwallis has constructed an imposing defensive perimeter around the town, encircling Yorktown in protective ditches, earthen mounds, and tall wooden fences composed of thick tree trunks. The forests around town have been felled to give his army a clear field of fire. The majority of the British and Hessian forces are concealed within Yorktown, along with the few thousand local residents and slaves who are also trapped by Washington's army.

Three hundred yards outside the town, Cornwallis has also built tall earthen forts known as redoubts to keep the Americans at bay. A typical redoubt is capable of holding one hundred men and is armed with cannon, and, because it is fabricated by digging a deep, wide ditch and using the earth to build a wall behind it, an attacker must first descend into the ditch then attempt to scramble up the sloping face of the redoubt. Long pointed stakes poke outward from each bulwark to further impede progress. The ground in front of the ditch is also lined with felled trees with branches still attached — an entanglement designed to further slow any assault.

Cornwallis has had two months to prepare. His defensive position is formidable, though Washington's force outnumbers that of the British by more than two to one. Washington's reconnaissance makes clear what he already knows: a ground attack on Yorktown is not possible.

Thus, the general makes plans to build earthworks and trenches of his own. General Rochambeau conceives a design that will run parallel to the British positions, one thousand yards from Yorktown. The trench will be ten feet wide and four feet deep, with room for thirteen artillery batteries.

A line of pine boards a half mile long is laid on the ground to mark where the trenches will be dug. Hundreds of soldiers are sent into the woods to gather vines and sticks, which are then woven into thousands of baskets. These are filled with stones and dirt, and formed into a protective wall to deflect enemy cannonballs. Work parties cut timber for shoring up the trenches, and oxen drag heavy cannon toward the front lines — but the moment has not yet come for these big guns to fire.

For a time, General Washington's army is no longer a fighting force but, rather, a construction crew. Planning for the digging of "the First Parallel," as the trench will become known, dominates every aspect of camp life. All the pre-attack preparations are carefully scrutinized and inspected by George Washington. Despite the French Navy's fast-approaching deadline for departure, the general realizes that haste could be ruinous. There can be no mistakes.

Inside Yorktown, malaria sweeps through the British Army, further reducing Cornwallis's beleaguered force.* With no need

*The Tidewater region of Virginia, where Yorktown is located, was known for being malarial. The gestation period for malaria is one month between the date of the mosquito bite and the onset of the illness. Having been in Yorktown for two months, the British had long been exposed to the malarial *Anopheles* mosquito. The Americans and French had been in the Tidewater region for only a few weeks during the Siege of Yorktown, and suffered far fewer instances of malaria.

for horses inside the tight confines of the town, the animals are slaughtered for food and their butchered corpses thrown down the bluff to rot in the river. The citizens of Yorktown cannot flee, and take refuge from the coming bombardment in the bush. Cornwallis himself makes similar preparations, noting the presence of a stone cave along the waterline that will provide protection from American shells.

Not that the British are passively awaiting the rebel onslaught. Cornwallis has assured his troops that the Americans lack the big cannon necessary to defeat them, and he launches coordinated artillery attacks of his own. The British open fire on the American positions to stop the construction that will spell their doom. The shelling continues around the clock, at ten-minute intervals. One shot comes so close to Washington and an army chaplain that dirt from the impact coats the reverend's hat.

"See here, General!" the terrified chaplain complains, eager to flee to safety.

"Mr. Evans," Washington replies. "You had better carry that [hat] home and show

---

However, one such American death was that of John Parke Custis, George Washington's twenty-six-year-old stepson.

it to your wife and children."

Day five, October 3.

Washington receives the welcome news that Banastre Tarleton's horsemen have been roundly defeated in a skirmish with French cavalry, suffering the death of one officer and eleven dragoons. Tarleton was thrown from his horse in the course of the action, but managed to mount another and gallop to safety. He will not fight again.

The conflict took place at Gloucester, on the opposite side of the York River from Yorktown. Tarleton and his men fled back to the safety of the British outpost along the waterfront. However, Washington had the forethought to position French and American troops on that shore. As in Yorktown, these forces hemmed the British in on three sides, with the river at their back. There was no place for Tarleton's cavalry to gallop their horses, and little forage with which to feed them. In time, Tarleton would order the slaughter of a thousand horses rather than let them fall into American hands.

Day eight, October 6.

Under the cover of rain and darkness, the digging of the First Parallel begins. General Washington makes a great show of symbolically taking a single swing of a pickax to mark the beginning of construction. The offensive line is anchored on the right by the river, wheeling in a slow arc to the Hampton Road. Fifteen hundred men swing pickaxes and entrenching tools, working through the night, throwing the dirt up onto the northern shoulder of the trench to form a protective barrier between themselves and the British cannon. Another twenty-five hundred soldiers fan out to protect the diggers. It is George Washington's hope that the rain will muffle the sound of the digging, thus preventing a surprise British artillery barrage to thwart the construction.

By sunrise, the trenches are all but complete. The hard work of moving the artillery into place will take three more days, but Washington and Rochambeau now have a secure line within easy striking distance of Yorktown.

And still the American guns are silent.

Day eleven, October 9, 3:00 p.m.

The trenches are shored up with timber. The seventy-three cannon, mortars, and howitzers are aimed and loaded, among them the devastating sixteen- and twenty-four-pound cannon. Stacks of ammunition, more plentiful than any man can remember ever seeing, are stacked and ready to be launched.

Finally, it is time to open fire.

In yet another symbolic act, George Washington "put the match to the first gun," as one American private will remember.

The cannonball from Washington's eighteen-pounder quickly finds its mark, smashing into a house where a British general and three officers are eating an early dinner. The barrage is devastating. Within seconds, French and American cannon up and down the line launch round after round. The attack is withering, an inferno of iron death emanating from almost one hundred guns. The firing continues almost nonstop for days.

There is nowhere for a British soldier to hide. Yorktown itself is being destroyed as cannonballs open enormous holes in homes and businesses. Writing about the trapped citizens of Yorktown, one Hessian soldier will report that "many were seriously and fatally wounded by the broken pieces of bombs that were exploding, partly in the air, partly on the ground, which broke arms and legs, or killed them."

Thick dust brought forth by the destruction chokes Yorktown. Rather than man the lines, many British soldiers huddle in basements, sometimes evicting residents to do so.

Death comes in many forms.

Even as the demoralized British deal with the effects of malaria, a new smallpox epidemic engulfs Yorktown. Also, food is in short supply. It is now the Americans who enjoy a hot meal and a good night's sleep when not on duty.

On Cornwallis's orders, the British attempt to fire back. But the nonstop American and French cannon fire is destroying many of their guns. Thirty-six hundred rounds per day now fall on Yorktown. So fierce is the allied attack that the barrels of their artillery pieces glow orange from overheating.

"On the evening of [October] 9th the enemy opened their batteries and have since continued firing without intermission," Lord Cornwallis writes to Clinton in New York.

On the night of October 10, the French Army delivers a cruel blow to British hopes. Cannonballs are heated over a flame until red hot, then launched at the few remaining British ships anchored off Yorktown. These vessels represent hope to Cornwallis, the vaunted power of the British Navy on full display — and perhaps an avenue of escape.

The French gunners find their mark. The frigate HMS *Guadeloupe* escapes, but not so the *Charon,* which becomes "enwrapped in a torrent of fire," in the words of one American eyewitness, "spreading with vivid brightness among the combustible rigging and running with amazing rapidity to the tops of several masts, while all around was thunder and lightning from our cannon and mortars."

General Cornwallis feels hope running out.

"We have lost about seventy men, and many of our works are seriously damaged," he writes in a desperate plea to General Clinton. "With such works, on disadvantageous ground, against so powerful an attack, we cannot hope to make a long resistance."

Day thirteen, October 11.

George Washington moves in for the kill.

No longer content to bombard the British from the First Parallel, he orders General von Steuben forward to dig a second trench. This line, called the Second Parallel, will be just three hundred fifty yards from Yorktown — close enough for the artillery gunners to fire more precisely. Instead of firing cannonballs at an arc to cover the long range, they will be close enough to ricochet them along the ground, smashing artillery pieces and severing arms and legs as they roll.

There is a problem, though. Even as the Baron's men work with spades and hoes to dig the new trench, their close proximity to enemy lines makes them easy targets for enemy cannon. In particular, a pair of British redoubts that the allies have numbered "nine" and "ten" make the completion of the Second Parallel impossible. British cannoneers, using withering cannon fire, zero in on von Steuben's construction crews.

Progress on the Second Parallel slows. The tense standoff between American and British forces, many of whom venture out into no-man's-land to snipe at one another after dark, grows more personal by the day. The anonymous nature of the siege, with its long-distance cannon blasts and passive resistance, is no more.

The French fleet is now just days away from sailing for the West Indies. Admiral de Grasse is eager to be away. General Washington knows that he cannot delay the construction of the Second Parallel for even a day. For this reason, he orders a bold attack on Redoubts 9 and 10. The French will attack 9. The task for capturing Redoubt 10 will fall to the Americans.

Washington has his choice of commanders. And he can think of no better men to lead the assault than Lt. Col. Alexander Hamilton and the Marquis de Lafayette.

Day sixteen, October 14.

General Washington offers quiet encouragement to Alexander Hamilton's four-hundred-man force as it prepares to attack Redoubt 10. Artillery units take aim at the British force within, seeking to soften the target. Lafayette had requested a more seasoned French soldier to lead the way, but Washington personally overruled the marquis to choose Hamilton.

It is 8:00 p.m. as three rockets light the evening sky. This is the signal to advance. Lieutenant Colonel Hamilton and his men begin the march across the open ground between the First Parallel trenches and Redoubt 10. Among his force are African American soldiers of the First Rhode Island Regiment. To Hamilton's left, advancing through the darkness at the same time, is an equally large French force, bound for Redoubt 9. Even after the rockets fade away, the night is clear enough to allow the men to see the planets Venus and Jupiter shining brightly. Sappers armed with axes move forward to hack away at the thick branches surrounding the British fortifications. Hamilton's men have not loaded their guns, knowing that close-quarter fighting will be more effective with the bayonet.

As Hamilton marches his men through no-man's-land, the sounds of fighting from Redoubt 9 can already be clearly heard. A Hessian sentry sensed the French approach and opened fire. The French are pressing the attack at an enormous loss of life — ninety-six French officers and enlisted men will die tonight, but Redoubt 9 will be taken.

"Things went very unmercifully that night," one Frenchman will write. "One screamed here, the other there, that for the grace of God we should kill him off completely. The whole redoubt was so full of dead and wounded that one had to walk on top of them."

Hamilton orders his old friend Lt. Col. John Laurens to march around to the back side of Redoubt 10 with a force of eighty men. Hamilton will attack directly from the front with the remainder of the force. Lafayette has remained behind to command his division at the right side of the American lines. This particular redoubt is square, and as the sappers sneak into position to remove obstructions from the perimeter, the British open fire with muskets and grapeshot. The advance unit drops thick bundles of sticks into the dry moat, allowing Hamilton's soldiers to walk over the abyss. These same men then hoist ladders up the side of the redoubt, allowing the American forces to climb up and over — and into the thick of the fighting.

George Washington watches from a distance, aware that the fate of his siege may well depend upon whether these redoubts are taken. He is still close enough to the action that a cannon shot might take him down.

"Sir, you are too much exposed here, had you not better step a little back?" an aide suggests.

"If you are afraid, you have liberty to step back," Washington replies.

Meanwhile, Lt. Col. Alexander Hamilton is so eager to prove his bravery that he does not wait for the sappers to finish their work. He orders his men to race up and over the walls with all speed, not wishing to waste a single ounce of momentum.

Climbing over the steep defensive walls, knowing that enemy bayonets await on the other side, is a bold act on the part of Hamilton. But his subsequent descent into the chaos of the redoubt confronts him with a more brutal reality, for this is the first time the twenty-four-year-old lieutenant colonel has the chance to kill with his bare hands.

Hamilton has fired upon men from a distance as an artillery officer, and witnessed death at George Washington's side in many a battle. But now he feels the adrenaline-fueled hyperawareness that comes from death's being just a bayonet or musket ball away.

As Washington pensively looks on from a distance, Alexander Hamilton and his men swing musket butts and thrust bayonets, ruthlessly hacking and killing the small band of defenders. Cries for mercy mingle with the moans of the dying. There are fewer than sixty British and Hessians defending Redoubt 10, and while they put up a strong fight, they are no match for the superior American forces swarming over the parapets.

In those nine minutes between the start of the attack and the moment Redoubt 10 falls, Alexander Hamilton engages in a rare battlefield emotion: pity.

It is a characteristic the British and Hessians have not shown the Americans in their moments of victory. But as it becomes clear that this battle is won, Hamilton intends to demonstrate that the Americans fight their wars differently.

"The killed and wounded of the enemy did not exceed eight," he will specify in his report. "Incapable of imitating examples of barbarity, and forgetting recent provocations, the soldiery spared every man who ceased to resist."*

But while Hamilton's men produce a minimal number of casualties, the fury of the British and Hessian fighters is such that Hamilton suffers nine dead from the daring frontal assault.

"Few cases have exhibited stronger proofs of intrepidity, coolness and firmness than were shown upon this occasion," Washington will write later approvingly in his journal.

*The "recent provocations" to which Hamilton refers is the slaughter of surrendering American soldiers during Benedict Arnold's raid on New London, Connecticut, six weeks earlier. Due to the British believing the rebels to be traitors, they sometimes showed little mercy. As one British officer wrote after a battle earlier in the war, "The Hessians and brave Highlanders gave no quarters, and it was a fine sight to see with what alacrity they dispatched the rebels with their bayonets after we had surrounded them so they could not resist."

■ ■ ■ ■

Day nineteen, October 17.

Construction of the Second Parallel trenches changes everything. The American and French gunners can now demolish targets with ease. Inside Yorktown, the British artillerymen can barely return fire, for their stores of ammunition are almost gone. Today is the fourth anniversary of British general John Burgoyne's surrender at Saratoga, and the Americans sense that another victory is close.

Inside Yorktown, the air reeks of rotting flesh. There is not a building left unscarred. There is no hope of escape and little reason to carry on.

Lord Cornwallis has no choice.

At ten o'clock on this Wednesday morning, a drummer can be seen standing atop the parapet separating the British and American forces. The field in front of him is pocked with deep craters, the results of shelling. There has been no attempt to bury the dead during the long siege, and decomposing corpses stretch across the bloody plain.

The drummer in his dusty red uniform can be seen but not heard, due to the continuous boom of French and American cannon. He is playing a universally recognized tune for a parley, a cease-fire. The drummer is closely followed by a British officer waving a white flag. Up and down the line, this signal of truce causes the crews of the big guns to halt their fire.

The officer approaches the American lines. He is hand-delivering a note from Lord Cornwallis to George Washington, a man the British once refused to acknowledge by rank, believing him their militarily inferior.

"Sir, I propose a cessation of hostilities for twenty-four hours and that two officers may be appointed by each side to meet at Mr. Moore's house to settle the terms of surrender for the posts of York and Gloucester," the appeal reads.

George Washington agrees — but on one issue the general is firm: the surrender will be on his terms and his terms alone.

Day twenty-one, October 19.

It is 2:00 p.m. Gen. George Washington and Gen. Jean-Baptiste Rochambeau signed the British surrender documents three hours ago, putting pen to paper, appropriately enough, inside a bloodstained redoubt. Cornwallis had requested that his army be allowed to sail home to England but Washington has refused this courtesy, knowing that the British could then replace them with fresh troops. Cornwallis was also denied the dignity of having his troops march out with colors flying, since the British did not extend the same treatment to the Americans after the fall of Charleston.

Instead, the British will be prisoners of war. They will be stripped of their weapons and regimental colors. Their disgrace will be complete. Ever mindful that history is made of small symbolic moments, Washington added a postscript to the surrender agreement in his own handwriting: "Done in the trenches before York, October 19th, 1781."

Now all that remains is for Article 3 of the Articles of Capitulation to be enacted: "The garrison of York will march out to a place to be appointed in front of the posts, at two o'clock precisely, with shouldered arms, colors cased, and drums beating a British or German march. They are then to ground their arms, and return to their encampments, where they will remain until they are dispatched to the places of their destination."*

*The captured British and German troops were

Now two long lines of soldiers face each other on a country road. On the right side are the French, dazzling in their glistening uniforms and military countenance. Despite their regal bearing, the foreigners have suffered grievously: two-thirds of the 389 allied casualties are French.

On the left side stand the rebels, many dirty and nearly barefoot. "The Americans, though not all in uniform or their dress so neat, yet exhibited an erect soldierly air, and every countenance beamed with satisfaction and joy," an eyewitness reports.

At the end of the columns, waiting to receive the official sword of surrender from Cornwallis, Generals Washington and Rochambeau wait on horseback. Admiral de Grasse, the man whose vessels made a British escape by sea impossible, is too sick to attend. Thousands of soldiers and locals have come to see this momentous occasion.

---

assigned to prison camps in Maryland and Virginia. Cornwallis was treated well as a general officer, being granted a parole by George Washington to join the British garrison in New York and eventually allowed to sail home to England. Benedict Arnold was a fellow passenger on that voyage, with both men reaching Portsmouth in January 1782.

But though the French bands played up-tempo marching music during the period of assembly, their instruments are now still. Observers will later remark on the complete silence reigning over what will come to be known as "Surrender Field."

Soon, the tattoo of British drums announces the arrival of the defeated army. Some eight thousand British troops are about to become prisoners of war. Marching eyes right, focusing on the French while ignoring the Americans, the entirety of Cornwallis's army advances down the road. Their newly issued uniforms are amazingly clean and bright, a supply of new clothing somehow surviving the shelling of Yorktown.

The British soldiers do not step with their typical precision. Their faces are haggard and insolent. "Their step was irregular, and their ranks frequently broken," one American later noted.

In a display of ego, Lord Cornwallis has chosen not to attend the public surrender personally. In his place on horseback, leading the British column, rides Gen. Charles O'Hara, the British second-in-command.

Upon arriving before Washington and Rochambeau, O'Hara extends his sword to the French general.

Rochambeau refuses to accept it, motioning for O'Hara to give the weapon to General Washington. O'Hara does so.

But Washington will not tolerate the British insolence. Instead of accepting the sword from O'Hara, he motions to Gen. Benjamin Lincoln, his own second-in-command. Not incidentally, it was Lincoln who, one year ago, remained in Charleston at the behest of the local populace and endured an embarrassing surrender to the British.

Lincoln accepts the sword — and then hands it back, an act of chivalry allowing O'Hara the honor of not leaving the surrender in disgrace.

Now it is time for each remaining British and Hessian also to surrender.

The scene is deliberately emotional, but it is the final moment of the British march that brings many to tears. For, in addition to the two hundred cannon and two thousand swords that Washington has captured, each British soldier must lay down his personal arms. Some cry as they hurl their muskets to the ground in great piles. Others grow angry when the order "ground arms" is given.

"Many of the soldiers manifested a sullen temper, throwing their arms on the pile with violence, as if determined to render them useless," one eyewitness later states.

■ ■ ■ ■

But the war is not yet over.

The rebels now control almost all of America, but General Clinton and his seventeen-thousand-man force are still hunkered down in New York. For once, the man who managed every detail of the war for so many years allows himself to enjoy the moment.

His Excellency George Washington immediately writes to inform Congress that Cornwallis has fallen. He then hands the missive to a trusted aide, who will ride night and day to deliver the shocking news.

The killing of England is almost complete.

29

Philadelphia, Pennsylvania
October 24, 1781
10:00 A.M.

Congress is jubilant.

An exhausted and feverish Lt. Col. Tench Tilghman stands at the front of their meeting room, reading aloud General Washington's report from Yorktown. As ordered, Tilghman has traveled three hundred miles nonstop to Philadelphia. He is Washington's longest-serving aide and has been entrusted by the general with ensuring that Congress quickly receive word of Cornwallis's surrender.

Lieutenant Colonel Tilghman has succeeded. The officer who once marveled of Washington that "the weight of the whole war may justly be said to lay upon his shoulders" now shares the joyous news that that burden has been lifted.

Tilghman galloped into Philadelphia shortly after midnight. He was nearly arrested, but upon sharing his good news with the city's watchmen, the word was shouted on street corners in the early morning darkness. Church bells soon pealed. Cannons fired at dawn. In order not to delay the celebration, Congress has decided to convene one hour earlier than usual.

As Tilghman speaks, the members sit quietly in their seats, savoring each word. This is the same chamber in which the Declaration of Independence was signed, but the original patriots left the Congress years ago. In their place is a new generation of American legislators, among them a Virginian named James Madison. In just a few short months, Alexander Hamilton will also serve in this chamber.

"A reduction of the British Army under Lord Cornwallis is most happily effected," Washington's letter begins.

There is more — another few hundred words of description and platitudes — but the delegates in Congress know all they need to know.

Once Tilghman finishes reading the letter, they stand as one and cheer. Cries of "huzzah" fill the air. A proclamation is issued, calling for a national day and night of celebration and thanks. The members then vote to march together to the local Lutheran church "and return thanks to Almighty God."

But the war is not over. George Washington remains vigilant, even conducting the grim business of hanging nine American deserters found among the new British prisoners of war. The general spares the lives of twelve other deserters, but orders that they be tied to a post and lashed one hundred times across their bare backs.

Washington lingers in Yorktown in case British reinforcements sailing from New York City arrive. But while an enemy fleet does appear off the Virginia coast on October 24, the British soon sail back to New York after learning of Cornwallis's surrender. That same day, October 29, sees the last of the British prisoners of war turned over to the authority of the Virginia militia for imprisonment.

Within two weeks of the battle, Washington knows it is time to return north. He sends two brigades of his army south to assist Gen. Nathanael Greene, who is still flushing the British out of South Carolina. The remainder of the army will march north to New York, among them General von

Steuben.

Admiral de Grasse and the French fleet have long overshot their deadline for returning to the West Indies. Informing "Mon Petit General," as the six-foot-two de Grasse refers to Washington, that it is time to leave, the admiral orders his ships south. It is November 4 when the French saviors finally sail away.

General Rochambeau, however, remains in Virginia. The climate suits him, and he is in no hurry to return to New York for the winter. So, the French stay behind as the Continental Army returns to the Hudson River Valley.

Sensing that there is no longer a role for him in the rebel army, the Marquis de Lafayette obtains permission from Congress to sail home for France.

"The end of this campaign is truly brilliant for the allied troops," he writes to his wife shortly after the siege, giving perhaps the best description of Yorktown.

"There was a rare coordination in our movements, and I would be finicky indeed if I were not pleased with the end of my campaign in Virginia. You must have been informed of all the toil the superiority and talents of Lord Cornwallis gave me, and of the advantage that we then gained in recovering lost ground, until at length we had Lord Cornwallis in the position we needed in order to capture him.

"It was then that everyone pounced on him."

On November 5, George Washington departs Yorktown. His stepson is about to die from malaria, and the general must return to Mount Vernon to be with a grieving Martha. He saddles his horse Nelson and rides home. However, he will not stay long, planning to winter in Philadelphia with Martha, enjoying months of congratulatory parties and festive balls as the celebration spreads throughout the colonies.

But George Washington is still a battle commander. And he will remain so until he hears from King George.

30

King George remains defiant.

Just two days ago, the news arrived from General Clinton in New York that Yorktown had fallen. It was Lord Germain, the cabinet secretary in charge of America, who received the shocking news first. There had been no previous communication about a potential defeat at Yorktown, or even about a joint American-French offensive against the British.

Unsure of how to proceed, Lord Germain traveled by carriage to the homes of two other cabinet ministers to seek advice. Within the hour, the three of them presented themselves to the prime minister, Lord North, at his official residence on

Downing Street. Speaking directly, Lord Germain informed the prime minister that Yorktown had fallen. North could not have been more distraught, pacing back and forth anxiously, flapping his arms wildly. "Oh, God," he cried. "It is all over!"

When later asked to describe the look on North's face, Germain will state that it was no different than "as if he had taken a ball in the breast."

The timing could not have been worse. With the opening of Parliament just two days away, and support for the war already waning, the king's opening speech would have to be rewritten. The current draft promises that the war will soon come to an end, resulting in a British victory.

Parliament must soon vote to continue funding British troops in America. Without money, British ships will cease to supply General Clinton in New York, and it will then be only a matter of time before Manhattan Island falls to a siege just like that at Yorktown.

A messenger is dispatched to the palace at Kew, where King George is spending the weekend with family. The man returns quickly with a reply. The king understands that the speech must be rewritten but issues blunt orders: "I trust that neither Lord

Germain nor any Member of the Cabinet will suppose that it makes the smallest alteration in those principles of my conduct, which have directed me in past time, which will always continue to animate me under every event, in the prosecution of the present contest."

King George will not give up.

The final draft of the new speech, written by Lord North and Lord Germain, arrives at midnight on the eve of the opening of Parliament. The king refuses to accept it. He will not deliver any speech unless it states clearly that his government will never accept defeat in America.

The king enters the House of Lords on November 27. He settles into his throne and begins his speech before the restless gathering. Of Cornwallis's loss, King George says very little, referring to the debacle as "very unfortunate."

He then continues, making it clear that he will not stop fighting. He demands "the firm concurrence and assistance of Parliament, in order to frustrate the designs of their enemies, which were equally prejudicial to the real interests of America, and to those of Great Britain."

But the lords in attendance do not support the king this time. In the subsequent debate taking place after George's departure, the antiwar Whigs assume the majority.

King George does not yet know, or perhaps does not want to admit, that it is finally over.

31

Benjamin Franklin knows the British are done and is about to exact revenge.

Four months after King George learns of Cornwallis's defeat at Yorktown, Dr. Franklin receives British diplomat Richard Oswald in his Passy home. It is Monday morning, and Oswald has spent the last week traveling from London, having just arrived yesterday afternoon. Like the Doctor, the Scottish-born Oswald, who made part of his fortune as a slave trader, is an elderly man. He is blind in one eye. Both men are in their eighth decade and have lived their many years in both England and America.

Oswald informs Franklin that the British government has given him no special instructions but is open to informal negotiations to end the war. But while the British are finally willing to discuss peace, Franklin is far more interested in payback. Since the war began, the British have burned homes and businesses and treated captives without the dignity usually afforded prisoners of war. They have also looted and plundered at will. In short, they have treated Americans with nothing but contempt. The issue to Franklin is not just peace, but compensation for these wrongs.

Franklin himself has suffered much at the hands of the British. There is no amount of money to recompense the public humiliation he experienced in London, or the loss of his once-close relationship with his son William. So, realizing that Great Britain's empire is tottering, Franklin presents an obstacle to Oswald's proposed negotiation with the utterance of one simple word: Canada.

The British path to peace began on February 27, when a resolution was passed in the House of Commons calling for King George to end the war. Despite his earlier threats to abdicate, out of shame for losing the colonies, the king defers. On March 4, the members get their response: George is in agreement.

That same day, Parliament passes a second resolution confirming that Great Britain's offensive war in America is over. The resolution reads:

This house will consider as enemies to his Majesty all those who shall endeavour to frustrate his Majesty's paternal care for the ease and happiness of his people by advising, or by any means attempting, the further prosecution of offensive war on the continent of North America for the purpose of reducing the colonies to obedience by force.

For good measure, the Parliament takes even more aggressive action on that day, recalling Gen. Henry Clinton from New York. In Clinton's place is a new commander in chief, Sir Guy Carleton. After returning to England, both Lord Cornwallis and Gen. Benedict Arnold allied themselves against Clinton, blaming the loss at Yorktown on his strategic ineptitude.

Surprisingly, Arnold has become a celebrity in London. No less than King George has been seen holding long conversations with the traitor in the royal gardens. The king finds an ally in Arnold, both of them believing the fight should not be abandoned.

But in the streets of London, the public response to Parliament's ending the war is so enthusiastic that George is fearful rioting might break out if he dissents.

Yet, while the British no longer wish to fight, they remain too proud to admit defeat.

This makes Benjamin Franklin wary. Writing to George Washington on April 2, the Doctor urges vigilance:

> The English seem not to know either how to continue the war, or to make peace with us. . . . I think we should not therefore relax in our preparations for a vigorous campaign, as that nation is subject to sudden fluctuations; and though somewhat humiliated at present, a little success in the West Indies may dissipate their present fears, recall their natural insolence, and occasion the interruption of negotiation and a continuance of the war.

Benjamin Franklin does not plan to make things easy for England. His contention that the king should give the colony of Canada to America for restitution is an outrageous demand. Canada is not Oswald's to give; nor does Franklin really expect it. Instead, the Doctor's audacious request is a statement to the British that the Americans will not be content with simply gaining independence.

"We do not consider ourselves as under necessary bargaining for a thing that is our own — which we have bought at the expense of much blood and treasure — and which we are in possession of."*

So it is that the seventy-seven-year-old Pennsylvanian, living comfortably in a Paris suburb, now holds power over the British Empire.

For Dr. Benjamin Franklin, revenge is indeed sweet.

*While Franklin did not gain Canada for America, he did get fishing rights for the United States — a privilege that exists to this day.

32

The British and their Loyalist sympathizers are trapped.

As peace talks continue in Paris, Benjamin Franklin's son William panics. Like many Loyalists, he has come to New York City seeking sanctuary. But Article 10 of Lord Cornwallis's capitulation agreement at Yorktown strips the Tories of all protection from justice.* When the British inevitably sail home, the Loyalists will be treated not as prisoners of war but as traitors. Now, here at New York's Assembly Hall, the younger Franklin gathers with other Loyal-

*In America, a Tory was an American colonist supporting the British cause. In Parliament, a Tory was a conservative voting in favor of King George's policies.

ists to write a petition requesting the king's protection.

"Great Britain thus permits her friends to be sacrificed," writes one New York Loyalist. "A halter will be the only reward a great many of them will receive for their loyalty."*

William Franklin longs to make his home in London, but his request to leave New York was denied by Gen. Henry Clinton before the general's departure three months ago. Franklin serves as president of the Board of Associated Loyalists and is so popular that one group of Loyalists has nicknamed their corner of New York City "Fort Franklin." Clinton believed that Franklin's presence in New York would bolster Loyalist spirits, sending a defiant message that all was not lost. Indeed, acting on his own authority as president of the board, William Franklin sentenced a captured American soldier to death to avenge the hanging of a Loyalist.

That action outraged General Washington, who now demands that Franklin be handed

*A halter is draped around the head of a horse to guide its movements. It is often synonymous with a hangman's noose. Most infamously, Judas Iscariot is thought to have hanged himself with a halter after his betrayal of Jesus.

548

over to the Americans to stand trial. Washington has established headquarters in Newburgh, fifty-five miles north of New York City. Though he is still wary of the British, His Excellency is comforted by the fact that American prisoners of war are now being loaded on board ships to be returned from England. That knowledge, plus the imminent departure of the French general Rochambeau and his men for the West Indies, is making it obvious to Washington that his invasion of New York City will be impossible. Thus, he begins ordering that all wagons and horses that were borrowed by the military be returned to their rightful owners, a sure sign that the war is coming to an end.

It has been years since New York City, nestled on the southern tip of Manhattan island, has seen any military action, but the island city has suffered terribly from over-crowding and deprivation. A fire in 1776, set by fleeing Americans bent on denying New York to the British, destroyed a fourth of the city, which has never been rebuilt. Two fires in later years burned additional sections. Soldiers live largely in tent camps and hut villages outside of the city, but the army nonetheless requires large amounts of storage space for food, fuel, hay, clothing, equipment, and munitions. All of the army's administrative activities are centered in the city, requiring the presence of staff officers, clerks, and countless others. All of these people need housing, as do the thousands of refugees who have flocked to the city. Hundreds of craftsmen and laborers maintain the navy's ships and the army's wagons, arms, and equipment.

Even though many inhabitants fled the British occupation, there is a constant struggle to find quarters for everyone. The crowded conditions resulted in problems with sanitation and crime. Every space in every building is put to use, some rented, some appropriated by the army, some taken by opportunists. American army prisoners of war are crammed into the Sugar House, a large warehouse in the middle of town; naval prisoners suffer on old ships anchored in the harbor. Hulks of abandoned merchant vessels litter the shoreline. Bored soldiers, sailors, and refugees find alcohol cheap and plentiful, and it fuels abuses that military policing can never fully restrain.

But as difficult as life in New York might be, for the British the city is vital. Its harbor and location make New York the hub of all British commerce. For this reason, King

George maintains a strong military presence in Manhattan. Even if America is granted independence, the king would very much like to continue occupying New York — forever.

On August 10, with George Washington still demanding William Franklin's arrest, a group of Loyalists gathers and votes that it would be best for their cause if Franklin sailed to England and presented their petition for protection personally to the king.

A few days later, William Franklin departs for London, never again to return to America.

Benjamin Franklin's son is finally safe from George Washington's hanging noose, but for those who remain in New York City, there is little safety and little hope.

33

Thomas Jefferson is grief-stricken.

The Virginian has hovered at his wife's bedside for four months. Since the birth of a daughter in June, Martha has failed to regain her health. Jefferson has personally administered his wife's medicines and nursed her, aided by his sister and sister-in-law. It has been this way all through the heat of the summer. When Martha sleeps, Jefferson spends his time writing in a small room just off her bedroom, making sure to be near if she calls out in need.

Jefferson has long known that his wife will die young. Martha knows it, too, and has extracted a promise from him that he never remarry. She "could not die happy if she thought her . . . children were ever to have a stepmother brought in over them."

Jefferson agreed.

Now, at the instruction of his sister (also named Martha), slaves help a devastated Thomas Jefferson leave his wife's bedchamber. His sister believes his grief will be so great as to kill him, should he witness the death of his wife.

In her final days, Martha struggled to copy a quotation on death from her favorite novel, Laurence Sterne's *The Life and Opinions of Tristram Shandy, Gentleman.** As Thomas Jefferson begins the process of burning all her letters to protect forever the privacy of their love from the world, he wraps this last piece of her handwriting in a lock of her hair and hides it in his writing desk, so that Martha will always be with him.

Martha Skelton Jefferson, thirty-four years old, passes away from complications of childbirth. She leaves behind three daugh-

*The Life and Opinions of Tristram Shandy, Gentleman, was a novel in nine volumes based on the life of a fictitious narrator. Despite its lightweight tone and often graphic subject matter, its metaphysical bent led German philosopher Arthur Schopenhauer to describe it as one of the greatest novels ever written.

ters and a husband who will never break his deathbed vow.

It is weeks before Thomas Jefferson has the will to rise from bed to face the world. As the autumn of 1782 descends over Monticello, he begins wandering the estate aimlessly, sometimes attended to by his nine-year-old daughter, Martha. In time, she will become his steadfast companion and confidante, privy to his innermost thoughts. One day, when her father becomes president of the United States, young Martha will be formally known as the First Lady.

But now, as the leaves fall at Monticello, settling onto the graves of her mother and three siblings, buried in the nearby family cemetery, Martha is only a young girl bearing witness to the depths of her father's pain.

Late in 1782, an event occurs that will change the path of Thomas Jefferson's life. Congress requests that he sail to Paris to help Benjamin Franklin negotiate the peace with Great Britain.

In the past, Jefferson would have denied Congress, for his devotion to his wife and children always came first. But the time has come for him to reinsert himself into public life and his once-prominent position at the forefront of independence.

Thomas Jefferson accepts.

34

Paris, France
January 21, 1783
Day

Thomas Jefferson never reaches Paris. Foul winter weather prevents the Virginian from making the twenty-five-day sail across the Atlantic. Nonetheless, he has reengaged with public life.

Therefore, John Jay, U.S. ambassador to Spain, and John Adams, ambassador to Holland, have traveled to the French capital to assist in negotiating the end of the war. But it is the tireless Benjamin Franklin, now in his eighth year as America's diplomat in Paris, who leads the way through the labyrinthine peace talks.

Two years ago, Franklin was sharply critical of the prickly Adams's confrontational negotiating style. But their time together has been restorative for the two signers of the Declaration of Independence. The past few months have seen a return of their friendship.*

It has taken almost a year for the specifics of the treaty to be worked out, but now Franklin pens a historical letter to Congress:

"The preliminaries of peace between France, Spain, and England were yesterday signed, and a cessation of arms agreed to by the ministers of those powers, and by us in behalf of the United States. I congratulate you and our country on the happy prospects afforded us by the finishing so speedily this glorious revolution."†

*The American delegation was to have numbered five men. In addition to Franklin, Adams, Jay, and the waylaid Jefferson, Henry Laurens of South Carolina was unable to attend due to ill health after spending a year imprisoned in the Tower of London. Laurens was captured at sea by a British warship. He was released in a prisoner exchange with General Cornwallis three months after the Battle of Yorktown.

†America and Great Britain signed a separate preliminary peace treaty on November 30, 1782. This document did not include the other powers involved in the war, and thus did not guarantee a cessation of fighting.

■ ■ ■ ■

It is Valentine's Day in London as King George finally admits defeat.

Despite a series of surprising British naval victories against the French in the West Indies that could prolong the war, the king bows to public pressure and issues a proclamation calling for an end to the fighting.

"We do hereby strictly charge and command all our officers, both at sea and land, and all other our subjects whatsoever, to forebear all acts of hostility, either by sea or land, against . . . the United States of America."

Two months later, the Continental Congress meets in Philadelphia to discuss the news from Europe concerning peace.

A resolution is put forth, requesting whether "it be our will and pleasure that the cessation of hostilities between the United States of America and his Britannic Majesty should be conformable." The measure goes on to state, "We hereby strictly charge and command all our officers, both by sea and land, and other subjects of these United States, to forebear all acts of hostility, either by sea or land, against his Britan-

George Washington, aged by war

nic Majesty or his subjects."

The motion passes by a unanimous vote.

April 19, 1783, will mark eight long years to the day since the Revolutionary War began in Lexington and Concord, Massachusetts.

George Washington is now fifty-one. The war has aged him. He is well over two hundred pounds, far from the lean, athletic horseman he was in the years prior to taking command. He has grown weary of the pressures of command and longs to return to Mount Vernon, where Martha has been ill with ongoing abdominal problems. There is also the matter of recapturing his many slaves, who either ran off during the war or took refuge with the British.

Yet, those matters, while pressing, do not preoccupy the general's mind today. Instead, he writes a letter from his headquarters in Newburgh, New York, where he has spent the last year. Washington has written thousands of letters over the course of the war, but none as wondrous as the missive he now composes. Directed by Congress to formally declare the end of fighting to his men, His Excellency allows his innermost emotions to flow onto the page.

"The Commander in Chief orders the cessation of hostilities, between the United States of America and the King of Great Britain," he begins. "The Commander in Chief, far from endeavoring to stifle the feeling of joy in his own bosom, offers his [most] cordial congratulations, on the occasion, to all the [officers] of every denomination, to all the troops of the United States in general, and in particular, to those gallant, and persevering men, who had resolved to defend the invaded rights of their country, so long as the war should continue . . ."

He then orders that the letter be read aloud on the anniversary of the Battles of Lexington and Concord, to every regiment and brigade in the Continental Army.

He also orders a reward: "An extra ration of liquor, [is] to be issued to every man, tomorrow, to drink [to] perpetual peace, independence, and happiness — to the United States of America."

The successful treaty that Benjamin Franklin, John Adams, and John Jay cobbled together now means that America officially extends as far west as the Mississippi River and that the fishermen of New England have unlimited access to the thriving Canadian fishing waters. More important, the Treaty of Paris can best be summed up in the opening sentence, a string of once-heretical words first suggested by the pen of Thomas Jefferson in 1776.

"His Britannic Majesty acknowledges the said United States," Article 1 begins, "to be free sovereign and independent states, that he treats with them as such, and for himself, his heirs, and successors, relinquishes all claims to the government, propriety, and territorial rights of the same and every part thereof."

With that sentence, the American War of Independence is over.

35

Almost three months after the Treaty of Paris is signed, General Washington finally retakes New York.

That event will go down in history as "Evacuation Day." The sun is shining brightly, although a sharp northwest wind makes Washington pull his cloak tightly about his shoulders. The general is astride his stallion Blueskin, leading a column of eight hundred American soldiers from Harlem to the Bowery. This army is no longer a band of rebels, but the true fighting force of the United States of America. Each man wears a black-and-white ribbon affixed to his military cocked hat in commemoration of the alliance with France.*

For Washington, this is to be a day of celebration, soon to be remembered for drinking at Fraunces Tavern, a night of bonfires and fireworks, and the adoring applause from rebel refugees returning home after years in exile — some now bereft to find their former dwelling burned to the ground or plundered of every stick of furniture. The crowds line the streets or look down from balconies and windows, all clamoring for a glimpse of this famous hero — the famous George Washington — whom they have only read about in the newspaper.

To the British and their followers, this is a time of shame and misery. After several delays, the army and their Loyalist civilian followers are finally fleeing the city. Ships will carry the soldiers home to England in defeat.

As for the Loyalists, they face uncertainty. The wealthy will be allowed to enter England, but the remainder will be taken by ship to either Nova Scotia or the West

*The black-and-white ribbon, called a cockade, was worn by both armies. Cockades were generally worn on military hats, but a special design was used to commemorate the alliance with France.

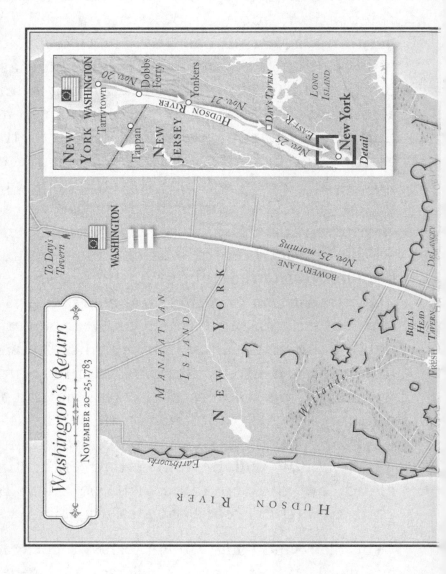

Washington's Return

NOVEMBER 20–25, 1783

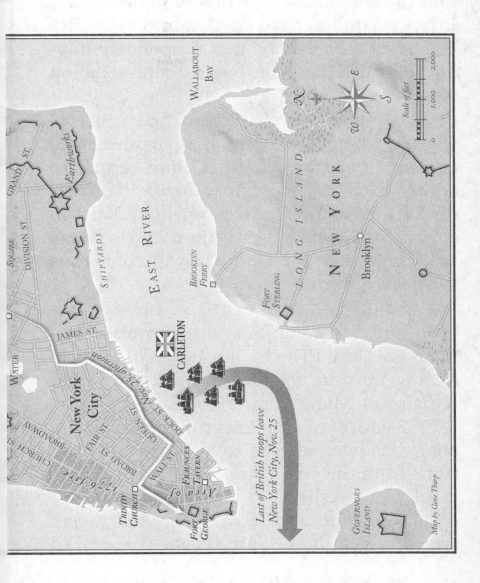

Map by Gene Thorp

Indies, to start a new life. Bitter and no longer welcome in the new United States, Loyalist families have flooded into New York City with their belongings, desperately hoping to find a place on board the evacuation vessels.

Many black Loyalists who fled a life of slavery to fight for the British have also chosen to sail away rather than return to servitude. Some travel to Canada, and others return to their ancestral homeland in Africa. In all, twenty-five thousand soldiers and thirty-five thousand Loyalist civilians are fleeing from New York.*

Washington's arrival at the Bowery has been timed to coincide with the precise moment the last British ship leaves the dock, leaving no time for looters to destroy what remains of Manhattan.

The route of Washington's triumphal entry has been altered to avoid the charred ruins from the Great Fire of 1776, but there is plenty to shock him. The streets are covered in filth and trash. Many businesses are shuttered; homes are vacant and devoid

*In Nova Scotia, the town of Shelburne, Canada (also known as Port Roseway), became a haven for white Loyalists. Black Loyalists founded nearby Birchtown.

of furniture, windows, doors, and other fixtures. Fences and church pews have been burned as firewood. Abandoned ships litter the waterfront. Everywhere there is damage from years of overcrowding.

But none of that matters now. The most vital port and city in America is finally in patriot hands.

As a last defiant taunt, the British have left the Union Jack hanging over Fort George, at the southern tip of Manhattan. The ensign is nailed to the top of the flagpole, which has been heavily greased. New Yorkers rush to rip it down and hoist the Stars and Stripes, but there is not a man strong enough or a ladder tall enough to accomplish this. Muskets are fired at the flag, which defies all attempts at destruction. Finally, a young sailor wearing a pea coat and a canvas hat who has served since the beginning of the war, surviving time on a British prison ship and in the jails of New York City, runs to a nearby hardware store. There, twenty-six-year-old Jack Van Arsdale buys the equipment that will allow him to improvise the same sort of cleats he might have used for climbing a ship's mainmast.

As George Washington looks on, Van Arsdale ascends the pole and rips down the

British flag.

In its place, as cannon boom a thirteen-round salute, one for each colony, the flag of the United States of America is raised over New York City.

With New York finally in American hands two years after Yorktown, there remains just one more obligation for George Washington before he can return home to Mount Vernon and his wife.

The general's war is over. It is unlikely that any other senior officer on either side has spent as many days in uniform. It has been a lonely life, with Washington spending nights in more than two hundred different homes and taverns over the course of the fighting. Having recently learned that his plantation is failing due to neglect, he is eager to return to Virginia.

The general is famous throughout America, lauded as a hero wherever he goes. But His Excellency does not crave power; nor does he long for more acclaim. Instead, he seeks to return to the quiet life of a gentleman farmer.

But first, George Washington must fulfill this last duty.

On December 4, Washington says an emotional good-bye to three hundred of his officers. He has delayed his departure from New York because the British remained on Staten Island one week longer than expected, and he refused to leave until they were gone. However, Washington has promised Martha that he will be home by Christmas, so he must be away.

George Washington's going-away party is held at Fraunces Tavern, where he has lodged this past week. "With a heart full of love and gratitude, I now take leave of you and now most devoutly wish that your later days be as prosperous in your future lives as your former ones have been glorious and honorable. . . . I cannot come to each of you but shall feel obliged if each of you will come and take me by the hand."

One by one, the officers come forward to shake the general's hand. It is a scene of unfiltered emotion, and many of these tough men actually break down and cry.

The next morning, Washington begins the long ride home. His fame makes it impossible for him to travel quickly, for news of his journey precedes him. The residents of every town and village along the route cheer him, an outpouring of affection decidedly distant from the horrific apathy of the war years, when so many Americans turned their backs on Washington and his men.

The journey takes Washington through Philadelphia, where he is lionized and feted at dinners and balls. The public outpouring of warmth is tinged with a second emotion — a national longing that George Washington lead the country. There is now a power vacuum. The Congress was never intended to be the sole legislative authority it has now become. As with Julius Caesar, Frederick the Great, Charlemagne, and so many other military leaders down through history, it seems only natural that General Washington take command of America.

But Washington has a better plan.

On December 23, he stands in a small room in the Maryland State House in Annapolis. The Congress has temporarily relocated to this port city, making it America's de facto capital.* Members of the Congress now sit before Washington. Above and behind the general, a gallery of spectators looks on. To his right, against the wall, sits Thomas Jefferson, newly returned to Congress.

Earlier in the day, Washington dictated his

---

*The move to Annapolis was made for social reasons. The lively waterside Maryland city was known for its entertainments.

last document as commander in chief. The letter was to Baron von Steuben, thanking him for his "zeal" and "meritorious service."

George Washington believes in the unique promise of America and that military rule is at odds with the virtues of democracy. Now, as evidence of that deeply held tenet, the man who once longed for the Congress to grant him a commission to lead the armies of the United States against the sovereign power of Great Britain stands before Congress to resign that commission.

"Having finished the work assigned me, I retire from the great theater of action. And bidding an affectionate farewell to this august body under whose orders I have so long acted, I hereby offer my commission and take my leave from all my employments of public life."

It is Christmas Day, 1783. George Washington gallops through the gates of his Mount Vernon estate. His Excellency's duty to his nation is complete.

Or so he thinks.

EPILOGUE

George Washington raises his right hand.

Since dawn, thousands have crowded around the Federal Building in Lower Manhattan, eager to witness the swearing-in of America's first president. Washington is in plain view, standing on the second-floor balcony overlooking Wall Street. His hair is powdered white for the occasion, and he wears a brown suit, white silk stockings, and shoes with silver buckles. A ceremonial sword hangs down at his hip. Washington's left hand rests on a Bible opened to the book of Genesis.

Robert Livingston, the chancellor of New York, stands opposite him, ready to administer the oath of office.*

"Do you solemnly swear that you will faithfully execute the office of President of the United States and will, to the best of your ability, preserve, protect, and defend the Constitution of the United States?"

George Washington is a restless man, one who quickly grew bored of his retirement in Mount Vernon. In the years immediately following the war he traveled into the American wilderness, revisiting lands he initially surveyed more than thirty years before. As befitting a man who had labored so diligently to forge the United States of America, Washington closely followed the actions of the Congress. In May 1787, he traveled to Philadelphia to represent Virginia at what would become known as the Constitutional Convention. The meetings took place inside the same room of the Pennsylvania State House where the Declaration of Independence had been approved, and

*The thirty-seven words for the Presidential Oath of Office, which have been used to swear in every American president since Washington, are written into the U.S. Constitution. They were penned in 1787 by delegates to the Constitutional Convention.

where Washington once accepted his commission as commander in chief of the Continental Army. The familiarity of the surroundings was reinforced by Washington's reunion with Alexander Hamilton, a growing force in national politics, and with Benjamin Franklin, now returned from Paris.*

Much to Washington's surprise, he was elected president of the convention.

The delegates met throughout the summer. Washington's leadership was evident to all: he kept the group on task despite several polarizing arguments that could have derailed the proceedings. The result was a document that reinvented the nascent American government, adding a second body to the Congress, establishing a judicial branch, and creating a role for a single individual to act as formal head of state. As with his wartime service, Washington was proud of his role in helping to create the U.S. Constitution.

All the while, George Washington was deeply in debt and struggling to pay the bills for his Mount Vernon estate. The time had

*Thomas Jefferson took over Franklin's role as minister to France. Alexander Hamilton was appointed to Congress, representing New York.

come to restore a measure of financial stability for himself and Martha by concentrating on making a profit from his plantation.

Then, in September 1788, Alexander Hamilton wrote Washington, imploring him to take part in the election of America's first chief executive, which was to take place between December 15, 1788, and January 10, 1789.

"If I should receive the appointment," Washington replied to Hamilton with dismay, "the acceptance would be attended with more diffidence and reluctance than I ever experienced before in my life."

In the end, however, Washington did allow his name to be placed on the ballot, along with those of seven other men: John Adams, John Hancock, John Jay, John Rutledge, Samuel Huntington, Benjamin Lincoln, and New York governor George Clinton.

The people voted overwhelmingly for Washington. John Adams came in second, and thus won the job of vice president. The Electoral College, another by-product of the Constitution, showed its approval of Washington by a unanimous vote.*

*The popular vote had strict rules. Only landowners over the age of twenty-one could cast a ballot.

It was not until April 14 that a horseman galloped to Mount Vernon to inform the general of his victory. Two days later, George Washington set out for New York, this time to lead his nation.

"I do solemnly swear," Washington states, repeating the oath back to Chancellor Livingston, "that I will faithfully execute the office of President of the United States and will, to the best of my ability, preserve, protect, and defend the Constitution of the United States."

Washington pauses before adding, "So help me God."

He then bends over the Bible and kisses its pages.

"It is done," Livingston announces to the crowd. "Long live George Washington, President of the United States!"

As the crowd cheers lustily, thirteen can-

In some states, only certain Protestant denominations could vote, and everywhere, women, immigrants, servants, and slaves were prohibited from taking part. Out of a U.S. population of nearly four million, it is estimated that fewer than forty-four thousand Americans voted in the first election.

non are fired in the distance.

America has its first president. The destiny of the republic is under way.

POSTSCRIPT

George Washington served two terms as president of the United States. He remains the only American chief executive never to have lived in the White House. Though in debt at the start of his first term, he initially refused a salary but changed his mind when Congress asked him to set a precedent for those who would follow him into office. The general returned to Mount Vernon in 1797, at the conclusion of his second term, and briefly came back on the national scene on July 4, 1798, when war with France seemed imminent. He accepted President John Adams's offer of a commission as commander in chief should that war occur. It did not. Thus, Washington resumed his plans to live out his days at Mount Vernon with Martha. However, on December 12, 1799, he spent the day on horseback, enduring snow and freezing rain as he inspected his property. Despite waking up with a sore throat the following morning, he once again rode through the snow to inspect his holdings. He awoke that night unable to breathe or swallow due to constriction of his throat. The affliction proved fatal. George Washington died on December 14, 1789, at the age of sixty-seven. Despite early efforts to place his body in a crypt below the Rotunda of the Capitol Building in Washington, DC, his remains are interred in a tomb at Mount Vernon. **Martha Washington** rests alongside her husband. Upon his death, she closed up their bedroom and moved to a separate upstairs bedchamber as a sign of mourning. She died on May 22, 1802, at the age of seventy after years of ill health.

After the war ended, **Thomas Jefferson** served as minister to France and then returned home to take the position of secretary of state during George Washington's first term in office. Jefferson also served as vice president under President John Adams, whom he later defeated for the presidency in the election of 1800. Jefferson and John Adams were good friends throughout their long careers but had a major falling-out over political differences in the 1790s. They reconciled in 1812, thanks to the efforts of Abigail Adams and fellow

Founding Father Benjamin Rush. For the rest of their lives, Adams and Jefferson engaged in lengthy correspondence about politics and world events. Thomas Jefferson died on July 4, 1826, at Monticello, where he is buried. **John Adams** died just hours later, in Quincy, Massachusetts, successfully making good on a personal pledge to remain alive until the fiftieth anniversary of the Declaration of Independence. Not knowing of his friend's death, Adams said shortly before his death, "Thomas Jefferson still survives" — a reference to the fact that they were among the oldest remaining signers of the Declaration. Adams is interred at United First Parish Church in Boston alongside **Abigail**, who died before him, in 1818.

Benjamin Franklin succumbed to pleurisy on April 17, 1790, in Philadelphia at the age of eighty-four. He was laid to rest alongside his wife, **Deborah**, in Christ Church Cemetery. He was busy almost to the end, serving as a member of the Constitutional Convention upon his return home from France in 1785, and then as president of Pennsylvania for three years afterward — a position similar to that of governor. More than twenty thousand people attended Franklin's funeral.

William Franklin moved to England in 1782, where he lived for the rest of his life. He wrote to his father in 1784, requesting a reconciliation. It never occurred, although Benjamin Franklin did leave his son a small piece of property in Nova Scotia in his will. William Franklin died in 1813. He is buried in St. Pancras Old Church cemetery in London, but the site of the grave has since been lost.

Alexander Hamilton rose to prominence in American politics after the Revolutionary War. An ardent proponent of the U.S. Constitution, he served in Congress and then as secretary of the treasury during George Washington's first six years in office. During that time, Hamilton was responsible for founding the U.S. Mint and the National Bank. He was famously blackmailed for a brief affair with a married woman in the early 1790s, an act for which his wife, **Elizabeth Schuyler Hamilton**, eventually forgave him. In 1804, Hamilton engaged in a pistol duel with his longtime rival Aaron Burr, who was at that time the vice president of the United States. At issue were Hamilton's beliefs that Burr was "despicable" and "a dangerous man," opinions Hamilton had expressed in private but that were later printed in a New York newspaper, the *Albany Register*. The duel took place on a New Jersey bluff overlooking the Hudson River on July 11, 1804. Hamilton fired first, with some later believing he intentionally aimed high to miss Burr. But the vice president shot straight, and the lead ball entered Hamilton's torso just above the right hip before ricocheting off his ribs and lodging in his spine. He was taken home, where he died the following day. He was forty-seven years old. Alexander Hamilton is buried in Trinity Church Cemetery at Broadway and Wall Streets in Manhattan. Elizabeth Schuyler Hamilton survived her husband by fifty years, dying in 1854 at the age of ninety-seven. She is also buried on the grounds at Trinity Church.

Hamilton's friend and ally during the Revolutionary War, the **Marquis de Lafayette,** led a stormy life upon his return to France. The nation's unstable political climate saw Lafayette thrown in jail, exiled, and even burned in effigy for his outspoken views and opposition to Emperor Napoleon Bonaparte. Lafayette returned to the United States in 1824 for a two-year tour of the nation in anticipation of its fiftieth-anniversary celebration. He observed the tumultuous election of 1824, in which John Quincy Adams was elected president over Andrew Jackson. Among the places Lafayette visited was the Bunker Hill battlefield, where he laid the cornerstone for a monument and scooped up dirt from the site, which was later sprinkled over his own grave. Lafayette died in 1834 at the age of seventy-six. He is buried in Picpus Cemetery in Paris. Upon hearing the news of Lafayette's death, President Andrew Jackson ordered both houses of Congress draped in black bunting for thirty days in memoriam.

One other veteran of Valley Forge also received the respect of a grateful nation. **Baron von Steuben** never returned to Germany, preferring to remain in New York with his companion, William North. He formally adopted North and another aide-de-camp, Benjamin Walker. In the absence of a wife and children, these two men became von Steuben's heirs. The U.S. Congress granted him an annual pension, and the state of New Jersey showed its thanks by giving him title to a home and estate. After a series of financial misadventures, von Steuben moved to upstate New York, where he settled in the town of Rome. Upon his death in 1794, the estate was passed down to his heirs, North and Walker. It is still traditional in many parts of the United States to celebrate Von Steuben Day, in honor of the Baron's September 17 birthday. In fact, the parade scene in the movie *Ferris Bueller's Day Off* memorably honors Von Steuben Day and the Baron's German heritage.

Lord Charles Cornwallis sailed for England after the surrender of Yorktown, never returning to America. He was roundly criticized for his battlefield strategies but refused to retreat from public life. In America, his name will forever be synonymous with his loss to Washington, but his postwar actions would lead to a different legacy in England. Cornwallis went on to serve successfully for seven years as governor-general of India and then lord lieutenant of Ireland, a position he held from 1798 to 1801. Cornwallis returned to India, where he died in 1805. He is interred in an elaborate monument in Ghazipur, overlooking the Ganges River. Lord Charles Cornwallis was sixty-six years old.

Among those on Cornwallis's ship home was **Benedict Arnold**, who hoped to make a new start in England. For a time, Arnold was a celebrity, seen taking garden strolls with King George III, who delighted in speaking with someone who shared his views on the war in America. But Arnold's decision to betray his country soon came back to haunt him. He was jeered in public and attacked as a money-crazed mercenary in the British press. One political cartoonist in London depicted him as a serpent. The traitor's life became a series of failed businesses, recurring debts, and other misadventures. Eventually, he moved to Canada, hoping again to start his life anew, but that didn't work out, either, and he eventually returned to London. Benedict Arnold's health declined and he died penniless in 1801, at the age of sixty. He is interred in St. Mary's Church on the banks of the Thames River in Battersea, England. **Peggy Shippen Arnold**, who remained with her husband throughout his life, survived him by just three years, dying of cancer at the age of forty-four. She is interred within the same crypt.

A memorial to **Col. John André** was erected in the nave of Westminster Abbey in 1782, paid for by King George III. Benedict and Peggy Arnold were observed paying a visit to the site in the winter of that year. In 1821, André's body was exhumed from its resting place in America and reburied in front of the memorial on November 28 of that year. A small stone marks the grave. The wooden box that carried André's bones home to England can still be found within the abbey's triforium, unavailable for public viewing. However, "this remarkable repository of monumental statues and sacred relics," as the triforium has been described, is in the midst of a major renovation, the completion of which will allow many such hidden artifacts to be put on display.

Banastre Tarleton, a man no less notorious than Benedict Arnold, returned to England a hero. The noted British artists Thomas Gainsborough and Joshua Reynolds both painted his portrait, and the one by Reynolds still hangs in London's National Gallery. Tarleton was elected to Parliament in 1790, where he staunchly defended the slave trade while still remaining a member of the British military, being promoted to major general in 1794. He maintained a fifteen-year affair with Mary Robinson, the former lover of King George IV, before finally marrying an illegitimate daughter of the Fourth Duke of Ancaster in

1798. Banastre Tarleton died in 1833 at the age of seventy-nine and is buried in Lancaster Cemetery in Lancashire, England.

The rivalry between **Francis "Swamp Fox" Marion** and Tarleton was the basis for the highly fictionalized Mel Gibson film *The Patriot*. Marion returned home after the war and lived a thoroughly normal life for the remainder of his days. A bachelor before the fighting, he married on April 20, 1786, at the age of fifty-four. He rebuilt his plantation, which had been burned in the war, and there he died in 1795, at the age of sixty-three. Marion is buried in the Belle Isle Plantation Cemetery in Berkeley County, South Carolina. His plantation, Pond Bluff, now lies at the bottom of nearby Lake Marion.

A visitor to London can find the tomb of **Lord William Howe** in Twickenham, in a cemetery called the Holly Road Garden of Rest. Howe requested a formal inquiry in Parliament to clear his name of any impropriety for failing to follow orders and link up with General Burgoyne in Saratoga. He was successful, but criticism over Saratoga would follow him for the rest of his life.

Like William Howe, **Elizabeth Loring** left America before the war ended. She and her two children moved to England to live with her father-in-law, and there is no evidence that she saw Howe again. Her husband, Joshua, joined her in England in 1783, and they had three more children at their new home in Reading. After her husband's death in 1789, Loring petitioned the king for a pension to support herself. Thanks to a recommendation from William Howe, the petition was granted, providing Elizabeth Loring an income until her death in 1831.

After the loss at Yorktown, British commander in chief **Sir Henry Clinton** was replaced and sailed home to England in 1782. He wrote a book blaming the defeat on Lieutenant General Cornwallis but otherwise did little after his return but serve in Parliament. Clinton died two days before Christmas in 1793, at the age of sixty-five. He is buried in St. George's Chapel at Windsor Castle, where many members of British royalty are laid to rest.

King George III lived to the age of eighty-one, dying in 1820 after fifty-nine years on the throne. At the time of his death, the madness that had begun to manifest itself decades earlier finally incapacitated him, and he was no longer acting as king. The reign of George III is remembered largely for the loss of the colonies. George's beloved wife, **Queen Charlotte,** died two years before her husband and is buried with him in the Royal Vault at St. George's Chapel in Windsor.

The burial of **John Paul Jones** was not as exalted as the king's. Unable to gain a command in the Continental Navy at the end of the war, he found work as an admiral for the Russian empress Catherine the Great. This posting lasted for one year, whereupon Jones settled in Paris. He was found dead in his apartment in the summer of 1792, the result of an infection that caused kidney failure. John Paul Jones was buried in the Saint Louis Cemetery, a property owned by the French royal family. In 1905, after a long investigation, the then U.S. ambassador to France, Horace Porter, discovered the site of Jones's grave. The body was exhumed, and Jones's remains were transferred to American soil. John Paul Jones now rests in a crypt beneath the chapel at the U.S. Naval Academy in Annapolis, Maryland.

■ ■ ■ ■

An estimated 400,000 Continental soldiers and state militia fought on the American side through the course of the war. There is no exact number.

It is thought that almost 7,000 American soldiers were killed in action during the war, with many more deaths coming from disease or from the harsh conditions endured as prisoners of war. Those mortality figures are roughly 17,000 and 12,000, respectively, bringing the total casualty figure to an estimated 36,000.

British casualties were estimated to be 24,000 killed in battle, missing in action, and dead from disease. Of the 30,000 Hessians who fought in the war, one-fourth either were killed in action or died from illness. Some 5,500 Hessian soldiers chose to remain in America following the war.

Many soldiers who fought in the Revolutionary War were given tracts of land by the new federal government, settling America and continuing the growth made possible by their service.

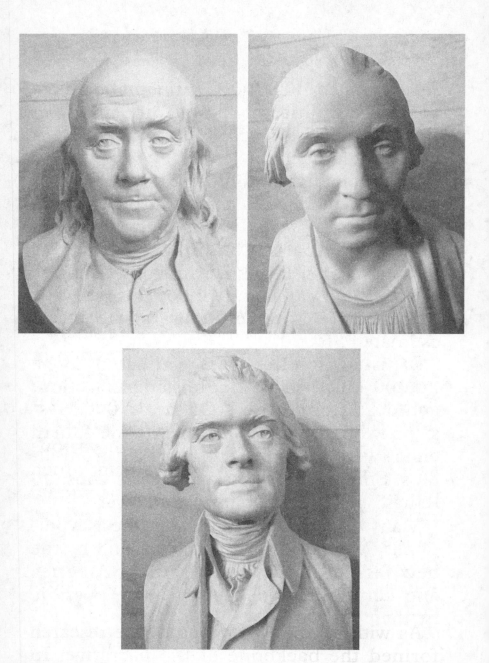

Busts of Benjamin Franklin, George Washington, and Thomas Jefferson located in the White House. Photographs by Bill O'Reilly.

SOURCES

Killing England presented a unique research experience. The Revolutionary War was, of course, a time without video, photographs, or YouTube to help describe a scene. Likewise, there were no sound recordings allowing us to hear the charisma or inflection in our subjects' spoken words. Very often, the mythologizing that builds around great historical figures became an impediment of its own, forcing us to sift through various accounts to see which are real and which have been built upon a fable constructed years after a character's death. George Washington, for instance, did not chop down the cherry tree, and Martha Washington did not name her tomcat after Alexander Hamilton.

As with all the *Killing* books, the research formed the backbone of the narrative. In the case of *Killing England,* online searches ran the gamut from the Central Intelligence

593

Agency website to queries about colonial toilets, malarial mosquitoes, and how to load a musket. The Internet cookies we've left behind should see intriguing spam email for years to come.

The *Killing England* investigation took us beyond libraries and the Internet to battle-fields, archives, graveyards, museums, and even the British Parliament, where we were granted a behind-the-scenes tour and access to centuries-old documents in the Parliamentary Archives. It's worth noting that the Royal Collection Trust has also placed an enormous amount of George III's personal papers online for future scholarship. These papers dating from 1755 to 1810 were originally meant "to be destroyed unread," an act that was luckily never carried out. While in London, we requested the chance to enter the Royal Vault in St. George's Chapel at Windsor Castle, where King George III and many other sovereigns dating back centuries now rest. Due to the personal nature of the vault, that request was politely denied by royal officials.

It was refreshing to find that some frustrating research questions could be resolved with a single phone call. So a word of thanks to the folks at Valley Forge, Monticello, Mount Vernon, and Independence Hall for taking the time to share their insights into the more arcane bits of American history. In every case, when those on the other end of the line did not have the answer at their fingertips, they pointed us to someone who did.

Other research required a bit more leg-work, for instance when we looked for the graves of British generals from the Revolutionary War. Included in this search were Benedict Arnold and his wife, Peggy, whose gravesite remains in the cellar walls of St. Mary's Church, Battersea, in London, England. However, the church has changed over the centuries. The basement that houses their burial vault is no longer a crypt but a collection of offices and a children's play area. The church asks that anyone wishing to see the tomb should phone ahead for an appointment.

In that spirit, the reader is encouraged to undertake their own hands-on exploration of American history. It is one thing to read about what took place in these locations and quite another to walk in the footsteps of the men and women who so courageously fought to form a nation in the face of unfavorable odds. Sites such as Mount Vernon, Monticello, Independence Hall, Boston's many historical sites, and the various battlefields maintained by the National Park Service should be required visiting for all patriots. Yorktown, in particular, is mind blowing. Both Yorktown and Philadelphia are now home to vast new museums devoted to the Revolutionary War.

Most sites described in this book are well known and heavily visited. However, there is one historical location in America that is hidden in plain sight but almost completely overlooked: the Old Senate Chamber inside the Maryland State House. Located in Annapolis, the room has been carefully restored to appear as it did on the day George Washington resigned his commission at the end of the war, complete with a life-size statue of General Washington and an interactive display. The room looks just as it did on that day, with no curtains or electric lights and a wooden floor joined with dowels instead of nails. While you're in town, make sure to visit John Paul Jones's crypt beneath the chapel at the U.S. Naval Academy.

It is helpful when writing history to read the works of others who have already researched and written about a topic. This becomes the jumping-off point, allowing us to expand our own research as the story guides us down countless new rabbit holes.

Literally hundreds of books, articles, and archival websites were referenced in the writing of *Killing England,* but several works deserve the highest praise and should be on any Revolutionary War reading list. Among them are the enthusiastically researched *Braddock's Defeat* by David L. Preston; *The Battle of Brooklyn, 1776* by John J. Gallagher; *The Swamp Fox: How Francis Marion Saved the American Revolution* by John Oller; *1776* by David McCullough; and *William Franklin: Son of a Patriot, Servant of a King* and *The Making of a Patriot: Benjamin Franklin at the Cockpit* by Sheila L. Skemp. Many a writer has peered into the mind of Benjamin Franklin, but the thorough scholarship of Dr. Skemp suggests a lifetime devotion to this subject.

Books aside, an intimate and enlightening way to read about the period of time recorded in *Killing England* is by reading the letters of the great men themselves. Founders Online, a section of the U.S. National Archives website, features a digitized collection of writings by George Washington, Thomas Jefferson, Benjamin Franklin, Alexander Hamilton, John Adams, and James Madison. Their personalities, hopes, fears, daily chores, and dreams come through powerfully. And because of the breadth of these letters, sometimes spanning decades, the reader can see the growth of not just the individual but also the nation itself — through their eyes.

ACKNOWLEDGMENTS

Stephen Rubin, the best publisher on the planet, and his muse Gillian Blake — an editor with a great eye.

Eric Simonoff, who puts the deals together and guides the process.

Marty Dugard, the best writing partner a person could have.

Finally, my fourteen-year-old son, Spencer, who loves history and keeps me on my toes!

— BILL O'REILLY

Thanks to Bill O'Reilly, for his vision and genius. Thanks also to the team that makes the *Killing* books possible: Steve Rubin, Gillian Blake, Chris O'Connell, and the intrepid Eric Simonoff. And to Calene and the Bongo Boys, with much love.

— MARTIN DUGARD

599

ILLUSTRATION CREDITS

Maps by Gene Thorp
Page 31: Image in the public domain via Wikimedia Commons
Page 63: Public domain
Page 89: DeAgostini/Getty Images
Page 112: © The Huntington Library, Art Collections, and Botanical Gardens/ Bridgeman Images
Page 182: Public domain
Page 230: Granger, NYC — all rights reserved
Page 237: Smith Collection/Gado/Getty Images
Page 276: Smith Collection/Gado/Getty Images
Page 287: Gift of George Washington Custis Lee, University Collections of Art and History, Washington and Lee University, Lexington, Virginia
Page 316: MPI/Getty Images
Page 335: Drawing provided by Designpics

.com: First Meeting of George Washington and Alexander Hamilton, by Alonzo Chappel, from *Life and Times of Washington,* volume 1, published 1857

Page 349: Photograph by Will/ullstein bild via Getty Images

Page 352: Musées de la Ville de Paris, Musée Carnavalet, Paris, France/Archives Charmet/Bridgeman Images

Page 383: Granger, NYC — all rights reserved

Page 402: Pictorial Press Ltd./Alamy Stock Photo

Page 444: North Wind Picture Archives/ Alamy Stock Photo

Page 473: Granger, NYC — all rights reserved

Page 559: Print Collector/Hulton Archive/ Getty Images

ABOUT THE AUTHORS

Bill O'Reilly is the trailblazing TV journalist who has experienced unprecedented success on cable news and in writing thirteen national number-one bestselling nonfiction books. There are currently more than 17 million books in the *Killing* series in print. He lives on Long Island.

Martin Dugard is the *New York Times* bestselling author of several books of history, among them the *Killing* series, *Into Africa,* and *The Explorers.* He and his wife live in Southern California.